THE WHEEL OF THE LAW
BUDDHISM

THE WHEEL OF THE LAW
BUDDHISM

ILLUSTRATED FROM SIAMESE SOURCES

THE MODERN BUDDHIST,
A LIFE OF BUDDHA,
AND
AN ACCOUNT OF THE PHRABAT.

BY
HENRY ALABASTER, ESQ.,

INTERPRETER OF HER MAJESTY'S CONSULATE
GENERAL IN SIAM,
MEMBER OF THE ROYAL ASIATIC SOCIETY.

GYAN

Published by

Gyan Publishing House
5, Ansari Road
Daryaganj, New Delhi-110002
Phone: 011-47034999, 9811692060
E-mail: books@gyanbooks.com

Distribution Network
gyanbooks.com
India, USA, Canada, UK, Australia, France

ISBN : 978-81-212-2504-5 (HB)
First Published, 1871

2nd Impression 2021

Printed at: Gyan Press, Delhi.

The Wheel of the Law, Buddhism
Author: Henry Alabaster

THE WHEEL OF THE LAW.

BUDDHISM

ILLUSTRATED FROM SIAMESE SOURCES

BY

THE MODERN BUDDHIST,

A LIFE OF BUDDHA,

AND

AN ACCOUNT OF THE PHRABAT.

BY

HENRY ALABASTER, Esq.,

INTERPRETER OF HER MAJESTY'S CONSULATE GENERAL IN SIAM,
MEMBER OF THE ROYAL ASIATIC SOCIETY.

LONDON:
TRÜBNER & CO., 60 PATERNOSTER ROW.
1871.

TABLE OF CONTENTS.

b

NOTES TO THE LIFE OF BUDDHA.

PART III.

THE PHRABAT, OR HOLY FOOTPRINT.

CHAPTER I.

CHAPTER II.

CHAPTER III.

APPENDIX.

INDEX.

PREFACE.

ALL Buddhists, throughout the wide range of countries where the doctrines of Buddha prevail, call their religion the doctrine of "The Wheel of the Law." I have adopted the name for this book, because it is peculiarly appropriate to a theory of Buddhism, which the book in some degree illustrates. I refer to the theory that all existence of which we have any conception is but a part of an endless chain, or circle, of causes and effects; that so long as we remain in that wheel there is no rest and no peace; and that rest can only be obtained by escaping from that wheel into the incomprehensible Nirwana. Buddha taught a religion of which the wheel was the only proper symbol; for his theory, professing to be complete, dealt with but a limited round of knowledge; ignored the beginning, and was equally vague as to the end. He neither taught of a God, the Creator of existence, nor of a heaven, the absorber of existence, but restrained his teaching within what he believed to be the limits of reason.

The wheel of the law, or Buddhism, is in this volume illustrated by three distinct essays or parts, which exemplify the sceptical phase, the traditionary phase, and the ultra-superstitious phase.

The first part is a revised and enlarged edition of the "Modern Buddhist," the short essay in which I, last year, introduced to European readers a summary of the ideas of an eminent Siamese nobleman on his own and other religions. The Buddhism it teaches, though it has a strong party in favour of it, rejects many superstitions, and so differs from the Buddhism of the generality of educated Siamese, which is illustrated by the second and third parts.

The second part, which illustrates the traditionary phase, is a Buddhist Gospel, or "Life of Buddha," commencing with events previous to his last birth, and ending with his attainment of the Buddhahood. I have translated it from a popular Siamese work, "Pathomma Somphothiyan," the "Initiation, or First Festival of Perfect Wisdom."

My translation is free or literal, according to my judgment. In many parts I have cut out tedious descriptive passages; in one or two places, duly referred to in the notes, I have corrected presumed errors in my Siamese manuscript; and in chapter x. I have substituted a simple for a confused arrangement. In order that the story of the Life may convey a thorough idea of the doctrines of traditionary Buddhism, I have in the notes dilated on every point of Buddhist teaching referred to in the text; and I believe that text and notes combined may be considered to give a fair idea of the Siamese view of the character of their great teacher, the principles of the law which he taught, and the observances becoming in his followers.

The third part, which illustrates the ultra-superstitious phase of Buddhism, is an account of the "Phrabat, or Siamese Footprint of Buddha," a curious and gross superstition, which offers a very thorough contrast to the ideas of the "Modern Buddhist." In the description of my journey to visit it will be found some notices of the Siamese people, monks, and temples, as they are.

When I introduced to the readers of Europe the speculations of a Siamese nobleman on his own and other religions, I looked forward, in the event of that essay being successful, to bringing out a new edition with the corrections and additions of the Siamese author, Chao Phya Thipakon, himself. His much-to-be-lamented death has prevented this, and I am left to re-edit it by myself.

I venture to preface it with some remarks, conceived, so far as such is possible for me, in sympathy with, and as a development of, the ideas of the author, particularly intended to show that practical application of his principles which has a personal interest for Europeans.

The "Modern Buddhist," in his endeavours to justify his religion in the eyes of Europeans, has enunciated a form of Buddhism which must be of considerable interest to many who, in these days of criticism and doubt, have lost all the faith and hope that was in them, and search in vain for some foundation on which to rebuild their belief. The "Modern Buddhist" is sceptical, but his scepticism is not of that demolishing character, the evil nature—I may perhaps say, untruth—of which is shown by the misery it brings to those who are plunged in it.

Happy are they that sleep! and happy are they who,

with unshaken faith, follow the religion of their ancestors, and console themselves for all the trials they experience in this life by the glad hope of a life immortal! Evidently miserable are most of those whose hopes are bounded by the day they are ever approaching, who believe in no reward for virtue unless it be an immediate one, whose aspirations to do good for future times only call up the sad thought that it is useless, and who, panting for an immortality they cannot see the reason of, chill the promptings of their spirit by such words as those of the poet—

> "No man lives for ever,
> And dead men rise up never."

The theories of the "Modern Buddhist" are better than such hopelessness.

The "Modern Buddhist" assumes religion to be the science of man, and not the revelation of God. He does not think that the comprehension of the Deity, or the firm persuasion of the exact nature of heaven, is of so much consequence as that just idea of one's own self which he believes he finds in Buddhism purged of superstitions.

He is a deeply religious man, but his ideas of religion differ so much from English ideas, that it is difficult to state them without giving offence.

Strange to us are his teachings on the subjects of God and eternity; yet throughout his work there is a spiritual tone which shows, that with him, as with us, religion is the link which connects man with the Infinite, and is that which gives a law of conduct depending on a basis more extensive than the mere immediate present.

The ordinary man, whatever his religion may be, whatever he believes in, whatever he doubts, acknowledges himself, and acknowledges infinity, and longs to connect the two.*

In his endeavours, he either works from himself towards the Infinite, as does the Buddhist, or by a bold definition of the undefinable, he assumes the nature of the Deity, and by a declaration of the laws which accord with that nature, he governs his religion. Such is the practice of the followers of the great religions of Christ, Mahomet, and Brahma.

Man, who cannot conceive the Infinite in any one of its aspects—who grows appalled as he looks at the sky, and utterly, hopelessly fails to find a limit to his look and his thought, cannot, and does not, of himself pretend to have so fearful a knowledge. But man, listening to a craving that is in him, welcomes the heaven-promising teachings of those he believes to have been inspired, and so in many cases learns sufficient for his satisfaction.

At the same time, there are many men who cannot believe that which they cannot comprehend ; and still more cannot accept as revealed truth those writings which appear to them to be the work of men very imperfectly acquainted with the laws of nature, inclined to write history from a rather partial stand-point, and often teaching very bad morality.

These sceptics must either cease to occupy their minds with religion, or must assume that it is the

* I do not here refer to the teachings of philosophers, but to the ideas of those who have learnt no metaphysical subtleties. Some Buddhists, like followers of other philosophical schools, emphatically deny their own existence, professing to believe in the maxim, "Neither I am, nor is aught mine."

subject of some law; for if it is not governed by some law, any attempt to reason on it would be waste of time.

If religion is the subject of law, it must be believed that the law which rules it is a law of perfect justice. Belief that we are ruled by an unjust law, or by an unjust God, capable of having ever reserved His special love for peculiar people, or of visiting on children the sins of their fathers, is too horrible.

If there is a law of perfect justice, then the "Modern Buddhist" argues that, from the different conditions and fortunes of men, we must conclude that there have been previous states of existence, and will be future states, which, taken together, will balance the good and bad luck, the happiness and misery of all beings. He, with a mathematical mind, cannot by any process balance one finite existence againt infinity. He cannot believe that a bad life of, say fifty years, shall be punished eternally, or a good life of fifty years blessed eternally. Fifty years is nothing when compared with infinite time, and there is no justice in allowing so short a period to perceptibly affect one that is long beyond all comparison with it. It seems to him, as it will seem to many others, that proportion is inseparable from justice; that limited time cannot bear any proportion to infinity; and that, in fact, infinity can only be affected by infinity. He can balance an infinite past, spent in innumerable states of transmigration, against an infinite future; he can also believe that life is but a phenomenon of disturbance; that the principle of equalisation existing in it will cause the rise and fall of the waves of disturbance to be proportionate to one another, acting and re-acting until the disturbance disappears in perfect rest. But he cannot believe that the short span of one life shall, by itself, determine the nature of our eternity.

Throughout his main arguments there is at least an appearance of reason. As the mathematician begins from a conceivable definite unit, and works towards infinity, rather than beginning with infinity in order thence to evolve his unit, so does the "Modern Buddhist" work from his apparently comprehensible unit man towards the incomprehensible eternity of existence, and does not begin by defining the eternity of existence, and other problems of infinity therewith connected, and thence argue as to the state of man. He observes that many men pass through a great deal of sorrow during their lives, whilst others are comparatively happy; that evil men, owing to the favourable circumstances of their birth, are prosperous, while good men, born in a less fortunate grade of life, often struggle vainly against adverse fortune. He believes all this must be balanced and equalised, and he thinks it natural that the equalisation should be obtained by the man that has suffered becoming, or having been, happier in another state of existence, and the man who has misused advantages afterwards suffering reverses. He sees in the different conditions of life a proof that there must be a transmigration of the spirit from existence to existence, that the beggar of yesterday may be the millionaire of to-day, and the prince of to-day the dog of the future.

Supposing he is right—that the merit and demerit of man accounts for his present existence and will shape his future; supposing that, whether or no we have a soul, there is a something we create,—our destiny—which will hereafter reap the benefit of our good actions and the punishment of our wickedness, then I think his teaching has at least one of the most valuable characteristics of religion, in that it affords a strong motive to be virtuous, and a very manifest reason to endeavour to benefit the world, whose pleasures and sufferings we shall by our destiny continue to partake of.

Many will object that the motive above stated is a selfish one, and therefore a bad one. We have, all of us, a prejudice against everything to which the word selfish can be applied; we like the thoughtless, liberal prodigal, better than the careful man who takes care of his future, and whom we call selfish. I venture to think that selfishness is not objectionable in so far as it makes man act on the presumption that his first duty is to take care of himself. It becomes objectionable when, exceeding its proper bounds, it interferes with the due performance of man's second duty, which is his duty to promote the general happiness. The Buddhist principle would increase man's readiness to perform this second duty, by its recognition that it is indeed a part of his first duty; that, in fact, his only way to act with a view to his own future benefit is to strive for the amelioration of the condition of all human beings. Selfishness producing unselfishness cannot be very seriously condemned. When we study the lives of Buddhists, we do not find that their religion has made them objectionably selfish. Those I have lived amongst are kind, charitable, and hospitable, and the life of the founder of their religion, given in this volume, is a remarkable instance of self-abnegation.

The theory that the various conditions of men and

animals is caused by good and bad acts and thoughts in previous generations, is orthodox Buddhism; but the argument, as used by the "Modern Buddhist," seems to me to tend to a somewhat latitudinarian belief.

If we are to dispense with "inner consciousness" and revelation, and belief in those venerable traditions which were introduced into our minds in our infancy, or before our minds were capable of fairly judging them; if we are to ignore all this, and deduce our belief in future existence merely from the conditions of present existence, then it appears to me to follow naturally, that as from the conditions of visible existence we have drawn a belief in future existence, and the advantage of a virtuous life, so also from the same conditions of visible existence we must ascertain what a virtuous life is—that is to say, what will conduce best to the happiness of all creatures, any one of which we may hereafter chance to be.

True it is the "Modern Buddhist" does not go so far as to assert this, but declares that Buddha, the wise one, has already taught the nature of a virtuous life. Nevertheless he does not attempt to set up the wisdom of Buddha as a bar to further progress in the way of wisdom. He has a firm faith that whatever truths science may reveal, none will be found opposed to the vital points of Buddhism. He freely criticises his sacred books by such small lights of science as he possessed. He states his opinion that Buddha, although he knew everything, was careful not to teach that which the people of his age were not ripe to understand, and therefore refrained from many topics he might have referred to had he lived in a more advanced age.

It may be denied that such ideas are consistent with orthodox Buddhism, but orthodox or unorthodox, they at least prove that Buddhism does not cramp the mind, as some of its antagonists have declared. They show that Buddhism does not hold men in such an iron grip that they dare not let their reason travel beyond its so-called canonical dogmas. They show that there is in that religion a suitability to the natures of many progressive men; that it will lead them well so far as it goes, and will not offer to those whose intelligence, rightly or wrongly, perforce carries them forwards—so terrible a ruin of all their previous ideas and aspirations, that they can lament that they are reasoning beings.

Chao Phya Thipakon was regarded as a very pious Buddhist by a nation of Buddhists, so it is scarcely for us to question his orthodoxy; yet he teaches doctrines which go a long way towards the belief that the highest religious duty of man is the reverential study of social and political science.

The teachings of Chao Phya Thipakon are at an end. In the text of the "Modern Buddhist," I mention that he had been for some years blind. In hopes of recovering his sight, he underwent an operation for cataract. He never recovered his sight, and sank under his afflictions in the summer of last year, before he had had the opportunity of criticising my version of his book, or had even learnt the pleasure with which his vindication of his religion was received by liberal-minded critics in Europe. I will tell one anecdote of my intercourse with him. Many years ago, when I first acquired some little facility in speaking Siamese, but had no real knowledge of Buddhism, I used sometimes to visit His Excellency of an evening, and converse on science and religion. One night I expounded to him part of the Sermon on the Mount, and he seemed so pleased with those beautiful maxims, that I thought him half a Christian, and hoped soon to convert him. Then it was that he told me of the beauty of Buddha's teachings, and showed me how hopeless was the task which the missionaries had undertaken in his country.

The missionaries again and again feel hopeful that the day of conversion is at hand, yet are ever doomed to disappointment. I cannot but think that the money and energy expended on their work is in great measure lost, and that the labour of many of them would be better employed in their own country. It is a pity to see good men, who might be of use in their own country, doomed to a life of disappointment in an unhealthy and enervating climate. It is a pity to see good Buddhists turned into bad Christians ; and I am afraid that the Protestant missionaries could not produce one good Siamese Christian for each ten thousand pounds that has been devoted to their work. They may have a few sincere and intelligent Chinese and Burmese converts, but Siamese converts, if any, are very rare.

I hope this will not be misunderstood to be an attack on the missionary body. They have not succeeded as missionaries, but they have done, and still do, much good in the country as physicians, teachers, and pioneers. There are too many of them, and the work of most of them is wasted, but some of them are among the most useful members of the foreign community. To one of them (who supports himself without drawing a salary from any missionary body) the Siamese are indebted for many useful publications, including the Siamese laws, and several volumes of semi-historical works. From another who has exiled himself to the Laos country, we may expect valuable information concerning the Laos language and people. While speaking of their useful works, I must mention the excellent schools of two of the lady members.

In the first edition of the "Modern Buddhist" I omitted a few passages which were of some importance, but which referred to subtleties of Buddhism that would, in my opinion, have made the essay unsuitable to the class of readers I designed it for. As an unknown man, seeking a publisher, I had to endeavour to make my work easily appreciable. I was fortunate enough to find in Mr Trübner a publisher who took a personal interest in the literature of Oriental religions, and he at once took charge of my essay, and has since urged me to extend my selections from the writings of Chao Phya Thipakon. I have therefore in this edition given to my readers all that seems to me worth translation in the book of Chao Phya Thipakon. I have not complied with the desire of some of my critics, that I should quash the "Modern Buddhist," and give a literal translation of the text of the Siamese author in its entirety, for I know that such a translation would scarcely find readers. I myself find literal translations of Oriental works intolerably tedious; and I am not alone in my opinion, for otherwise the original edition of the "Lotus de la Bonne Loi," the work of Burnouf, the most illustrious of European scholars of Buddhism, would not now be procurable uncut from its publishers.

One more remark, and I shall end this preface to the "Modern Buddhist." Some men appear to believe that, in publishing that book, I have perpetrated a literary hoax, and invented a Siamese author. I do not think that any careful reader of the book would do me this injustice, for it seems to me that there is a quaintness of thought and manner in the writing of Chao Phya Thipakon which I have in some measure happily rendered in the translations, while I have quite failed to imitate it in my remarks. In this edition I have been careful to mark all the translated passages by inverted commas, and my readers may rest assured that all passages so marked are purely Siamese. It is as a translator and exponent of the thoughts of the Siamese that I seek for credit, and I altogether decline the honour of being considered a clever forger.

I will now make some prefatory remarks on the second part of this work, the "Life of Buddha."

The "Life of Buddha" has been translated several times, from different sources; but I believe Bishop Bigandet's translation from the Burmese is the only "Life" now procurable in England.

The most classical translations I have read are Turnour's and Foucaux's—the first from the Pali classics of Ceylon, the second from the Thibetan "Rgya Tcher Rol Pa," compared with the Sanscrit "Lalita Vistâra." Turnour's translations, published in his "Pali Annals," are elegant and concise; Foucaux's work, though valuable for reference, is the literal reproduction of a long and tedious book, which not even the skill of M. Foucaux can render pleasant reading.

Bishop Bigandet's compilation from Burmese sources is interesting, and in one sense complete; for whereas my Siamese manuscript concludes with the attainment of omniscience, he had materials which enabled him to continue the story to the death or Nirwana. So far as we travel over the same ground, I prefer the Siamese version to the Burmese : it is not only more poetical, but in those points where there is a difference as to fact, it may be considered more accurate, inasmuch as when the same circumstance is mentioned in the Pali annals, it is generally in accordance with the Siamese version. Bishop Bigandet's work has very much assisted me in my labours, and should be read by all who take an interest in Buddhism.

There is an ample "Life of Buddha," compiled from Singhalese sources, in the Rev. Spence Hardy's "Manual of Buddhism," which, I believe, is out of print. I have not the good fortune to possess a copy, but when I read it, it appeared to me that, although the narrative of events was ample, it was deficient in those explanatory notes which Spence Hardy's great knowledge of Buddhism would have rendered it easy for him to supply, and it seemed altogether to lack the poetical character which marks the "Life of Buddha" in the native texts. To translate agreeably, one must to a certain extent sympathise with the feelings of the author one translates from, and not serve up our glowing Oriental feasts with a cold chill on them.

I believe that Csoma de Körös and Hodgson, men eminent among Buddhist scholars, have also published abstracts of translations of the "Life of Buddha," but I have not seen that portion of their writings.

I do not expect to supply fresh materials to scholars. I rather write in hopes of popularising the knowledge of Buddhism, and giving a fair idea of Siamese literary style. I have taken some pains to make my translation readable, though I fear my success is but partial, and I have also endeavoured to elucidate every Buddhist expression by a note. Where there is no direct reference from the text, the index will generally direct the reader to an explanation. The index is not a verbal one, referring its consulter to every page of the book on which any word appears, but it is purposely limited to those references which are important to the understanding of the words entered in it.

Many of the notes have been written especially for my readers in Siam, who will, I hope, find that my hints open out to them a new interest in their study of the Siamese language, their participation in Siamese ceremonies, and their visits to Siamese temples. They will see that much that they may have hitherto regarded as meaningless formality, or fanciful painting, has a religious and historical significance that carries them back to the dawn of history. As instances, I may refer to the notes on the custom of giving money and lottery tickets in limes at cremations, the ceremony of pouring water on the earth, the ploughing ceremony, the gift of gold and silver flowers at coronations, &c. Some may perhaps be interested in the comparisons I have endeavoured to draw between Siamese and Sanscrit words. I was moved to attempt the comparison of Siamese and Sanscrit words by the complaint of a critic, who blamed me for not having done it in the "Modern Buddhist." He rightly presumed that I was "no Sanscrit scholar." I had not even begun to study that language; nevertheless, I did not discover in his criticism any Sanscrit words that were not known to me from miscellaneous reading; and, indeed, the simple examples he gave suggested to me the thought that scholarship was not required for such an undertaking. I therefore procured a Sanscrit dictionary, and by its aid I have been able to make numerous comparisons. I hope some day to return to the work with a better knowledge of Sanscrit to help me; in the meantime, I must ask Sanscrit scholars to excuse such errors as they may detect. The labour has proved interesting, as it has enlightened me as to the original meaning of many Siamese words, and has shown how much the Siamese language has been enlarged from the Sanscrit. The Siamese seem to have derived their religion, most of their state ceremonies, and (so far as I have yet examined) almost every word in their language which rises above mere savagery, from the ancient Aryans—"the respectable race"—of Central India.

The Siamese "Life of Buddha," as my translation shows it, contains a mixture of what seem to be several very distinct reverential (if not exactly religious) ideas.

We find a primitive form of Buddhism, with its four great truths, conveying the simple idea that as all states of existence which we can conceive are states of vanity, sorrow, and change, the object of the wisely pious must be to escape from them, and that it is possible to escape from them by eradicating all delight in worldly pleasure, and raising the mind to that intellectual state in which there is no longer any cleaving to existence, but a tranquil readiness to pass into the perfect rest of Nirwana.

We find monastic Buddhism sharing the fate which must attend all religions which encourage a professional class of monks, or men who lead unnatural lives, that is cumbered with dogmas and absurdities, the result of warped, fantastic, and prurient minds. We do not find an Athanasian Creed; for so far as this book enlightens us, we find that the Buddhist speaks of heaven rather than of hell, and never thinks of such uncharity as to damn everlastingly those who differ with him. But nevertheless we find that the professional religious class, in the absence of useful occupation, has invented an intolerable terminology, has multiplied ridiculous distinctions, has twisted the elementary principles into all manner of shapes, and has invented a system of meditation which, in lieu of expanding the mind, tends to contract it almost to idiocy.

We find Brahminical superstitions, a continual reference to Brahmin soothsayers and the Vedas, and an adherence to Brahminical rites in all matters pertaining to royal ceremonials. Those who know that by the Brahmins the Buddhists were extirpated from Central India, the birthplace of their religion, must wonder to see Brahmins and Buddhists pictured side by side in harmony. Yet this story gives no undue idea of the position of the royal Brahmins in Siam. On every great occasion the Brahmin soothsayers are consulted, in every state ceremony they are prominent personages; yet they are genuine Brahmins, and not Buddhists, and worship in their own Brahman temple, full of grotesque and lascivious gods.

We find Indra and Brahma, and other Hindu divinities, and indeed a cosmogony and mythology mainly drawn from the Hindus, and only altered in the divinity being denied. The gods are but mortal beings in a superior state of transmigration.

We find mention of the Naga or snake, powerful as the gods; we find a disc or wheel, Chakkra, reverentially brought into prominence as a mystic symbol; we find a Trinitarian idea represented as Buddha, the Law, and the Church; we find indications of relic worship associated with holy buildings, Topes,* or, as the Siamese call them, Phrachedis; we find one reference to the Suphasit or Confucian doctrines of propriety; and we find extraordinary importance attributed to the Sacred Feet.

We find what we may suppose to be local superstition in the mention of angels of gates and of trees; not but what these latter are also mentioned in the Nepalese "Life of Buddha," "Lalita Vistâra."

And lastly, we find, what I have seen in no other "Life of Buddha," a very curious passage representing Buddha offering adoration to a tree. I refer to the concluding passage in my translation.

Professor Fergusson's splendid work on "Tree and Serpent Worship" first drew my attention to the adoration of the tree at an early period of Buddhism; and I was much struck when I reflected on this illustrative passage. I am not yet inclined to go as far as Professor Fergusson, and call every sign of respect to an emblem a distinct worship; but I certainly believe the tree was an object of worship, and one of the very first objects of man's worship.

Some think that this sculpture-depicted worship of the tree, shown equally in the bas-reliefs of Assyria and India, was no more than the adoration now paid by intelligent Buddhists to their images of Buddha; the worship of an idea through an emblem, a vicarious worship; and they may be right. Yet it seems to me

* I mention Phrachedi (Chaitya) as the most common designation of a relic spire, but the word Tope is better reproduced in the word Sathup.

that before the mind of man was prepared for emblematic subtleties, for Arkite symbolism and other idolatries, while it was simple, straightforward, and uneducated, it would have led man to adore the tree. The primeval savage, pursued by a beast of prey, overtaken by a pitiless storm, or sinking under the fierce heat of the sun, would have found in some large tree a refuge excelling all others. On its branches was a hiding-place where he could rest safe from his fierce enemies; beneath its leafy canopy was shelter from the cutting hail or the intolerable heat. There was no dank smell, such as he found in his only other asylum, the caves, but a delicious fragrance offered itself for his enjoyment. Its ever-lovely foliage, lovely in the sun and lovely in the rain, inspired him with the sentiment of beauty; its size, its longevity, and its quiet majesty, inspired him with a sense of awe. It was beautiful, beneficent, and wonderful, and he venerated it. He picked up the fallen flowers that lay around, and placed them on a stone, so that they might not be trodden on. That act originated a worship, an altar, and a sacrifice.

Such seems to me a probable origin of the worship of the tree. The Pipul, Bodhi, or Bo-tree, the chief sacred tree of the Buddhists, has certainly some of the attributes which would account for its being selected above other trees as the typical tree of this worship. It is noble in dimensions and appearance. Its seeds have extraordinary vitality; and when a drop of moisture has caused them to shoot, even in a crack high in some lofty tower, they will not die, but forcing the thin air and the hard bricks to nourish them, they will send down their suckers to the earth; and then these suckers, growing into huge roots, will crack and rend the building, shiver and destroy it, and only preserve its memory by the huge fragmentary masses which it will for centuries retain clasped in its embrace. Its Sanscrit name, "Bodhi-tree," may be translated "The Tree of Wisdom." The same word, Bodhi, is also applied to the penetrating wisdom of a Buddha, and is said to be derived from a word, Budh, meaning to penetrate. If it obtained this name, Bodhi, independently, and not from connection with any religious myth, I suppose it may have originated in the above-described insinuating or "penetrating" character of its roots.

Great as is the variety of these elements, the more important points of Buddhism are not lost among them, but stand out with marked distinctness. When I say more important points of Buddhism, I do not mean points peculiar to, and originating in, Buddhism, but I mean points the belief in which is essential to all who would be called Buddhists.

It has been said that there is no special teaching in Buddhism, and that its tenets are the same as those of the Sânkhya and other schools of Indian philosophers. Certainly, as we read portions of the Sânkhya books, we recognise doctrines like those we meet in Buddhist books. In both we find that the great object of man is to destroy the misery inseparable from ordinary existence; in both we read the words, "Neither I am, nor is aught mine." Both systems are apparently grounded on ideas such as transmigration, &c., generally prevailing in India some two to three thousand years ago. Yet, as among other differences, we find that the Sânkhyas dwelt specially on the existence of a soul, while the Buddhists specially avoided all recognition of one, we cannot allow that the teacher or teachers of Buddhism felt bound by the principles of the early Sânkhya philosophy ascribed to Kapila. Still less could the Buddhists have valued the Yoga or theistical development of the Sânkhya system which asserted the existence of a God actively interested in the world, and making His law known by revelation,—beliefs incompatible with Buddhism.

Similarly with the Nyaya and other Indian sects, the metaphysical theories are at times identical, but the practical differences are radical.

The origin of these sects is, I believe, now considered to be posterior to the rise of Buddhism. The story of Buddha's life, however, assumes that there were philosophers before him, with whom he studied, and whose teachings were not opposed to his, but only failed in not going to the height of meditative science which he reached. In Buddhism there are eight degrees of the meditation called Dhyâna; these philosophers, we are told, could only attain to the seventh. The Yoga Sânkhyas have a system of Dhyâna meditation akin to that of the Buddhists, and possibly both drew the idea from the same source. I believe that Dhyâna was not a primitive institution of Buddhism; for though it has been associated with it long enough to be referred to several times in the "Life," I think the story would be quite complete if all those references were omitted. Dhyâna is not mentioned in the vital parts of the story.

The metaphysical system of Buddhism is now an important part of the religion; but we are by no means bound to believe that originally it was treated in any but a very broad way. A great many of the Buddhist classics—presumably the oldest—deal little in metaphysical niceties. Our oldest Buddhist records, that cannot have been corrupted, are the stone-cut edicts of King Asoka in the third century before Christ. Asoka, King of Magadha, desiring to extend the Buddhist religion, had edicts cut in stone in various parts of his dominions, of which several have been discovered, and deciphered by Prinsep and other scholars. Their teaching is marvellously simple. In one the King enjoins his subjects "not to slay animals;" in another, "to plant trees and dig wells by the road-sides, for the comfort of men and animals;" in another he desires "the appointment of teachers to superintend morals, and encourage the charitable, and those addicted to virtue;" in another he orders his subjects "to hold quinquennial assemblies for the enforcement of moral obligations—duty to parents, friends, children, relations, Brahmans and Sramanas (Buddhist monks)." "Liberality is good, non-injury of living creatures is good; abstinence from prodigality and slander is good." In others, he proclaims, "The beloved of the gods (himself) does not esteem glory and fame as of great value; for it may be acquired by crafty and unworthy persons." "To me there is not satisfaction in the pursuit of worldly affairs; the most worthy pursuit is the prosperity of the whole world. My whole endeavour is to be blameless towards all creatures, to make them happy here below, and to enable them to attain Swarga (heaven)."

Observe that it is not "Nirwana" which is to be sought, but heaven!

So free is the pious King from dogmatism, that though in one proclamation he declares that he has faith "in Buddha, the law, and the assembly," so far, at least, as to "the words which have been spoken by Buddha;" he in another edict declares himself no sectarian in the words, "ascetics of the different sects *all* aim at moral restraint and purity of disposition; but men have various opinions and various desires."

Such is an abstract of the Asoka edicts, and the picture they present of Buddhism, when compared with the picture of the metaphysical Buddhism of the monks, seems to me as cool and refreshing as is the "Sermon on the Mount" of our religion, compared with the Thirty-nine Articles and Creeds of our Church.

I will now give a sketch of the chief points of Buddhist belief and practice mentioned in the "Life."

The first essential idea is that of transmigration—transmigration not only into other human states, but into all forms, active and passive.

Gods and animals, men and brutes, have no intrinsic difference between them. They all change places according to their merits and demerits. They exist because of the disturbance caused by their demerits. How they began to exist is not even asked; it is a question pertaining to the Infinite, of which no explanation is attempted. Even in dealing with the illustrious being who afterwards became Buddha, no attempt is made to picture a beginning of his existence, and we are only told of the beginning of his aspiration to become a Buddha, and the countless existences he subsequently passed through ere he achieved his object.

The teaching on this point may be said to recognise the equality of all beings, at the same time that it provides against the mischievous results European Socialists draw from that doctrine; which it does, by declaring the compatibility of intrinsic equality of being with actual difference of condition and advantages. It teaches that the relative positions of all beings are perfectly just, being self-caused by the good and evil destiny created by conduct in previous existences. It teaches that if a good man is poor and wretched, he is so because he has lived evilly in previous generations: if a bad man is prosperous, he is so because in previous generations he lived well.

Having thus declared the fact of transmigration, and the principle which causes its various states, Buddhism teaches that there is no real or permanent satisfaction in any state of transmigration; that neither the painless luxuries of the lower heavens, nor the tranquillity of the highest angels, can be considered as happiness, for they will have an end, followed by a recurrence of varied and frequently sorrowful existences.

Here is one of the great distinctions, the irreconcilable differences, between Buddhism and Christianity. Christians, even priests, have been known to write of the similarity between their religion and Buddhism. They saw corrupt Buddhists, dressed in gorgeous raiment, going through mummeries, and as they, too, prided themselves on the gorgeous vestments in which they concealed their spiritual humility, and as they, too, were addicted to mummeries, they did not see much difference between the religions. Possibly they had false ideas of Christianity, and equally false ideas of Buddhism. Passing from outside show to inner belief, the distinction is radical. Take this one point alone: Christians profess that their existence is the effect of the benign providence of God, and that they have something to thank God for. The few who divide the hoarded wealth of former generations, people who are well off, have every reason to believe this; and the many who are taxed to pay the debts of former generations, the people who are not well off, are taught to believe this without any special reference to their own circumstances. But Buddhists, rich or poor, acknowledge no providence, and see more reason to lament existence than to be grateful for it.

Nirwana, the extinction of all this kind of existence, must therefore be the object of the truly wise man. What this extinction is may perhaps have never been defined. Certainly it has been the subject of endless contention by those who think themselves capable of dealing with the infinite, and analysing the beginning and the end. All I can see of it in this "Life" is that it is now considered to be peace, rest, and eternal happiness. The choicest and most glorious epithets are lavished on it by the Siamese (see Notes to "Life"—No. 6), but we are left as ignorant of it as we are of the heaven of Christians. We may call heaven an existence, but we are even less capable of realising that existence than we are of realising what Barthélemy St Hilaire calls, with professed horror, the annihilation or non-existence of Nirwana.

I believe that most men recognise sleep as a real pleasure. Certain it is that after a hard day's toil, bodily or mental, man longs for sleep; and if his overtasked body or too excited brain deprives him of it, he feels that the deprivation is pain. Yet, what is sleep? It is, to all intents and purposes, temporary non-existence, and during its existence we do not appreciate its temporariness. The existence during sleep, when sleep is perfect, appreciates no connection with the waking existence. When it is imperfect, it is vexed by dreams connected with waking existence, but that is not the sleep which men long for.

The ordinary Siamese never troubles himself about Nirwana, he does not even mention it. He believes virtue will be rewarded by going to heaven (Sawan), and he talks of heaven, and not of Nirwana. Buddha, he will tell you, has entered Nirwana, but, for his part, he does not look beyond Sawan. A man of erudition would consider this Sawan to be the heaven (Dewaloka) of Indra, a heaven that is not eternal. The ordinary Siamese does not consider whether or not it be eternal; it is at least a happy state of transmigration of vast duration, of which he does not recognise the drawbacks, and it is quite sufficient for his aspirations.

This Sawan is the Siamese form of the Sanscrit word used for heaven in those primitive records, the edicts of Asoka, mentioned above. It is the Sanscrit Svarga.

Whatever Nirwana may be, Siamese Buddhists assume it to be more desirable than anything they can define as existence, and the question they ask is not; "How shall it be defined?" but "How can it be attained?"*

Before giving their answer to this question, I must

* In Note 6, page 165, I have given an extract from Professor Max Müller's remarks on Nirvana, in his introduction to "Rogers' Buddhaghosha's Parables." I ought in the same place to have given Mr R. C. Childers' note on the subject, which appeared in Trübner's *Literary Record* of June 25, 1870. Mr Childers writes as follows:—"I venture to propose a theory of Nirvana, which may, perhaps, afford the true solution of that important problem. It is well known that in the

speak of the Buddhist idea as to what we call the soul.

The Buddhist who differs from us in recognising a law of nature, without seeking for a Maker of that law, also differs from us in assuming a continuation of existence, without defining a soul as that which is continued. For all practical purposes we may speak of a soul as that which passes from one state of existence to another, but such is not the Buddhist idea, at least, not the idea of Buddhist metaphysicians.

According to them, it is not the soul or self which is reborn, but the quality, the merit and demerit. Individual existence (Djâti) is but a part of general exist-

Buddhist books there are two distinct sets of epithets applied to Nirvana, the one implying a state of purity, tranquillity, and bliss, the other implying extinction or annihilation. This circumstance has given rise to endless discussions relative to the true nature of Nirvana, the result being that the most conflicting views have been held upon this question by European scholars. The theory I have to propose is one which, if true, will, I think, meet all difficulties, and reconcile expressions in the Buddhist texts, even the most opposite and antagonistic. It is, that the word Nirvana is applied to *two different things*, namely—first, to the annihilation of existence, which is the ultimate goal of Buddhism; and secondly, to the state of sanctification, or, as we should say, "conversion," which is the stepping-stone to annihilation, and without which annihilation cannot be obtained. According to this view, the term *Anupadhiçesha*, "void of all trace of the body" (see Burnouf, Int. p. 589), is not merely an epithet of Nirvana generally, but a *distinctive* epithet, distinguishing that Nirvana which is the extinction of being from *Upadhiçeshanirvâna*, "Nirvana in which the body remains," that is to say, the blissful state of one who is walking in the Fourth Path. I advance this theory not without hesitation, for though I have collected a great deal of evidence in support of it, I feel that I have not as yet proved it to my satisfaction. I am, however, actively prosecuting my inquiries, and I hope some day to return to this important subject."

The fourth path is that of Arhat, or perfect saint. Mr Childers has lately read an important paper on this subject before the Royal Asiatic Society, which will appear in their Journal. Vol. v., part ii.

ence (Bhava); and general existence is but the result of the pre-existence of distinction caused by merit and demerit. Commonly, merit and demerit, in the active potential condition, must have an effect in producing the general existence suited to them. I will not now enlarge upon the doctrine of Karma, as it is discussed at some length in the "Modern Buddhist."

In my explanation of Buddhist ideas, I at times use the word soul, because it facilitates the comprehension of the idea I want to convey, and because I have not been able to find any other way of conveying it. The Buddhist tells me there is no soul, but that there is continuation of individual existence without it. I cannot explain his statement, for I fail thoroughly to understand it, or to appreciate the subtlety of his theory. Perhaps it is to be understood by comparison with the "line" of a mathematician. The line is length, without thickness or breadth; but very few people can conceive it by such a definition. Again, the "line" is produced by the motion of a point; but a point has no dimensions. So we see a "line" arising from that which has no dimensions. And indeed, all the definiteness which we thought we saw in our carefully drawn geometrical problem passes into the difficult abstraction of relative motion and relative position.

This mathematical abstraction is assuredly true, and it seems to me that by analogy we may consider the "line" or continued individual existence to be made up of the motion or succession of points, which are separate individual existences. The point is nothing but an idea realising the rest or motion arising from any cause; and the soul is also but an idea realising the disturbance caused by merit and demerit.

The line is an infinite one; it is greater than any which has dimensions, yet we cannot recognise the dimension which is its only material quality—we have left only the abstract idea of direction or tendency.

Now for the answer to the above stated question, "How to obtain Nirwana?"

The answer is, that, as all that we define as existence is (within the limits of our thought) self-caused, is the result of a law that every act, word, or thought must be followed by its effect, we can annihilate such existence, by removing all cause for future action; and as this cause, that is to say, our every thought and word and act, is voluntary, or the result of desire, we must eradicate all desire, and shall then be free to enter Nirwana.

Tracing backwards the chain of causation, we find that ignorance is the first cause of which desire or worldly cleaving is but an effect. Ignorance is not really a first cause, for, as the modern Buddhist tells us, Buddha would not teach of the beginning, and Buddhism has nothing to do with first causes, which pertain to the infinite. But it is a first cause within the limits to which reason can penetrate; inasmuch as, but for ignorance, all beings would infinitely, before this time, have perceived that Nirwana was the only object desirable, and would have destroyed all that prevented its attainment, that is, would have destroyed existence.

The ignorance of those who lived before us, caused us to be born. Our own desire or affection for worldly things, causes existence to be continued. We come then to the means of destroying desire or affection for the world.

The four pre-eminent truths of Buddhism (see note 71 to Life), which declare the principles I have enlarged on in the preceding pages, do not help us much here. The fourth truth, instead of pointing out a means to attain a state of purity, simply asserts that purity is a consequence of entering into the paths of the saints, or the eightfold path of purity (notes to Life, Nos. 14 and 78). Extending our inquiry, we find that man by perseverance, continued through countless successive births, can of himself become a Buddha, a teacher of the paths, but that the majority of those who enter the paths are only led into them by the personal influence of a Buddha; and that when the earth is not enlightened by the teaching of a Buddha, the most remarkable religious attainments * will not lead men into the paths to Nirwana, but will only so far fit them for its reception, that after some further angelic and human experiences, they will, by the inherent power of their accumulated merit, be born to meet a Buddha, and by his teaching, be led into the paths of the saints.

The object of man must therefore be, the accumulation of merit, and repression of demerit, so as to fit himself to benefit by the teachings and influence of the next Buddha.

To this end, Buddhism inculcates a virtuous and self-denying life, the practice of charity, and the exercise of meditation.

Whether we read the opinions of the Wesleyan missionary, Spence Hardy, or the Roman Catholic Bishop, Bigandet, or the philosophic student of all religions, Max Müller, we find the highest praise

* See story of Kaladewila, in chap. iv. of the Life of Buddha.

awarded to the moral teachings of Buddhism. I believe this Buddhist gospel will confirm their views.

The main rules of a virtuous life, that is, the five principal commandments, are—

1. Not to destroy life.
2. Not to obtain another's property by unjust means.
3. Not to indulge the passions, so as to invade the legal or natural rights of other men.
4. Not to tell lies.
5. Not to partake of anything intoxicating.

Other commandments mentioned in the Life relate to the repression of personal vanity, greed, fondness for luxury, &c.; and among evil tendencies, especially singled out for reprobation, we find covetousness, anger, folly, sensuality, arrogance, want of veneration, scepticism, and ingratitude. These bad qualities are personified as leaders of the army of Mara, the evil one, who, with a curious parallelism to our story of Satan, is made out to be an archangel of a heaven even higher than that of the beneficent Indra.

Of the practice of charity, it is not requisite to say much here. The whole character of Buddha is full of charity, insomuch that, although his perfection was such that at almost an infinite period before he became Buddha, he might, during the teaching of an earlier Buddha, have escaped from the current of existence, which he regarded as misery, he remained in that current, and passed through countless painful transmigrations, in order that he might ultimately benefit, not himself, but all other beings, by becoming a Buddha, and helping all those whose ripe merits could only be perfected by the teaching of a Buddha.

Meditation is regarded by Buddhists as the highest means of self-improvement. It is referred to in the Life, under three classes, called Kammathan, Bhâvana, and Dhyâna, which are described in notes 87, 10, and 65.

The Kammathan meditation on the nature of elementary substances, leads to the thorough appreciation of their impermanence and unsatisfactoriness; the Bhâvana meditation on the characteristics of charity, pity, joy, sorrow, and equanimity, leads the mind to a pure state of intellectuality; and the Dhyâna meditation, each step of which is accompanied by a state of ecstacy or trance, is supposed, during its continuance, actually to remove him who is absorbed in it from subjection to the ordinary laws of nature; indeed, it is supposed to be such a proof of power in him who can achieve it, that he will, at the same time, become a master of magical arts, such as flying, changing his form, &c., &c. It is, in fact, a kind of spiritualism. We find that the modern Buddhist speaks of these magic powers with great contempt. He laughs at books which contain such stories, saying they are unprofitable reading; but perhaps his allusion is rather to secular than to religious novels. He, however, tells us that there are no saints now-a-days, and I think we may add, there are none who can achieve the state of Dhyâna.

With meditation is connected the system devised to facilitate its practice, monastic asceticism. The Life assumes that there were religious bodies, devoted to asceticism, before Buddha began to teach; it shows Buddha imitating them in the practice of extreme austerities, and after a long course of them, relaxing the severity of his discipline, and declaring a middle course to be the best. In one passage, the self-inflicted torture of some classes of ascetics, is particularly reprobated.

In Siam, the monastic vow is not binding for life, but can be, and is cancelled, by the authority of the superior of the monastery, whenever application is made to him. This rule leads to every Siamese man spending at least three months of his life in a monastery. While in the monastery, he is supported by the alms of the pious.

With a few words on prayer, I shall conclude this sketch of Siamese Buddhism.

Prayer is not a Buddhist practice, for the simple reason, that Buddhists have no divine being to pray to. What some writers designate as Buddhist prayers, are not prayers at all. Palligoix, in his "Grammatica Linguæ Thai," gives the Pali and Siamese text of what he calls "tres preces valdè in honore apud Siamenses," which, on examination, I find not to be prayers, but merely sentences for repetition. The first, is a simple list of the thirty-two elements, into which their philosophers resolve the body; the repetition of which is supposed to assist meditation on the vanity and misery of existence. The second, is a list of the epithets of Buddha, designed to help meditation on the excellence of Buddha. The third, is the creed or profession of belief in Buddha, his law, and his church. It is the habit of both monks and laymen to recite formulas of this kind, but that habit cannot properly be called prayer.

There is perhaps something of the nature of prayer in the request to a living Buddha, to reward an offering by some particular re-birth, such as is illustrated in our first chapter, by Maia's desire expressed to the former Buddha Wipassi—"May I be, in some after generation, the mother of a Buddha like thyself." I have also, in my translation, found it convenient to use the word prayer, for the practice of expressing a firm determination * or desire, addressed to no one in particular, but being an invocation of the power existing in him who prays, and dependent for its success on the inherent force of his merits and demerits. As an example, take the incident of Buddha throwing into the air the long locks he had just cut off, and crying, "If, indeed, I am about to attain the Buddhahood, let these locks remain suspended in the air;" and they remained suspended by virtue of his merits.

The Life, however, illustrates a real form of prayer, resulting from superstitions grafted on to Buddhism; we find it in the girl Suchada's prayer to the angels of the tree, to grant her a happy marriage and a male child; and we find it in the prayer of Maia's mother, "Hear me, all ye angels! In that I am old, and shall not live to see the child that this my daughter will bring forth to be the Holy Teacher, may I after death be re-born in the heavens of the Brahmas, and thence descend to listen to the teaching of the Wheel of the Law, and so escape further evils in the circle of transmigration."

Prayer of this kind is not uncommon; for the Siamese are angel worshippers as well as Buddhists, and many of them, ignorant of their own religion, without doubt pray not only to angels, but to Buddha, and worship him with offerings. They are encouraged in angel worship by their popular novels, from one of which I extract the following example:—"Then the

* In Siamese called Athithan.

queen, raising her hands over her head, did homage to the angels of all places who had power, possessions, and dignity, and called on them to be benevolent to her child, to help, protect, and shield him."

I have dilated somewhat on this subject of prayer, because I have been asked to explain it by men who, after a residence of some years in Siam, have failed to comprehend it. They have heard men fervently repeating these formulas, and to all appearance praying. They have read of the Northern Buddhists turning the praying-wheel, a box full of texts, the turning of which is supposed to be as efficacious as the actual repetition of them; and they naturally accept the dictionary translation of "suet mon" as to pray, rather than the, in my opinion, more correct interpretation "to recite mantras, *i.e.*, verses, or formulas."

. . . . .

My Essay on the Footprint of Buddha originated in this wise:—

About two years ago I was in very bad health, and, seeking change of air and scene, made a journey to the Footprint. I had no intention of publishing anything on the subject. I did not impose upon myself the task of inquiring closely into what I saw; and I did not make any notes.

Some twelve months afterwards, Mr Trübner, seeing a drawing of the Footprint in my possession, considered it of sufficient interest to warrant his publishing a photograph of it; and asked me to prepare a memoir to accompany it, for gratuitous distribution. I promised to do so. The memoir proved longer than Mr Trübner had anticipated, and by his advice was reserved for this book.

The Footprint superstition does not seem to me to

be one of much importance, and I can scarcely expect that any but residents in Siam will take much interest in my attempt to show its present state and probable origin.

The recollections of what I saw on my journey to Phra Bat (Holy Foot), which is the name both of the Footprint and the hill on which it is indented, will, I hope, be not altogether uninteresting to those who can care little about the Footprint itself.

. . . . .

I should have much preferred withholding, not only the Essay on the Footprint, but the whole of this book for revision with native aid in Siam. My return to Siam is, however, indefinitely postponed, and I have, therefore, sent my work to the printer in what may be called a rough state.

It is now my duty to mention some of those greater labourers in the field of Buddhism, whose works have been most useful to me, and are essential to the European student of that religion.

The most important of all are E. Burnouf's "Introduction a l' Histoire du Buddhisme Indien," Paris, 1844; and his "Lotus de la Bonne Loi," Paris, 1852; to which latter are attached twenty-one very important essays on various points of Buddhist scholarship. M. E. Burnouf was not only an extraordinary scholar, but also a beautiful writer, and it is remarkable that the original edition of his works should be still procurable uncut. His labours were mainly founded on the study of the Sanscrit classics, forwarded by Mr Brian H. Hodgson from Nepal; but he was also acquainted with some of the Pali classics of the Ceylonese or Southern Buddhists, and he was assisted by the preceding labours of Mr Hodgson, Csoma de

Körös, and the Hon. G. Turnour. Csoma de Körös was one of the most remarkable travellers that ever lived. Without any resources but his ability, he made his way overland from Hungary to Thibet, searching for the origin of the Hungarian race. In Thibet he devoted himself to the study of Buddhism, and finally made his way to Calcutta, where he was welcomed and enabled to make his knowledge known to the world.

The Hon. G. Turnour's principal contributions to Buddhism were translations from the Ceylonese Pali classics, with valuable essays accompanying them, published as "The Mahawanso," and "Pali Annals." I found the "Pali Annals," which contain a classical Life of Buddha, extremely useful when translating the Life from the Siamese. I was also indebted to Ph. E. Foucaux's French translation of the Thibetan Rgya Tcher Rol Pa, a version of the Sanscrit classic Lalita Vistâra. The work is tedious, for it is a close translation of a most tedious book. It is very agreeable to turn from it to M. Foucaux's charming Essay on Nirwana, a critique on the controversy between M Barthélemy St Hilaire, the attacker of Buddhism, and M. Obry, its learned defender.

I now come to the writer whose works are best known among those whose knowledge of Buddhism is gained from English sources, the Rev. R. Spence Hardy, a Wesleyan missionary, long resident in Ceylon, to whom all honour is due for his candour in dealing with that which he desired to destroy, and whose "Manual of Buddhism," and Eastern Monachism" are mines of information. These works are, if I am not misinformed, both out of print, and if so, the owner of the copyright might do well either to reprint them or to have a digest of the two works prepared for publication.

The Roman Catholic Bishop, Bigandet, who has studied Buddhism in Burmah, has published a very complete biography of Buddha, in his "Life or Legend of Gaudama, the Buddha of the Burmese," to which are added some interesting appendices.* The bishop is not merely tolerant, but generous, in his endeavours to do justice to Buddhism. I do not, however, always agree with his statements, as will be found by readers of this work.

I cannot attempt to give a complete biography of Buddhism; those who desire a convenient list of books and papers relating to this religion will find one in Otto Kistner's cheap little pamphlet, entitled, "Buddha and his Doctrines." † I think it a pity that such a title was given to the essay, which is only valuable for the list of books, papers, etc., it contains; and which has in it very little about Buddha and his doctrines, and that little very unsatisfactory. I should have liked the title for this book of mine.

Among the books which have been especially consulted by me whilst writing these pages, I must also mention Max Müller's translation of the "Dhammapada," from the Pali, with which is published Capt. Rogers' translation from the Burmese of "Buddhaghosha's Parables." ‡ The Rev. S. Beal's "Travels of Buddhist

* The Life or Legend of Gaudama, the Buddha of the Burmese, with Annotations, the Ways to Neibban, and Notice on the Phongyies or Burmese Monks. By the Right Reverend P. Bigandet, Bishop of Ramatha, Vicar-Apostolic of Ava and Pegu. 8vo. Trübner & Co.

† Buddha and his Doctrines. A Bibliographical Essay. By Otto Kistner. 4to, sewed, 2s. 6d. Trübner & Co.

‡ Buddhaghosha's Parables, translated from the Burmese. By Captain H. T. Rogers, R.E. With an Introduction, containing Buddha's Dhammapada, or Path of Virtue, translated from Pali. By E. Max Müller. 8vo, cloth. 1870. Trübner & Co.

Pilgrims," being the narrative (translated from Chinese) of the travels of enthusiastic Chinese Buddhists, in the fifth and sixth centuries, to increase their religious knowledge, and obtain books, in Central India, the Holy Land of Buddhism.* Professor Fergusson's "Tree and Serpent Worship." General Cunningham's "Bhilsa Topes," and "Geography of Ancient India." Mr R. C. Childers' translation from the Pali of the Khuddaka Patha, or lesser readings, a small but valuable pamphlet contributed to the Journal of the Royal Asiatic Society.

I have also used, and referred to in my notes to the Life, Pallegoix's "Grammatica Linguæ Thai," Bradley's "Bangkok Calendars," Skeen's "Adam's Peak," Colebrooke's "Essays on the Philosophy of the Hindoos," Low's "Essays on the Phra Bat, etc.," published in the Journal of the Royal Asiatic Society, and Bastian's "Reisen in Siam."

The most readable popular work on Buddhism that I have yet met with, is M. Barthélemy St Hilaire's "Bouddha et sa Religion." It is a beautifully written book, the production of a master of language, a most learned man, a member of the Institute of France. Mainly a compilation from the works of Burnouf, Foucaux, Stanislas Julien, and Spence Hardy, it contains much accurate information on Buddhism; but most unfortunately the learned writer, leaving the safe guidance of the eminent authorities above mentioned, has included in his book a critique on Buddhism and the civilisation of Buddhist nations, founded on apparent misinformation.

* Travels of Fah Hian and Sung Yun, Buddhist Pilgrims from China to India. Translated from the Chinese. By S. Beal, a Chaplain in H.M. Fleet, &c. Crown 8vo.

M. Barthélemy St Hilaire, who has perhaps never seen living Buddhists, has conceived a violent horror for what he describes as Atheism and Annihilation, and it has led him to attack Buddhism with a vigour of persecuting assertion, which must be wondered at by those who have read the tolerant writings of men who have lived among Buddhists for long periods—Bishop Bigandet, for example.

Whether Buddhism is truly a religion of Atheism and Annihilation is, to a certain degree, a moot point, for indeed it is doubtful what those words mean. The terms Theism and Atheism, Immortality and Annihilation, involve infinite considerations, which, in my humble opinion, we are so little capable of thoroughly comprehending, that I, though a Theist, am unwilling to apply to a Buddhist a term which is held in reproach. The word Atheist is among us a word of reproach, and I do not like to apply it to those who, so far as I see, do not deny the existence of a God, but only reverentially abstain from defining that which it is impossible to comprehend.

Nevertheless, as Buddhism (at least the Southern Buddhism) recognises no eternal, personal God, actively interested in the world, it is what most people would call Atheistic, and I shall not dispute the correctness of the epithet.

Also as Buddhism, according to my appreciation of it, regards the highest aim of man to be the peace resulting from the utter absence of all that we understand to be connected with existence, I cannot decline to allow the term Nihilistic to be applied to it.

I must accept it as being Atheism and Annihilation, only hoping that men will not too rashly believe that they thoroughly understand these terms, and hoping that they will, if interested in Buddhism, read the arguments of Obry, Foucaux, Max Müller, and Childers on these points.

While I accept so far M. Barthélemy St Hilaire's definitions of Buddhism, I cannot but lament that he should have been misled as to the practical effect of those beliefs on Buddhist nations, causing him to attribute to religious belief differences in civilisation which perhaps are due to other causes.

M. Barthélemy St Hilaire candidly acknowledges that he is a partizan writer. He commences his work with the acknowledgment that he is not attempting to do justice to a religion which it is difficult for Europeans to view without prejudice, but has one sole object, that is, to strengthen that prejudice. His opening words are—"En publiant ce livre sur le Bouddhisme, je n'ai qu'une intention : c'est de rehausser par une comparaison frappante la grandeur et la vérité bienfaisante de nos croyances spiritualistes."

To obtain the striking comparison, he simply misrepresents the civilisation of between three and four hundred millions of men, and coupling this misrepresentation with an ever-recurring appeal to prejudice, in the form of skilfully introduced "deplorable abysses of Atheism and Annihilation," he produces in some degree the desired contrast.

On page 180 of the edition of 1866, in a passage apparently referring to all Buddhists, but especially mentioning the Chinese, Tartars, Mongols, and Thibetans, he actually tells us that "These people have no books but those of their religion ; they have not let their imagination, ill-regulated as it is, wander to other subjects ; and the most part of Buddhist nations has no literature but that of the Church (Sutras).

Of Tartars, Mongols, and Thibetans, I am unable to speak, having no knowledge of their literature; but of Chinese and some other Buddhist nations I am able to assert (and to prove my words by catalogues, etc., existing in Europe), that they have a large secular literature. They have an extensive imaginative literature, including many novels of no small interest; they have histories, law-books, and treatises on medical and other arts; even the luxuries of literature, elaborately illustrated works on artistic design, are to be found in China; and not only do these things exist, but the arts of printing and woodcutting have, in China and Japan, made books very cheap, and given the poor great facilities for study.

Not satisfied with this misrepresentation as to the literary state of Buddhist nations, M. St Hilaire adds to it the charge that Buddhism has been unable to organise equitable and intelligent societies.

I will not say that Buddhism has organised such societies, for it has not that meddling propensity which marks some other religions, and it does not set itself up as the organiser of society; but it is clear enough that M. St Hilaire means, by his assertion, that the natives, where Buddhism is professed, have not been able to organise such societies.

The societies or systems of government now existing in China or Siam have fairly flourished for long periods, despite all their deficiencies. The people have not found it necessary to change their form of government once in every decate, nor even once a century. The Siamese Government manages to rule a country as large as England with a fair amount of comfort to its people, and little annoyance to its neighbours. Unwieldy China is ruled in a manner that certainly shows a great deal of intelligence. I grant that these governments cannot claim to be perfect models of equity and intelligence, but indeed, if a Siamese asked me to point out a perfect government in Europe, I should be unable to do so.

An Asiatic reader of M. St Hilaire's book would probably be interested to know what M. St Hilaire considers to be an intelligent and equitable government, for with the vagueness which not uncommonly characterises those who talk about "grandeur," he does not define what he means by his words. To which of the many governments that have during the last century ruled his spiritualistic country, does he prefer to ascribe that character?

Eminent philosophers have denied that the superior civilisation of Europe is attributable to the prevailing religion; and when we see the head of the Catholic Church fulminating orders in council against the exercise of men's intellects, we recognise a great testimony to the truth of these philosophers' views. The modern Buddhist, in reply to a missionary who boasted of European civilisation with its railways and telegraphs, acknowledged the advantage of those things, but pertinently asked, "Are Christians happier than other men?"

The terrible war that has lately raged, and a new outbreak of which can only be prevented by force, and not by civilisation, affords a very sad answer to the Asiatic philosopher's question. I am afraid that our religious education is not entirely blameless for these wars. We have given up that proud feeling of being the special children of God, as distinguished from other men, which characterised the old Jews; yet our earliest ideas are formed from the history of that nationally selfish race, and we are full of what seem to me to be very objectionable notions of patriotism. We encourage, rather than discourage, differences of race, language, and territory, and so organise nations that the wonder is, not that we fight so often, but that we do not fight oftener.

On such grounds, I think that we must not be too jubilant on the success of our civilisation as between nation and nation, nor too rashly adduce it as a proof of the "vérité bienfaisante" of spiritual ideas.

When I turn to our domestic condition, I still fail to find any very sufficient proof of M. Barthélemy St Hilaire's theory, and I fail also to find a satisfactory answer to the Buddhist's question. Much as my countrymen excel the Siamese in arts and sciences, which ought to promote the general happiness of all ranks, I cannot but feel that vast numbers of us, the poor, may well envy the corresponding class in Siam.

It may be answered that the difference in physical comfort is mainly due to climate, and I am ready to agree to the truth of this if I may, at the same time, ascribe to the same cause our greater physical strength and practical intellectual power.

Fairly to judge of the difference due to religious ideas, I believe one must judge of them as seen side by side.

It would not be fair to make the comparison between Buddhism and Christianity as seen in Siam, for, as I have before said, Christianity does not flourish there. It is, however, sufficient for my purpose to compare the Siamese Buddhists with their neighbours, the Malays, who, being Mahometans, ought, according to M. Barthélemy St Hilaire's theory, to have shown the superior civilisation due to spiritualistic belief.

While Siam has made remarkable progress, produced men like the late king, the modern Buddhist, and the present regent (under whose auspices his country is rapidly progressing), what progress has been made by the Malays, and what eminent men have they produced?

So far as I have seen, they have not produced one eminent man, and have not progressed one step beyond what has been forced on them by the Siamese Regent on the one side, and the British Government of Singapore on the other. The Siamese Buddhist materialist goes ahead, while the Malay Mahometan spiritualist, with all his grandeur of idea, drops behind in the race of civilisation. The Siamese materialists, modifying their laws as they find expedient, year by year strengthen their position. The Malay spiritualists —unable, apparently, to organise societies—are broken up into a number of small factious states mainly dependent on their better organised neighbours, the English, Dutch, and Siamese.

It is not fair to ascribe these differences to religion, for religion is but one of many causes. Race, climate, nature of the country, etc., have each of them had as much, if not more, effect than religion. Religions may differ widely in their solutions of the greatest of mysteries, but happily they differ less in their definitions of what is good and evil conduct. The more elastic a religion is, the more modifications it admits of, by so much the more likely is it to harmonise with the ever-changing necessities of civilisation. Buddhism does not seem to be inelastic or unsuitable to civilisation, and judged on the charges laid against it by M. Barthélemy St Hilaire, it appears to me to stand at least as well as its numerically greatest spiritualistic rival, Roman Catholicism.

Had M. Barthélemy St Hilaire personally studied Buddhism in Buddhist countries, had he lived some years in Siam or Ceylon, he would surely have had a different opinion, both of the present condition and the future capabilities of the followers of that wide-spread religion.

I have lived long among Buddhists, and have experienced much kindness among them. Above all things, I have found them exceedingly tolerant.

In recognition of their hospitality, tolerance, and other good qualities, I have attempted this defence of them and their opinions.

This book of mine is but the superficial work of a man who is no scholar, who has not learned the classical languages of Buddhism, Sanscrit, and Pali, and unfortunately whilst in Siam was unaware how acceptable the labours of local students would be to Europeans.

Should the chances of life take me back to the country where I shall be most usefully employed, though perhaps not for my own advantage, for its climate plays havoc with my health, I shall hope a few years hence to rewrite this book in a much more complete manner. The Pali Dictionary of Mr Childers, now being printed, will immensely decrease the labour of students of Southern Buddhism, and whether from myself or from another, will, I hope, in a few years, elicit a more thorough book on Buddhism than any that has yet appeared.

PART I.

THE MODERN BUDDHIST;

BEING

THE VIEWS OF A SIAMESE MINISTER OF STATE ON HIS OWN AND OTHER RELIGIONS.

THE MODERN BUDDHIST.

Of the three hundred and sixty-five millions of men, the third of the human race who, according to a common estimate, profess in some form the religion of Buddha, the four million inhabitants of Siam are excelled by none in the sincerity of their belief and the liberality with which they support their religion. No other Buddhist country, of similar extent, can show so many splendid temples and monasteries. In Bangkok alone there are more than a hundred monasteries, and, it is said, ten thousand monks and novices. More than this, every male Siamese, some time during his life, and generally in the prime of it, takes orders as a monk, and retires for some months or years to practise abstinence and meditation in a monastery.

The principal works on Buddhism in our language are uninviting to the general reader. The most able translators have not been able to render the Buddhist classics anything but tedious to read, and it is seldom that the great authorities go beyond the classics. Such pleasing and instructive discourses as Max Müller's late lecture on Buddhistic Nihilism are rare indeed, and the most familiar accounts of Buddhism depict it surrounded by, and almost buried in, the mass of superstitions which have been from time to time connected with it.

Such treatment is no more fair than it would be fair to describe Christianity as inseparable from every monkish fable which has from time to time found credence. Indeed, it is still less fair, for Christianity has always had some check kept on alterations of its teachings, by the fact that some of its earliest apostles committed their views to writing, but Buddhism having, for upwards of four hundred years,* from the days when Samana Khodom, Gotama, or Buddha first taught it, been transmitted by oral tradition alone, must, in the very nature of things, have been overwhelmed with ideas which were not those of its founder.

Our object is to show something of the religion of Buddha apart from its grosser superstitious surroundings, not by our own analysis, but by extracts from the writings of a thoughtful Ṣiamese Buddhist on his own and other religions.

Somdet Phra Paramendr Maha Mongkut, the late King of Siam, has been called the founder of a new school of Buddhist thought, having, while himself a monk, eminent among monks for his knowledge of the Buddhist Scriptures, boldly preached against the canonicity of those of them whose relations were opposed to his reason, and his knowledge of modern science. His Majesty was a man of remarkable genius and acquirements. His powers as a linguist were considerable, and enabled him to use an English library with facility. Had he been able to publish his ideas at

* Buddhists themselves say four hundred and fifty years, but this is improbable. Some modern scholars are inclined to believe that the period was much less.

a late period of his life, we might have had still more enlightenment shown, than appears in the book we are about to present to our readers; but his position as king was a bar to his doing such a thing; he could do no more than in some measure inspire his minister, whose ideas were less advanced.

Chao Phya Thipakon, better known to foreigners as Chao Phya Phraklang, successfully conducted the foreign affairs of Siam from 1856, when Sir John Bowring's Treaty opened the country to foreign trade, until two years ago, when he retired into private life stricken with blindness. The minister was greatly esteemed by those his duties brought him in contact with; he was always open to argument, and never let anything disturb the courteous urbanity of his demeanour. It was his wont, when with those who could converse freely in Siamese, to end every official interview with a private discussion on some theoretical or transcendental subject, therein differing from all the other leading men in his country, whose thoughts and inquiries were always about material, mechanical, and practical subjects. For instance, if gunpowder was alluded to, he would expatiate on the advantage civilised nations derived from it, or would speculate on its combustion changing a solid into gas, while any other nobleman would have discussed either the best proportion of its ingredients, or the best place to buy it, and the right price to pay for it.

By many years of verbal inquiry, and by reading the elementary tracts published by missionaries in Siam, he acquired such knowledge as he has of European science and of foreign religions.

The results of his speculations he published two

years ago in the "Kitchanukit:" "a book explaining many things," which, independently of its internal qualities, is curious, as being the first book printed and published by a Siamese without foreign assistance. He thus states his reason for becoming an author :—

"I propose to write a book for the instruction of the young, being of opinion that the course of teaching at present followed in the temples is unprofitable. That course consists of the spelling-book, religious formulæ, and tales. What knowledge can any one gain from such nonsense as 'O Chan, my little man, please bring rice and curry nice ; and a ring, a copper thing round my little brother's arm to cling'? jingling sound without sense,—a fair example of a large class of reading exercise. I shall endeavour to write fruitfully on various subjects, material knowledge and religion, discussing the evidence of the truth and falsity of things. The young will gain more by studying this than by reading religious formulæ and novels, for they will learn to answer questions that may be put to them. My book will be one of questions and answers, and I shall call it 'a book explaining many things.'"

We can, from our own experience, confirm the character thus given to the education of children in monasteries, which are the only extensive educational establishments in Siam. The pupils who remain long enough in them, learn to read and to write their own language, and also, if clever, the Pali language in the Kawm, or old Cambodian character; but when the language is mastered, the literature it opens to them is for the most part silly and unprofitable. To quote again from our author :—

"Our Siamese literature is not only scanty but

nonsensical, full of stories of genii stealing women, and men fighting with genii, and extraordinary persons who could fly through the air, and bring dead people to life. And even those works which profess to teach anything, generally teach it wrong, so that there is not the least profit, though one studies them from morning to night."

The work, though mainly devoted to the comparison of Buddhism with other religions, commences with an account of native and foreign methods of reckoning time, the construction of calendars, the author's views on astronomy, the nature of air and water, &c., prefaced by the modest remark—

"Though I may be wrong, still, what I write will serve to stimulate men's thoughts, and lead to their finding out the truth."

It seems to us that much of this is inserted for the purposes of showing that the absurd cosmogony of the "Traiphoom,"* a work which the old school of Buddhists regard as sacred, is not wholly an essential part of the Buddhist religion; but that Samana Khodom or Buddha, even if he did not teach the truths of modern science, taught nothing opposed to them. It is also written, to keep in some degree the promise of the first page, that it shall be a book of education for the young, a book about many things. It is not until the author has warmed to his work that the religious and controversial element takes the place of every other.

It is not our purpose to refer much to this first

* The "Traiphoom" is the standard Siamese work on Buddhist cosmogony, &c. It was compiled from presumed classical sources in A.D. 1776, by order of the Siamese King, Phya Tak.

part of the book. There is a great deal of useful information in it, strangely mixed up with nonsense. The author has been at times deliberately deceived by his informants, and gravely quotes some very foolish stories which there is no use in repeating. We prefer to give, as an example of his style, a part of his discourse on rain.

"Now as to the cause of the dry and wet seasons, I will first give the explanation as it stands in the 'Traiphoom.' When the sun goes south near the heavenly abode of the Dewa Wasawalahok, the Lord of Rain, the Dewa finds it too hot to move out of his palace, and so it is dry season. But when the sun is in the north, out he goes, and sets the rain falling.

"Another statement is that in the Himaphan forest there is a great lake, named Anodat, and that a certain kind of wind sucks up its waters, and scatters them about. Another statement is, that the Naga King,* when playing, blows water high up into the air, where it is caught by the wind, and falls as rain. There is no proof of these stories, and I have no faith in them, for I cannot see where Wasawalahok lives, and I don't know whether he can make rain fall or not. As for the wind sucking up the water in the Himaphan† forest, that forest lying to the north, all clouds must needs form in the north, but as in fact they form at all points of the compass, how can we say they come from Himaphan? As for the Naga playing with water, no one has seen him, so there is no proof of it. The Chinese say rain falls because the

* The King of the Nagas—hooded serpents of immense size and power. For an account of them see the Essay on the Phra Bat.

† Or Himalayan forest. The Buddhist fairyland.

Dewas* will it, or because the Dragon shows his might by sucking up the sea water, which by his power becomes fresh. They having seen that in the open ocean a wind sometimes sucks up the water transparently into the sky, and that thence arise clouds, believe that the Dragon does it. There is no proof of this. The Brahmins and other believers in God the Creator, believe that He makes the rain to fall, that men may cultivate their fields and live. I cannot say whether God does this or not, for it seems to me that if so, He would of His great love and mercy make it fall equally all over the earth, so that all men might live and eat in security. But this is not the case. Indeed, in some places no rain falls for years together, the people have to drink brackish water, and cannot cultivate their lands, or have to trust but to the dew to moisten them; besides, a very great deal of the rain falls on the seas, the mountains, and the jungles, and does no good to man at all. Sometimes too much falls, flooding the towns and villages, and drowning numbers of men and animals; sometimes too little falls in the plains for rice to be grown, while on the mountain tops rain falls perpetually through seasons wet and dry. How can it be said that God, the Creator of the world, causes rain, when its fall is so irregular? We now come to the idea of philosophers, who have some proof of their theory. They say rain falls somewhere every day without fail; for the earth, the sky, and the sea are like a still, and it is a property of salt water to yield fresh by distillation. The heat of the sun draws up steam from the sea, and wherever there is moisture. Do not pools dry up? This steam is not lost, it flies

* Angels of earth, trees, and the lower heavens.

to cool places above, and collecting in the cold skies, becomes solid like ice, then, when the hot season arrives, this ice melts, and forms into clouds, floating according to the wind, and when a wind forces a cloud near the earth, the hills and earth act on it like a magnet, draw it down, and there is rain. Hence it arises that rain water is cooler than other water, for it is formed by melting ice, and wherever the sun goes, there it is rainy season."

We also give his remarks on epidemic diseases, which, like the preceding passage, illustrate his idea of the perfect equality that should result from divine justice.

"How is it that in some years fevers prevail, in others not; in some, ophthalmia, small-pox, etc., arise as epidemics; and in some, animals are attacked by epidemics?

"Those who believe in devils say they cause them. Those who believe in God the Creator say He inflicts them as a punishment. The Mahometans say that there are trees in heaven, on each of whose leaves is the name of a human being, and whenever one of these leaves withers and falls, the man whose name it bears dies with it. Old Siamese sages held that some King of Nagas mixed poison with the air.* Those who do not believe in devils ascribe epidemic diseases to the change of seasons, the change from heat to cold, and cold to heat, disturbing the body, which is healthy enough when the season is well set in, and become thoroughly hot, or cold, or rainy, as is the case. They further say, the evil element in the atmosphere is a

* Among the supernatural powers attributed to Nagas is that of poisoning by their breath.

poisonous gas, affecting all those whose bodily state cannot resist its entry. Epidemics among animals can be accounted for by the poisonous gas finding an affinity for the elements of the animals. I find corroboration in the fact that exposure to bad air brings on sicknesses which those who remain sheltered do not suffer from. Moreover, the sea water, which is a coarse atmosphere, when it is discoloured and stinking kills the fish which are in it, but those which are strong enough to swim out of the foul part escape. The same is seen with fish in a basin, which die if fresh water is not given to them. So we find many people live to old age without having the small-pox, by always running away from any place where it has broken out. In the same way outbreaks of fever are local, and danger is escaped by moving to another locality where there is none. Now, if it was a visitation of God, there would be no running away from it. I leave you to form your own opinion whether it is the work of devils, or the visitation of God, or the result of the fall of the leaves in heaven, or of a Naga King's poison, or of a bad atmosphere."

The tides he explains by "lunar attraction, which can be demonstrated by mathematics, and is a more reasonable idea than that of the Brahmins, some of whom believe that they are caused by winds blowing back the water in estuaries, and others that they are caused by flames rising from time to time up a chimney in the middle of the ocean, and forcing the water back towards the coast and rivers."

We shall now compare our author's view of the probable manner of formation of mountains and islands, with the account given in the "Traiphoom" of the coming into being of a new group of worlds. First our author's view.

"It is said in our old books that the world arose from rain-water, which, drying up, left the earth floating about over it like a lotus-leaf, and the hills were caused by the water boiling up. The earth was left heaped irregularly, like rice at the bottom of a boiling rice-pot, and in time the higher parts became rock. Some think that the world was created by Allah for the use and advantage of mankind, but I cannot believe it, when I think of the terrible rocks on which ships are wrecked, and of fiery mountains, which are certainly not an advantage to man. How, then, can we ascribe it to a Creator? Those who say the higher parts became rock, do not say how they became so. Philosophers think that when the earth was first formed there was fire beneath the surface, and that hills are due to that cause. And it is observed in other countries, as well as our own, that mountains and islands generally lie either in groups or in lines.

"And there is an inference of fire to be drawn from the fact that we can melt earth with fire, and it will become like rock or glass. I mention this only as a suggestion, for if the fire existed when the earth was formed, it should exist now; but no one has seen any hills arise in this way, and no one saw the world come into existence, so we cannot say anything for certain."

The "Traiphoom" view is, that the whole of space has been for ever occupied by an infinite number of Chakrawans, or groups of worlds, all exactly similar, and each embracing a world of men, with a series of heavens and hells, &c. From time to time a billion of these groups are annihilated by fire, water, or wind and a void remains, until the necessity of giving scope to merit and demerit * causes the void to be again filled. First there appears an impalpable mist, gradually changing to an immense rainfall, continuing until a great part of the void is filled with water. Then arises a whirlwind, which shapes the system, and dries up part of the water, causing the mountains and plains to appear in slow succession. During this time the only inhabitants of the system are the Brahmas, the highest order of angels, glorious beings, whose own radiance illuminates the system, who need no food, and have no sensual feelings. These Brahmas have, in the course of thousands of previous transmigrations in pre-existing worlds, gradually improved, until reaching that angelic state which is next to perfection. They have then degenerated, and some will continue to degenerate until they reach the most unhappy forms of life. This degeneracy commenced by one of them craving for food, and being so pleased on tasting it, that he could not refrain from continually eating thenceforth. Others followed his example. Their glory and luminosity left them, and, by degrees, gluttony being followed by other desires, the distinction of sex arose, their forms decreased in beauty, and they became human, then brutal, and, lastly, devilish.

We revert to our modern Buddhist. Eclipses, comets, meteors, and will-o'-the-wisps are in turn treated of mainly according to European ideas, and the common Siamese idea of the intervention of spirits

* The subject of "merit" and "demerit" is treated of later in the book. See p. 47, *seq.*

is ridiculed; but he claims that the theory of eclipses being caused by the dragon Phra Rahu swallowing the sun or moon, may be regarded as a parable veiling the truth; and he makes the somewhat bold statement that the great noise made in his country whenever there is an eclipse, the frantic beating of gongs and firing of guns, is not an effort on his countrymen's part to frighten the dragon, and make him drop the sun from his jaws, but is a sign of the joy of all men that their mathematicians are able to predict the time of such extraordinary events. This ingenious explanation seems more like a saying of the late king than that of the author of this book, and was probably the plea by which His Majesty justified himself for allowing his cannons to be fired on these occasions.

He fully adopts the general views of astronomy he has learned from Europeans, even to the theory of the plurality of solar systems, and then imagines the question put, "Is not this contrary to the teaching of Buddha?" His argument in reply is lengthy, comprising, firstly, an abstract of the "Traiphoom" cosmography; secondly, an account of the chief religions of the world, which, he argues, were all as opposed to true astronomical teaching as Buddhism is supposed to be; and thirdly, an exposition of what he considers to be Buddha's teaching on the subject, from which he deduces that Buddha knew the truth, and that the "Traiphoom" and other books of the class are uncanonical. His abstract of the "Traiphoom" cosmography, being intended for those who have already read that book, is not very definite; we shall therefore give our own in its place.

The universe consists of an infinite number of solar

systems (Chakrawan), each depending on a central mountain named Phra Men, or Meru. Around this central mountain are eight circular belts of ocean, divided from each other by seven annular mountains (Satta Boriphan). Outside of all is an eighth ring of mountains, called the Crystal Walls of the World. On the ocean between the seventh mountain-chain and the walls of the world, which is called the Great Ocean, are four groups of islands, each consisting of a principal island and 500 satellites. The group to the south, called Jambudvipa (Siamese, Chomphu Thawip), is that inhabited by man; the groups to the north, the east, and the west, are inhabited by beings akin to man, but differing in appearance. On the annular mountains, and on and above Meru, are the six lower heavens, inhabited by Dewas, or ordinary angels, whose pleasures are of a sensual nature, and who are blessed with an immense number of wives. Above them are nine tiers of heavens, which are subdivided into sixteen heavens, wherein dwell the Brahma angels (Siamese, Phrom), superior angels, whose pleasures are simply intellectual or meditative, but who are yet mundane, in that they have bodies or forms. Above them are the four highest heavens of the spiritual, or formless Brahma angels. The Dewa heavens are attainable by virtue and charity, but the Brahma heavens are entered only by those who have devoted themselves to the abstract meditation called by Buddhists Dhyâna (Siamese, Chan). The sun and moon are Dewa angels living in gold and silver palaces, who travel round and round on the plane of the summit of the mountain range next to Meru, which is named Yukunthon. Beneath the earth, at a distance of 100 miles, is the nearest of eight places of misery, or hells. The whole system is held up by an ocean, in which are vast fish, whose movements cause earthquakes. The ocean is supported in space by wind.

About one-third of the region of men, Jambudvipa, is taken up by the Himaphan forest—the Buddhist fairyland.

In the "Traiphoom" this system is elaborated in a most tedious manner, and the strictest measurements are given of every thing and place referred to.

It will be convenient for a while to omit our author's account of the great religions of the world, excepting so far as bears on the point of astronomy. He first gives the Brahminical cosmography, which closely resembles that in the "Traiphoom," differing only in that it names a creating God as the cause. He then traces from Brahminism the religions of Abraham, Christ, and Mahomet, asking where any of these teachers taught astronomy correctly, and sums up in the following words:—

"When philosophers found out the truth, the disciples of Mahomet put them in prison because they taught that which was opposed to the teaching of 'the Exact One,' which made out the world to be a plain, with the sun and moon revolving about it, much as our 'Traiphoom' does. But after a while, there being too many witnesses of the truth of what the philosophers asserted, they then adopted their ideas, and incorporated them into their religion. The ancients, whether Brahmins or Arabs, or Jews or Chinese, or Europeans, had much the same idea of cosmography, and their present ideas on the subject are the work of scientific men in modern times."

We now come to the third point, what was Buddha's teaching on astronomy.

"When the Lord Buddha was born in the land of the Brahmins, he knew all that was just, and how to deliver the body from all ills. This he knew perfectly. And he journeyed and taught in Brahmin countries, the sixteen great cities,* for forty-five years, desiring only that men should do right, and live suitably, so that they might escape sorrow, and not be subject to further changes of existence. Those who have studied Pali know that the Lord taught concerning the nature of life, and the characteristics of good and evil, but never discoursed about cosmography. It is probable that he knew the truth, but his knowledge being opposed to the ideas of the 'Traiphoom,' which every one then believed in, he said nothing about it. For if he had taught that the world was a revolving globe, contrary to the traditions of the people, who believed it to be flat, they would not have believed him, and might have pressed him with questions about things of which there was no proof, except his allegations; and they, disagreeing with him, might have used towards him evil language, and incurred sin. Besides, if he had attacked their old traditions, he would have stirred up enmity, and lost the time he had for teaching all living beings. Therefore he said nothing about cosmography. When a certain man asked him about it, he forbade him to inquire; he would not teach it himself, and forbade his disciples to speak of it. This can be seen in

* Central India, the neighbourhood of Benares. This statement gives up the popular idea of the Siamese that Buddha visited their country.

various Sutras; and where there are references to heaven and earth and hell in the sacred books, I presume they have found their way in as illustrations, etc. Yet there is an expression in those old books pointing out the truth for future men as to the revolution of the earth. The Pali expression is Wattakoloko, which, translated, is 'revolving world;' and those who did not know this translation, explained it as referring to the sun and moon turning round the world, because they did not fully comprehend it. After the religion of Buddha had spread abroad, a certain king, desiring to know the truth as to cosmogony, inquired of the monks, and they, knowing the omniscience of Buddha, and yet fearing that if they said Buddha never taught this, people would say 'your Lord is ignorant, and admired without reason,' took the ancient Vedas, and various expressions in the Sutras and parables, and fables, and proverbs, and connecting them together into a book, the 'Traiphoom,' produced it as the teaching of Buddha. The people of those days were uneducated and foolish, and believed that Buddha had really taught it; and if any doubted, they kept their doubts to themselves, because they could not prove anything.

"Had the Lord Buddha taught cosmography as it is in the 'Traiphoom,' he would not have been omniscient, but by refraining from a subject which men of science were certain eventually to ascertain the truth of, he showed his omniscience."

Our author, nevertheless, will not give up the tradition that Buddha visited the heaven called Davadungsa, and there taught the angels. He believes that omnipotence may be gained by perfect virtue, abstinence, and thought, and does not think it impossible that it should enable a man to visit the starry heavens.

"It cannot be asserted that the Lord did not preach in Davadungsa, any more than the real existence of Mount Meru can be asserted. I have explained about this matter of Meru, and the other mountains, as an old tradition. But with respect to the Lord preaching on Davadungsa as an act of grace to his mother, I believe it to be true, and that one of the many stars or planets is the Davadungsa world. The Lord Buddha disappeared for a period of three months, and then returned. Had he been hiding, that he might pretend he had been preaching to the angels in heaven, he would have been seen by somebody, and could not have kept quite concealed. The disciples, who must have brought him food, would surely not have kept the secret. It would have become matter of conversation and rumour. In truth, nothing was said against it, but in consequence of it great respect was shown, and the religion spread far and wide. It cannot be authoritatively denied that many saints have visited the abodes of the angels, for the worlds of heaven are beyond the knowledge of ordinary men."

Henceforward the book deals with none but religious subjects. The first selections we shall give are from his criticism of missionary tracts, and his conversations with their writers. Many readers will be shocked at his apparent irreverence. We beg to remind such persons that he, from education, sees these matters in an utterly different light to what it is seen by believers in a God actively interested in the world, and also that he naturally feels justified in treating with ridicule the ideas of those foreigners who send to his country a body of missionaries, who spare little sarcasm or insult in their never-ceasing endeavours to bring his religion into contempt. He, as a Buddhist, might believe in the existence of a God sublimed above all human qualities and attributes, a perfect God, above love and hatred and jealousy, calmly resting in a quiet happiness that nothing could disturb, and of such a God he would speak no disparagement; not from desire to please him, or fear to offend him, but from natural veneration. But he cannot understand a God with the attributes and qualities of men, a God who loves and hates and shows anger, a Deity who, whether described to him by Christian Missionaries, or by Mahometans or Brahmins or Jews, falls below his standard of even an ordinary good man.

"I have studied the Roman Catholic book, 'Maha Kangwon'—the Great Care—and it seems to me that the priests' great cares are their own interests. I see no attempt to explain any difficult and doubtful matters. If, as they say, God, when He created man, knew what every man would be, why did He create thieves? This is not explained. The book tells us that all those virtuous men who have taught religions differing from the Roman Catholic, have been enemies of God, but it does not explain why God has allowed so many different religions to arise and exist. How much do this and all other religions differ on this point from the religion of Buddha, which allows that there are eight kinds of holiness leading to ultimate happiness! (*i.e.*, does not insist on Buddhism being necessary to salvation).*

"The American missionary, Dr Jones, wrote a book

* This strange passage does not at all accord with the general teaching of Buddhists as to the "eight paths," which I explain in my notes to the Life of Buddha.

called the 'Golden Balance for weighing Buddhism and Christianity,' but I think any one who reads it will see that his balance is very one-sided; indeed, he who would weigh things ought to be able to look impartially at the scales.

"Dr Caswell remarked to me that if the religion of Buddha prevailed throughout the world, there would be an end of mankind, as all men would become monks, and there would be no children. This, he urged, showed that it was unsuited to be the universal religion, and therefore could not be the true religion. I replied that the Lord Buddha never professed that his religion would be universal. He was but as a transient gleam of light, indicating the path of truth. His religion was but as a stone thrown into a pool covered with floating weeds; it cleared an opening through which the pure water was seen, but the effect soon died away, and the weeds closed up as before. The Lord Buddha saw the bright, the exact, the abstruse, the difficult course, and but for the persuasion of angels would not have attempted to teach that which he considered too difficult for men to follow. The remark of the doctor really does not bear on the question (*i.e.*, on the truth of the religion)."

This answer is less to the point than most of the arguments of the Modern Buddhist. Had I been in our author's place, answering from a Buddhist point of view, I should have said that as Buddha recognised that all existence in this world was unsatisfactory and miserable, the suggested cessation of the renewal of the species was not a matter to be at all deplored.

"Dr Gutzlaff declared that 'Samana Khodom only taught people to reverence himself and his disciples, saying that by such means merit and heaven could be attained, teaching them to respect the temples, and Bo-trees,* and everything in the temple grounds, lest by injuring them they should go to hell, a teaching designed only for the protection of himself and his disciples, and of no advantage to any others.' I replied, 'In Christianity there is a command to worship God alone, and no other; Mahomet also taught the worship of one only, and promised that he would take into heaven every one who joined his religion, even the murderer of his parents, while those who would not join his religion, however virtuous their lives, should surely go to hell; also he taught that all other religions were the enemies of his religion, and that heaven could be attained by injuring the temples, idols, and anything held sacred by another religion. Is such teaching as that fit for belief? Buddha did not teach that he alone should be venerated, nor did he, the just one, ever teach that it was right to persecute other religions. As for adoration, so far as I know, men of every religion adore the holy one of their religion. It is incorrect of the doctor to say that Buddha taught men to adore him alone. He neither taught that such was necessary, nor offered the alternative of hell as all other religions do.'

"The doctor told me that 'Jehovah, our Creator, although jealously desirous that men should not hold false religions, permits them to hold any religion they please, because in His divine compassion, doing that which is best for them, He will not force man's con-

* This Bo, or Bodhi tree, is the tree under the shade of which Buddha attained to omniscience. It is to be found in most, if not all, Siamese monasteries.

version by the exercise of His power, but will leave it to their own free will.' I answered, 'Why did the Creator of all things create the holy chiefs (teachers) of the religions of the Siamese, Brahmins, Mahometans, and others? Why did He permit the teaching of false religions which would lead men to neglect His religion, and to suffer the punishment of hell? Would it not have been better to have made all men follow the one religion which would lead them to heaven? Mahometans hold that Allah sent prophet after prophet to teach the truth, but that evil spirits corrupted their teaching, and made it necessary for him to send an emanation from himself in human form (Mahomet) to teach the truth as they now have it. Brahmins hold that God the Father, ordering the descent of Siva in various avatars, as Krishna, and others, has so given rise to various sects; but that, whichever of these sects a man belongs to, he will, on death, pass to heaven, if only he has done righteously according to his belief. The missionaries hold that God Jehovah made all men to worship in one way, but that the devil has caused false teachers to arise and teach doctrines opposed to God. Such are the various stories told by Mahometans, Brahmins, and missionaries. My readers must form their own opinion about them.'

"I said to the missionary, 'How about the Dewas the Chinese believe in—are there any?' He said, 'No; no one has seen them; they do not exist; there are only the angels, the servants of God, and the evil spirits whom God drove out to be devils, and deceive men.' I said, 'Is there a God Jehovah?' He answered, 'Certainly, one God!' I rejoined, 'You said there were no Dewas because no one had seen them; why then do you assert the existence of a God, for neither can we see Him?' The missionary answered, 'Truly, we see Him not, but all the works of creation must have a master; they could not have originated of themselves.' I said, 'There is no evidence of the creation; it is only a tradition. Why not account for it by the self-producing power of nature?' The missionary replied, 'That he had no doubt but that God created everything, and that not even a hair, or a grain of sand, existed of itself, for the things on the earth may be likened to dishes of food arranged on a table, and though no owner should be seen, none would doubt but that there was one; no one would think that the things came into the dishes of themselves.' I said, 'Then you consider that even a stone in the bladder is created by God!' He replied, 'Yes. Everything. God creates everything!' 'Then,' answered I, 'if that is so, God creates in man that which will cause his death, and you medical missionaries remove it and restore his health! Are you not opposing God in so doing? Are you not offending Him in curing those whom He would kill?' When I had said this the missionary became angry, and saying I was hard to teach, left me.

"Dr Gutzlaff once said to me, 'Phra Samana Khodom, having entered Niruana, is entirely lost and non-existent, who, then, will give any return for recitations in his praise, benedictions, reverences, observances, and merit-making? It is as a country without a king, where merit is unrewarded, because there is no one to reward it; but the religion of Jesus Christ has the Lord Jehovah and Christ to reward merit, and receive prayers and praises, and give a recompense.' I replied, 'It is true that, according to the Buddhist religion, the Lord Buddha does not give the reward of merit; but if any do as he has taught, they will find their recompense in the act. Even when Buddha lived on earth, he had no power to lead to heaven those who prayed for his assistance, but did not honour and follow the just way. The holy religion of Buddha is perfect justice springing from a man's own meritorious disposition. It is that disposition which rewards the good and punishes the evil. The recitations are the teachings of the Lord Buddha, which are found in various Sutras, set forms given by Buddha to holy hermits, and some of them are descriptions of that which is suitable and becoming in conduct. Even though the Lord has entered Niruana, his grace and benevolence are not exhausted. You missionaries praise the grace of Jehovah and Christ, and say that the Lord waits to hear and grant the prayers of those that call to Him. But are those prayers granted? So far as I see, they get no more than people who do not believe in prayer. They die the same, and they are equally liable to age, and disease, and sorrow. How, then, can you say that your religion is better than any other? In the Bible we find that God created Adam and Eve, and desired that they should have no sickness nor sorrow, nor know death; but because they, the progenitors of mankind, ate of a forbidden fruit, God became angry, and ordained that thenceforth they should endure toil and weariness and trouble and sickness, and, from that time, fatigue and sorrow and sickness and death fell upon mankind. It was said that by baptism men should be free from the curse of Adam, but I do not see that any one who is baptized now-a-days is free from the curse of Adam, or escapes toil and grief and sickness and death, any more than those who are not baptized.' The missionary answered, 'Baptism for the remission of sin is only effectual in gaining heaven after death, for those who die unbaptized will certainly go to hell.' But the missionary did not explain the declaration that by baptism men should be free from pains and troubles in their present state. He further said, 'It does at times please God to accede to the requests of those that pray to Him, a remarkable instance of which is, that Europeans and Americans have more excellent arts than any other people. Have they not steamboats and railways, and telegraphs and manufactures, and guns and weapons of war superior to any others in the world? Are not the nations which do not worship Christ comparatively ignorant?' I asked the doctor about sorrow and sickness, things which prevail throughout the world, things in which Christians have no advantage over other men, but he would not reply on that point, and spoke only of matters of knowledge. Where is the witness who can say that this knowledge was the gift of God? There are many in Europe who do not believe in God, but are indifferent, yet have subtle and expanded intellects, and are great philosophers and politicians. How is it that God grants to these men, who do not believe in Him, the same intelligence He grants to those who do? Again, how is it that the Siamese, Burmese, Cochin Chinese, and other Roman Catholic converts, whom we see more attentive to their religion than the Europeans who reside among us, do not receive some reward for their merit, and have superior advantages and intelligence to those who are not converted? So far as I can see, the reverse is the case: the unconverted flourish, but the converted are continually in debt and bondage. There are many converts in Siam, but I see none of them rise to wealth, so as to become talked about. They continually pray to God, but, it seems, nothing happens according to their prayer.' The missionary replied, 'They are Roman Catholics, and hold an untrue religion, therefore God is not pleased with them.' I said to the missionary, 'You say that God sometimes grants the prayers of those who pray to Him; now, the Chinese, who pray to spirits and devils, sometimes obtain what they have prayed for; do you not, therefore, allow that these spirits can benefit man?' The missionary answered, 'The devil receives bribes.' I inquired, 'Among the men and animals God creates, some die in the womb, and many at or immediately after birth and before reaching maturity, and many are deaf, dumb, and crippled: why are such created? Is it not a waste of labour? Again, God creates men, and does not set their hearts to hold to His religion, but sets them free to take false religions, so that they are all damned, while those who worship Him go to heaven: is not this inconsistent with His goodness and mercy? If He, indeed, created all men, would He not have shown equal compassion and goodness to all, and not allowed inequalities? Then I should have believed in a creating God. But, as it is, it seems nothing but a game at dolls.'* The missionary replied, 'With regard to long and short lives, the good may live but a short time, God being pleased to call them to heaven, and sometimes He permits the wicked

* Or, "a mere manufacture of dolls to play with."

to live to a full age, that they may repent of their sins. And the death of innocent children is the mercy of God calling them to heaven.' I rejoined, 'How should God take a special liking to unloveable, shapeless, unborn children?' The missionary replied, 'He who would learn to swim must practise in shallow places first, or he will be drowned. If any spoke like this in European countries, he would be put in prison.' I invite particular attention to this statement.

"Another time I said to the missionary Gutzlaff, 'It is said in the Bible that God is the Creator of all men and animals. Why should He not create them spontaneously, as worms and vermin arise from filth, and fish are formed in new pools by the emanations of air and water? Why must there be procreation, and agony and often death to mothers? Is not this labour lost? I can see no good in it.' He replied, 'God instituted procreation so that men might know their fathers and mothers and relatives, and the pains of childbirth are a consequence of the curse of Eve, for whose sin all her descendants suffer.' I said, 'If procreation was designed that men should know their relatives, why are animals which do not know their relatives, produced in the same manner? And why do they, not being descendants of Eve, suffer pain in labour for her sin of eating a little forbidden fruit? Besides, the Bible says, by belief in Christ man shall escape the consequences of Eve's sin, yet I cannot see that men do so escape in any degree, but suffer just as others do.' The missionary answered, 'It is waste of time to converse with evil men who will not be taught,' and so left me."

"Missionaries profess that Christianity teaches the

true nature of the beginning of man, his creation by God. The Lord Buddha did not know the origin of living beings, and taught about that which was already in existence, saying that it would continue to exist in various states of transmigration until the richness and perfection of its merits should cause it to be born in the world during the teaching of a Buddha, by whom it would be saved from farther sorrows."

"The Lord Buddha declined to discourse on the creation; he said that there was no beginning, and that the subject was unprofitable, as such knowledge was no help towards diminishing misery. I doubt not that he knew the truth, and would not tell it, because it would have shocked the prejudices of his hearers, Brahmins, who believed that various classes of men had sprung from different parts of the Creator's body, and who had instituted caste according to the more or less honourable part of the body from which they thought that certain classes had sprung. Those who believe in God the Creator tell us that the creation occupied six days, the sun, moon, and stars being created on the fourth. Now the number of stars is infinite, and each star or sun is greater than the earth by as much as a fortress is greater than a pea. How can we believe that God made this inconceivable infinity of immense things in one day, and yet required five days to make this little world, this mere drop in the great ocean?"

"Again the missionaries tell us that God brought all animals to Adam, that he might name them. How can we believe this when we find that in every language the names differ?"

"I asked a missionary, 'How it is that man, who was created after everything else, is able to give an account of that which was created before him?' He replied, 'Man knows, because God has revealed it to him.' I rejoined, 'If this is the revelation of God, why does your (scriptural) account of the creation differ from the teaching of philosophers, who show that the world is a revolving globe? Were not the first philosophers who held these views punished for them? And were not their views opposed until the number of their followers rendered further opposition vain?' The missionary answered, 'The knowledge of the revolution of the world was obtained by wisdom and intelligence given by God, which is the same as if God had revealed it directly. God did not reveal it before, because He considered men were too stupid.' Let those who are intelligent say whether such an explanation can be accepted!"

"I asked the Mussulmans and missionaries, 'If God created all things, and is Ruler of the world, and has spirit, and knowledge, and judgment to reward the good and punish the wicked, what merit did He make in former times that He should become the Great God of heaven?' They answered, 'Not by acquired merit, but by Himself did God exist. As in numbers you have two, and three, and four, upwards, but they all depend on the first, or one, and none can say whence comes one.' I asked, 'The elements of the world are endless, space is infinite, men and animals infinite, the worlds in space uncountable; if the Spirit of God is single, how can it fill them all and search out everything in the disposition of men, and watch the good and evil in every heart? Surely this idea is rather that there is an infinity of gods, than that there is but one God!' They replied, 'The power of God is great, wherever there is space God is.' I invite a comparison between this idea of a Divinity going about in all directions, and the (Buddhist) idea that the all-knowing Divine Bestower of rewards and punishments is Merit and Demerit, or Kam itself."

Nearly fifty pages of the "Kitchanukit" are taken up by the sketch of the religions of the world.

There are philosophers who say that all known sects may be classed under two religions only, the Brahmanyang and the Samanyang. All those who pray for assistance to Brahma, Indra, God the Creator, Angels, Devils, Parents, or other intercessors or possible benefactors—all who believe in the existence of any being who can help them, and in the efficacy of prayer, are Brahmanyang; while all who believe that they must depend solely on the inevitable results of their own acts, that good and evil are consequences of preceding causes, and that merit and demerit are the regulators of existence, and who therefore do not pray to any to help them, and all those who profess to know nothing of what will happen after death, and all those who disbelieve in a future existence, are Samanyang.

"Brahminism is," he writes, "the most ancient known religion, held by numbers of men to this day, though with many varieties of belief. Its fundamental doctrine was that the world was created by Thao Maha Phrom (Brahma), who divided his nature into two parts, Isuen (Vishnu), Lord of the Earth, and rewarder of the good, and Narai (Siva), Lord of the Ocean, and punisher of the wicked. The Brahmins believed in blood sacrifices, which they offered before idols with three faces and six hands, representing three gods in one. Sometimes they made separate images of the three, and called them the father, the son, and the spirit, all three being one, and the son being that part of the deity which at various times is born in the earth as a man, the Avatar of God."

After Brahminism he treats of Judaism.

"About 3000 years ago a Khëk,* named Abraham, who lived in Khoran (? Chaldæa), the son of a Brahmin priest, dreamt that the Lord Allah came and told him that it was not right to worship images, and that he must destroy his idols, and flee from that country, and establish a new religion, permitting no kneeling or sacrifice except to God alone. Animal sacrifice was to be retained, and the followers of his religion were to be circumcised instead of being baptized. For without circumcision none is a follower of Islam."

He continues with the story of Abraham and his trial, as told in the Bible, ending with the remark, "Thus the religion of Islam branched off from Brahminism." Next follows a short account of the separation of Christianity from Judaism, and the introduction of the rite of baptism, of which he observes:—

"Baptism was a religious rite from very ancient times, the Brahmins holding that if any one who had sinned went to the bank of the Ganges, and saying, 'I will not sin again,' plunged into the stream, he would rise to the surface free of sin, all his sins floating away with the water. Hence it was called baptism, or the rite of washing off offences, so that they floated away. Sometimes when any one was sick unto death,

* This word is applied to Jews and Mahometans, whatever country they are natives of.

his relatives would place him by the river, and give him water to drink, and pour water over him till he died, believing that he would thus die holy, and go to heaven. This was the old belief, the rite of circumcision being introduced by the prophet Abraham, and it is to be supposed that the holy man John (the Baptist) thought that the ancient rite was the proper one, and so restored it."

Next follows an account of the second great offspring of the religion of Abraham, Mahometanism, the rise of which, and its division into two sects, Soonnees and Mahons (Sheres), are treated of at some length. "This religion," he observes, "was not spread by the arguments of preachers, but by men who held the Koran with one hand, and the sword with the other." We will not occupy our readers' time by quoting the history of Mahometanism, which they can read elsewhere, but they may be amused by the account of the reason that pork is forbidden food.

"They say that when men first filled the world, Allah forbade them to eat any animals but such as died a natural death; and as the animals would not die as quickly as they wished, they accelerated their deaths by striking them, and throwing things at them. The animals complained to Allah of this treatment, and He sent His angel Gabriel to order all men and animals to assemble together, that He might decide the case. But the pigs were disobedient, and did not come. Then Allah said, 'The pigs, the lowest of animals, are disobedient, let no one eat them or touch them.'"

His remarks on other religions, we quote in his own words:—

"Another religion is what the Siamese call that of the Lord Phoot (Phra Phutthi Chao), and Europeans call that of Samana Khodom or Gotama, or Buddha. Its followers, some of them, walk reverently according to the rules, called Winya, others follow a relaxed code. In some countries Buddhist monks are treated as kings. The teaching of Buddha does not go back to the origin of life, but treats of that which already exists, showing that ignorance of the four truths is the cause of continued existence (in transmigration). These four truths are—1st, The perception of sorrow; 2d, The perception that sorrow is a consequence of desire; 3d, The perception of nirot, which is the extinction of sorrow, so that it has no further birth; 4th, Walking in the eight paths of holiness, which purify the disposition, and lead to a happiness beyond all sorrow. Such was the teaching of Buddha."

"Christianity is also a great religion. Christians were originally all Roman Catholics. The Roman Catholics believed in Jehovah and Christ, and Mary the mother, and in saints, and in the Pope, the great bishop of Rome, who they say is the substitute for Christ on earth, with power to absolve from sin, and to order doctrines. The priests of that religion, whom we call Bat Hluang, dress in black, and have no wives. After many centuries certain Germans considered that the Roman Catholic tenets were contrary to the Bible, so they formed a new sect, believing in God and Christ only. Their teachers are called missionaries, and dress like ordinary people, and have wives, and if their wives die, can marry again, though some hold that they should not do so. They do not worship Mary the mother, nor the saints; many left the old religion to join this sect. Another sect are the Mormons; they say that their religion arose from certain men dreaming that God in heaven took a golden plate, whereon was written the holy doctrine, and buried it in the earth. And those who dreamt thus dug, and found a scripture engraven on a plate of gold, according to their dream. Then they believed in God in heaven, and Christ, and polygamy, and doing as they pleased; the rules of their religion being much more lax than those of Roman Catholics or Christians (Protestants). And they believed that if they turned their thoughts to Christ when at the point of death, Christ would take their souls to heaven. All these three sects worship the same God and Christ, why then should they blame each other, and charge each other with believing wrongly, and say to each other, 'you are wrong, and will go to hell, we are right, and shall go to heaven?' It is one religion, yet how can we join it when each party threatens us with hell if we agree with the other, and there is none to decide between them. I beg comparison of this with the teaching of the Lord Buddha, that whoever endeavours to keep the Commandments,* and is charitable, and walks virtuously, must attain heaven." A few remarks on the worship of Vishnu (Juggernauth), fire-worship, Confucianism, spirit-worship, and unbelief, and a sketch of the principal localities of each religion, conclude this subject.

The next question is, Out of so many religions, how shall a man select that which he can trust to for his future happiness?

"He must reflect, and apply his mind to ascertain

* For an account of the Five Commandments, see page 57.

which is most true. This is a subject of constant dispute, every one upholding his own religion. Even the lowest of mankind, devil worshippers, have faith in their own belief, and will not hear those who would teach them differently. It is very hard for men to relinquish their first ideas and habits. Those who do change their religions are either poor people who do it out of respect to those who have helped them when in difficulties, or those who have been persecuted and forced to change, or those who are induced, by observing the superior skill and knowledge of the followers of any religion, to believe that their religion must be the true one; or those who change their religion for that of some one whom they respect as much wiser and better than themselves, and sure to be right in everything, or those who do it to get help when they have lawsuits,* and to obtain protectors against oppression. Also there are those who, having listened to teaching, are enlightened, and see clearly that form and name are not realities, and must be considered as sorrows, and that there is no help to be had from any one, but that good and evil are the result of merit and demerit. Some there are who have become Buddhists on these considerations."

On this subject he quotes one of the Sutras, supposed to be a sermon of Buddha:—

"There is a Buddhist Sutra which pleased me much when I read it, and I have remembered it, and will repeat it here, begging to be excused for variations, omissions, and additions, as it is intended for those

* This refers to Catholic priests, supported by French Consuls, interfering with the ordinary course of Siamese law when Christians are concerned.

who are not learned in the holy religion of Buddha. It is as follows:—On a certain occasion the Lord Buddha led a number of his disciples to a village of the Kalamachon, where his wisdom and merit and holiness were known. And the Kalamachon assembled, and did homage to him and said, 'Many priests and Brahmins have at different times visited us, and explained their religious tenets, declaring them to be excellent, but each abused the tenets of every one else, whereupon we are in doubt as to whose religion is right and whose wrong; but we have heard that the Lord Buddha teaches an excellent religion, and we beg that we may be freed from doubt, and learn the truth.'

"And the Lord Buddha answered, 'You were right to doubt, for it was a doubtful matter. I say unto all of you, Do not believe in what ye have heard; that is, when you have heard any one say this is especially good or extremely bad; do not reason with yourselves that if it had not been true, it would not have been asserted, and so believe in its truth. Neither have faith in traditions, because they have been handed down for many generations and in many places.

"'Do not believe in anything because it is rumoured and spoken of by many; do not think that it is a proof of its truth.

"'Do not believe merely because the written statement of some old sage is produced; do not be sure that the writing has ever been revised by the said sage, or can be relied on. Do not believe in what you have fancied, thinking that because an idea is extraordinary it must have been implanted by a Dewa, or some wonderful being.

"'Do not believe in guesses, that is, assuming something at hap-hazard as a starting point draw your conclusions from it; reckoning your two and your three and your four before you have fixed your number one.

"'Do not believe because you think there is analogy, that is a suitability in things and occurrences, such as believing that there must be walls of the world, because you see water in a basin, or that Mount Meru must exist, because you have seen the reflection of trees; or that there must be a creating God, because houses and towns have builders.

"'Do not believe in the truth of that to which you have become attached by habit, as every nation believes in the superiority of its own dress and ornaments and language.

"'Do not believe because your informant appears to be a credible person, as, for instance, when you see any one having a very sharp appearance, conclude that he must be clever and trustworthy; or when you see any one who has powers and abilities beyond what men generally possess, believe in what he tells. Or think that a great nobleman is to be believed, as he would not be raised by the king to high station unless he were a good man.

"'Do not believe merely on the authority of your teachers and masters, or believe and practise merely because they believe and practise.

"'I tell you all, you must of your own selves know that "this is evil, this is punishable, this is censured by wise men, belief in this will bring no advantage to one, but will cause sorrow." And when you know this, then eschew it.

"'I say to all of you dwellers in this village, answer

me this. Lopho, that is covetousness, Thoso, that is anger and savageness, and Moho, that is ignorance and folly,—when any or all of these arise in the hearts of men, is the result beneficial or the reverse?'

"And they answered, 'It is not beneficial, O Lord.'

"Then the Lord continued, 'Covetous, passionate, and ignorant men destroy life and steal, and commit adultery and tell lies, and incite others to follow their example, is it not so?'

"And they answered, 'It is as the Lord says.'

"And he continued, 'Covetousness, passion, ignorance, the destruction of life, theft, adultery, and lying, are these good or bad, right or wrong? do wise men praise or blame them? Are they not unprofitable, and causes of sorrow?'

"And they replied, 'It is as the Lord has spoken.'

"And the Lord said, 'For this I said to you, do not believe merely because you have heard, but when of your own consciousness you know a thing to be evil, abstain from it.'

"And then the Lord taught of that which is good, saying, 'If any of you know of yourselves that anything is good and not evil, praised by wise men, advantageous, and productive of happiness, then act abundantly according to your belief. Now I ask you, Alopho, absence of covetousness, Athoso, absence of passion, Amoho, absence of folly, are these profitable or not?'

"And they answered, 'Profitable.'

"The Lord continued, 'Men who are not covetous, or passionate, or foolish, will not destroy life, nor steal, nor commit adultery, nor tell lies, is it not so?'

"And they answered, 'It is as the Lord says."

"Then the Lord asked, 'Is freedom from covetousness, passion, and folly, from destruction of life, theft, adultery, and lying, good or bad, right or wrong, praised or blamed by wise men, profitable and tending to happiness or not?'

"And they replied, 'It is good, right, praised by the wise, profitable, and tending to happiness.'

"And the Lord said, 'For this I taught you not to believe merely because you have heard, but when you believed of your own consciousness, then to act accordingly and abundantly.'

"And the Lord continued, 'The holy man must not be covetous, or revengeful, or foolish, and he must be versed in the four virtuous inclinations (Phrommawihan), which are, Meta, desiring for all living things the same happiness which one seeks for one's self; Karuna, training the mind in compassion towards all living things, desiring that they may escape all sorrows either in hell or in other existences, just as a man who sees his friend ill, desires nothing so much as his recovery; Muthita, taking pleasure in all living things, just as playmates are glad when they see one another; and Ubekkha, keeping the mind balanced and impartial, with no affection for one more than another.'"

From another Sutra is extracted the following passage:—

"Consider! Can you respect or believe in religions which recommend actions that bring happiness to one's self by causing sorrow to others, or happiness to others by sorrow to one's self, or sorrow to both one's self and others?

"Is not that a better religion which promotes the

happiness of others simultaneously with the happiness of one's self, and tolerates no oppression?'

"This better religion, exercising an excellent influence on the natures of those who walk according to it, has produced holy men of the eight grades of sanctity, called the four ways and four fruits. These holy men have taught the importance of the four Satipatthan, or applications of reflective power; of the four Sammappathan, or reasonable objects of continued exertion; of the four Itthibat, or effectual causes; of the five Intri, or great virtues (moral powers); the five Phala, or forces; and the seven Photchangkas, or principles of all knowledge, which are the illuminators of the mind. They have also taught that those persons who, on due consideration of form, sensation, perception, idea, and intelligence (which are the five elements of existence), conclude that they are unreal, full of sorrow, and perishable, may be called 'flourishing in intelligence;' that those who have no longer any desire for worldly pleasures, or evil feelings towards others, may be called 'firm in intelligence;' and those who have entirely freed themselves from desire, anger, folly, revenge, ingratitude, giving blow for blow (?), envy, avarice, deceit, resistance (?), desire to excel others, pride, intoxication, and heedlessness, all which are vices, are said to have a 'crushing intelligence.' This is the state of mind which sets the spirit and body free from all entanglement, which makes the nature of man bright and pure, and leads to calm and happiness. Is not this teaching good?"

In the above passage, full of monastic technicalities, the most noticeable feature, in my opinion, is that these dogmatisms are not attributed to Buddha, who, in a previous passage, is said to have simply taught the four truths, but are attributed to the saints. By this neat distinction our author avoids the appearance of heresy. The twenty-nine qualities mentioned in the text, with the eight ways and fruits, constitute what Buddhists call the thirty-seven constituents of Buddha's wisdom. Those who wish to investigate more thoroughly the tedious and, to many of us, stupid subject, must consult note 174, at the end of the notes to the Life.

The next subject we deal with is the future state:—

"Some men believe that merit and demerit cause successive re-births of the soul until it becomes perfect, when it is not born again. Others believe that after death the soul is next born in heaven or hell, and has no further change. Others believe that man is re-born as man, and every animal born again in its kind for ever. Others believe that there is no resurrection of the dead. I have pondered much on this subject, and cannot absolutely decide it. If we were to believe that death is annihilation, we should be at a loss to account for the existence of mankind.

"If we were to hold with those who believe in God the Creator, it should follow that (the impartial justice of God) would make all men and animals equal in life and similar in nature, which is not the case. We observe that some die young, others live to old age; some are born great, others not; some rich, others poor; some beautiful, others ugly; some never suffer illness, others are continually ill, or blind, or deaf, or deformed, or mad. If we say that God made these, we must regard Him as unjust, partial, and ever changing; making those suffer who have never done anything to deserve suffering, and not giving to men in general that average of good and bad fortune which attends even the speculations of the gambler. But if we believe in the interchange and succession of life throughout all beings (*i.e.*, the transmigration of souls), and that good and evil arise from ourselves, and are the effects of merit and demerit, we have some grounds for belief. The differences of men and animals afford a very striking proof, clear to our eyes."

The argument here is, that as some men and animals have a superior lot to others, there must needs follow other successive states to compensate those whose present condition is inferior, unless we suppose the difference of present condition to be caused by the merits and demerits of a previous existence. Either supposition, he considers, affords proof of his proposition, and requires only one presumption, viz., that the law of the world is perfect justice :—

"Those who believe that after death the soul passes to hell or heaven for ever, have no proof that there is no return thence. Certainly, it would be a most excellent thing to go direct to heaven after death, without further change, but I am afraid that it is not the case. For the believers in it, who have not perfectly purified their hearts and prepared themselves for that most excellent place, where there is no being born, growing old, and dying, will still have their souls contaminated with uneradicated evil, the fruit of evil deeds, for where else can that evil go to ?

"That there is a place of perfect happiness, where there is no being born or growing old, or dying, was known only to Him who attained the perfection of holiness. He said that there is really such a place, but none of us have seen it, and we know not the condition of his soul. We can only judge of it by analogy.

"The worker in gold cannot make anything of his gold until he has refined it from all impurities. Subsequent meltings will not then affect it, because it is pure. In like manner the Lord, before he ceased to breathe, had repressed and cleared away all evil from his soul,* so that it could not return, and there remained nothing but good. Being pure, we can conceive that, like the pure gold, it might pass to where it would be affected by no further change. How is it possible that those who have not cleared away the evil disposition from their soul should attain the most excellent heaven, and live eternally with God the Creator? and of those who are to remain in hell for ever, many have made merit, and done much good. Shall that be altogether lost?

"The Lord Buddha taught, saying, 'All you who are in doubt as to whether or not there is a future life, had better believe that there is one; that there is another existence, in which happiness and misery can be felt. It is better to believe this than otherwise, for if the heart believes in a future life it will abandon sin and act virtuously; and even if there is no resurrection, such a life will bring a good name, and the regard of men. But those who believe in extinction at death will not fail to commit any sin that they may choose because of their disbelief in a future; and if there should happen to be a future after all, they will be at a disadvantage —they will be like travellers without provisions.'

* Possibly I have erred in using the term soul in this passage. The Siamese terms are chitr and chitr-borisut—*i.e.*, perfectly pure chitr. For the usual meaning of chitr see note 155.

"Buddha, seeing the doubt in some men's minds as to birth and extinction, was pleased to preach thus."

This argument is followed by stories from the sacred books illustrating transmigration, and by several anecdotes of the present time of children who, as soon as they could speak, have asserted and given proofs of their having previously existed as men or animals.

"In the sacred books we read of a certain rich Brahmin of Sawatthi named Tothai, who was not a Buddhist, and whose death-bed thoughts were only about his money. The result of his merit and demerit caused him to be born as a puppy in the very house that had belonged to him when a man, and of which his son was now master. One day, as Buddha passed the house collecting alms, the puppy ran to the gate and barked, and the Lord called to it, 'Tothai! Tothai!' and it ran and lay down at his feet. Then was the son very angry at the insult he considered to have been cast against his father, by using his name to a dog; and he remonstrated with Buddha. Buddha asked him, 'Have you yet found the money your father buried during his life?' He answered, 'Only a part of it.' 'Then, if you would indeed know whether or not this puppy is Tothai the Brahmin, treat him with great respect for several days, and then ask him where the treasure is, and he will show you.' And the young man did so, and the dog indicated the place where the treasure was hid. And from thenceforth the son of Tothai followed the teachings of the Lord Buddha." This story is an old one, handed down from the days of Buddha, and people must attach just so much credit to it as they think due.

"Another instance is that of the child of a Peguan,

at Paklat (a town near Bangkok), who, as soon as he learned to speak, told his parents that he was formerly named Makran, and had been killed by a fall from a cocoa-nut tree, and that as he fell his hatchet fell from his hand and dropped into a ditch. And they, seeing that his story coincided with something that had happened within their knowledge, tried the child by making him point out the tree, and he pointed out the tree, and his story was confirmed by their digging up the hatchet from the ditch."

The next question is, What is it that is re-born?

"It is difficult to explain whether it is the same or another life which is born again in a future state. It may be compared to the seeds of plants which sprout and grow, and produce more seed; can the succeeding tree and seed be said to be the same as the original tree and seed? So it is in this case. To dwell on the subject would be tedious. Again, is the echo the same sound as that to which it answers, or another sound? The condition in which the new birth will take place must be dependent on the necessity which the being has itself caused by the state of its disposition, for merit and demerit are the orderers of the manner of the new birth, and the preparers of increasing happiness or misery.

We are next told that all entry into a new state is effected in one of four ways—*i.e.*, by production in the egg, by ordinary birth, by life resulting from emanations of earth and water, and change of leaves, &c., as vermin results from filth, fish from emanations in new pools, insects from fruits, and snakes from a certain vine; and fourthly, by spontaneous appearance without birth, as angels and devils originate.

The subject of a future life will be again reverted to after our readers have had set before them the nature of the directing influence of merit and demerit, of that law of nature or guiding power with which Buddhists supply the place of God. The Siamese call this Kam,* and it is sometimes translated as fate or consequence. We shall use the word Kam in preference to any translation.

We may aid our readers to comprehend this Kam, by giving a short account of its action before proceeding further with quotations.

Buddhists believe that every act, word, or thought has its consequence, which will appear sooner or later in the present or in some future state. Evil acts will produce evil consequences—that is, may cause a man misfortune in this world, or an evil birth in hell, or as an animal in some future existence. Good acts, etc., will produce good consequences; prosperity in this world, or birth in heaven, or in a high position in the world in some future state. When we say every act, etc., has its effect, we must make the exception that where several acts, etc., are of such a nature that their result will be the same in kind, and due at the same time, then only one of the said acts, etc., will produce an effect, and the others will be neutralised, or become "Ahosikam." Sometimes even single acts may become effectless, or "Ahosikam," as will be explained further on.

There is no God who judges of these acts, etc., and awards recompense or punishment; but the reward or

* Kam is the same as the Sanscrit word Karman (action). The Siamese, while they pronounce it Kam, spell it as if it should be pronounced Karma.

punishment is simply the inevitable effect of Kam which works out its own results.

Our author first draws a distinction between the causation called Kam and that called Nisai.*

"Nisai causation is that which can be calculated or foreseen, and results from intention, such as where a speculation is entered into, because one knows that it will be profitable, or work is done for the king, because one knows that it will be rewarded. These two instances are nisai causation of a meritorious kind. The demeritorious kind is illustrated by a wilful breach of the law leading to the punishment known to be due to it. These are instances of Nisai, and are not called Kam."

"Kam causation gives rise to that which is not foreseen. It is illustrated by the story of Phra Maha Chanok, who, escaping from a wrecked ship, fell asleep in the woods, and on waking was received in a royal chariot and made king of the country. This happening without any plan or foreknowledge on his part, was Kam causation of the meritorious kind. The demeritorious kind is illustrated when an innocent man is punished for another's crime. And we have instances of both kinds of Kam in the cases where, when two men were bathing together, a crocodile devoured the one and left the other; and when two men were equally liable to execution, the judges condemned the one and set free the other."

Our author next quotes from the ancient canonical commentaries, "Attha Kathâ;" adds some passages from the "Attanomati" (a work I am unacquainted with,

* Nisai is, I presume, the Sanscrit Niçchaya, meaning ascertainment, certainty, design.

but which is probably a Siamese commentary on part of the "Attha Kathâ"), and interposes with much deference a few explanations of his own :—

"The meritorious and demeritorious Kam, which living beings have caused to exist by their own acts, words, or thoughts, are, whether their fruits be joy or sorrow, to be classed under three heads.

"The first is Thittham Wethaniya Kam, that is the Kam of which creatures will have the fruits at once, in their present state of existence.

"The second is Upacha Wethaniya Kam, that is the Kam of which creatures will have the fruits in the next state of existence.

"The third is Aprâpara Wethaniya Kam, that is the Kam of which creatures will have the fruits in future states of existence from the third onward.

"Merit or demerit will cause a tendency of the soul in one direction sometimes to as many as seven births and deaths, which will be followed by a relapse in the opposite direction for six, five, or less times; such is the way of the soul.

"The merit of a single act of charity, or the demerit of the slaughter of a single ant, will be certainly followed by one of these three Kams.

Then follow anecdotes of Thittham Wethaniya Kam, telling how men have been rewarded for a distinguished act of goodness by a sudden change from poverty to wealth; and how for an act of cruelty horrible sufferings have been almost instantaneously experienced.

"Merit or demerit of this class must have their fruit in the present existence. If they do not, they will become 'Ahosikam,' lost altogether. They will be like a bowshot which misses the animal it is aimed at, or like fruit which a man has gathered and forgotten to eat until it has turned rotten.

"Meritorious Upacha Wethaniya Kam, of which the fruits appear in the next existence (that following the one in which the works which caused it were done), is produced by the eight states of pious meditation (Samabatti),* and will assuredly cause re-birth in the superior heavens; but as any one of the eight would of itself be followed by this Kam, and cause the same heavenly birth, and as the effect is one which can happen in the second and in no other existence, it follows that he who has attained all the eight Samabatti will but receive the result of one, and the other seven will be lost or Ahosikam.

"Demeritorious Upacha Wethaniya Kam is caused by parricide, matricide, killing saints, defiling Buddha with blood,† and dispersing monks. Any one of these will cause re-birth in hell, and the commission of more than one of these sins will make no difference. The others will be lost or Ahosikam, for they have no power in any other existence.

"Aprâpara Wethaniya Kam differs from the preceding, in that it can never be lost or Ahosikam. Every act of which the Kam is of this class, whether meritorious or demeritorious, will certainly have its fruits in some generation, from the third onward, whenever the suitable time may come.

"The 'Attanomati' states, 'This present existence,

* See Notes 38 and 65.

† Our author remarks that as Buddha has passed to Nirwana, and there are now no saints, it is no longer possible to commit these two sins.

from the time that Kam is incurred until death, is the domain of Thittham Wethaniya Kam; when it has power, it produces its effects within this limit; when it has not enough power to produce its effects within this limit, its domain is ended by death, and it becomes Ahosikam. The whole of the second existence is the domain of Upacha Wethaniya Kam; when it has power enough, it gives its fruits within that time, but when it has not power enough to do so, it becomes Ahosikam. From the time of entering on the third existence and onwards, is the domain of Aprâpara Wethaniya Kam, which ends only with the attainment of Nirwana, the cessation from further change.'"

Kam is again divided under four heads—Khru, Pahula, Âsanna, and Kottâ,—according to the time when its effects will appear, which depends on comparative importance. The more important the act, the sooner will the effect come. First of Khru Kam :—

"The most powerful of all demeritorious Kam is the result of the five before-mentioned sins (parricide, &c.); when any one of these has been committed, not even a hundred years of merit-making will secure happiness, or prevent the soul going to hell at death. The most powerful meritorious Kam results from the eight states of Samabatti (pious meditation)."

We omit, as of less interest, the remarks on Pahula and Âsanna Kam; the first, meaning Kam which is important from its nature, the second, Kam which is rendered important by the circumstances of the action giving rise to it, as a good or bad act done at the point of death; and we quote the account of Kottâ Kam, the lightest Kam :—

"Kottâ Kam is light, small, not made at the point

of death, and made in ignorance of its being meritorious or demeritorious. As, for instance, when men not knowing that they are doing a meritorious act, remove a stake or thorn, or tile from the road, lest it may hurt any one passing along, or, seeing any kind of filth lying in a public place, remove it, and cleanse the place; or when a child, seeing its parents make offerings and bow to a Phrachedi,* imitates them, this is meritorious Kottâ Kam.

"Demeritorious Kottâ Kam arises when men, not knowing that they are doing wrong, kill or strike small animals, regarding them as vegetables; and when children playfully do mischievous tricks, and when any wrong is committed in ignorance. In the absence of other Kam, this Kam will operate at some stage of existence, causing happiness or sorrow according as it is meritorious or demeritorious."

The aforementioned divisions of Kam, under three heads and four heads, refer to time and gravity; it is also divided into four classes according to the nature of its action. They are Chanaka Kam, Uphatamphaka Kam, Upa-pilaka Kam, and Upakhâthaka Kam. The first is the Kam which causes birth or existence in any particular state of happiness or sorrow; the second modifies that state by causing its premature cessation or prolongation; the third modifies it by reducing the amount of happiness or misery; and the last violently opposes itself to any existing Kam, so as to destroy its effects. This last Kam is illustrated by the story of "Angkuliman."

* Phrachedi are spires in temples, generally covering a relic, or image of Buddha, and supposed to lead the thoughts to the teachings of the Great Teacher.

"Angkuliman, whilst yet a layman, committed nine hundred and ninety-nine murders, but afterwards, by attaining to saintly perfection, he obtained an Upakhâthaka Kam, which cut off the Kam of the murders he had committed. He acquired meritorious Upacha Wethaniya Kam, of which he would enjoy the fruits in his next generation, and meritorious Aprâpara Wethaniya Kam, of which he would enjoy the fruits in the third and subsequent generations. There was left only Thittham Wethaniya Kam, by which his murders could have any effect; and it did have effect, causing him, after he had attained his saintly condition, to be accidentally pelted with sticks and lumps of earth."

Such are the eleven Kam of the Attha Kathâ Chari, the last eight being only the same as the first three, but differently described. Next follows a passage comparing the idea of Kam with that of a divine judge.

"These Kam we have discoursed about have no substance, and we cannot see where they exist; nor when they are about to have effect do they come crying, 'I am the Kam, named So-and-so, come to give fruits to such-a-one.' This I have only adverted to for comparison with the belief of some that there is a creating God who causes existences. Those who so believe cannot see the Creator better than others see the Kam. It is a matter for the consideration of the wise, whether we should say there is a creating God, the Lord and Master of the world, or should say that it is Kam which fashions and causes existences. Neither has a visible form. If we believe that Kam is the cause, the creator, the arranger, we can get hold of the end of the thread, and understand that the happiness and misery of living beings is all caused by natural sequence. But if we assert that a creating God is the dispenser of happiness and misery, we must believe that He is everywhere, and at all times watching and trying, and deciding what punishments are due to the countless multitude of men. Is this credible? Moreover, we are told that the Creator made animals to be food for man; these animals enjoy happiness and suffer misery, like as human beings do. How can we, then, say that the Creator does not grant them justice, and give them also a future state of reward and punishment?

From this disquisition on Kam, we pass to the duties of a good Buddhist. The question is put, "If a man believes in a future existence governed by Kam, how shall he make merit to save himself from future misery?" The answer to this is, of course, "By following the teachings of Buddha, the holy and omniscient; the teaching which praises kindness, and compassion, and pleasure in the general happiness of all beings, and freedom from love or dislike to individuals, and which forbids hatred and jealousy, and envy and revenge; the religion which teaches Than, or almsgiving, Sin, or rules of morality, and Bhawana, or simple meditation; which, with fidelity and other virtues, are the merits of an ordinary class; and the firm observance of the rules of the priesthood, which is merit of the highest class."

Than, or almsgiving, is explained as follows:—

"Than is the voluntary gift of anything not injurious. If there is no intention to give, or the gift is harmful (as poison or spirits), it is not Than. Furthermore, there must be either the desire to assist, or the desire to show gratitude.

"The desire to assist is manifested when a layman gives food to monks, reflecting that monks must starve unless laymen feed them; also when a man, from compassionate motives, gives anything to a beggar; and also, in a lower degree, when a man gives food to animals merely from the knowledge that without his assistance they would die.

"The desire to show gratitude is manifested in gifts to parents, and others entitled to respectful regard, especially to holy and distinguished men.

"It is not Than when gifts are given from other considerations, as when animals are fed that they may be used, or presents are given by lovers to bind affection, or given to slaves to stimulate labour.

"Sages and religious men have observed that Than is an universal merit, existing at all times and in all countries. It was a practice of old, it is a practice now, and it will be a practice in future in all countries and among all people, sometimes more, sometimes less, sometimes having much fruit, and sometimes not being genuine and having but little fruit. I now beg to speak of it as practised at the present day, and to point out what is praiseworthy, and what censurable, according to my own observation. The following descriptions of almsgiving are very meritorious :—

"Firstly, When a man, reflecting that his present wealth is but the result of causation in previous existences, and that it is his duty to make merit for future existences, and not hoard up that which is unstable; and that so long as there are wearers of the yellow robe, the religion will exist, but that if none assist them the monks must die out—eagerly devises means to promote the religion of Buddha, and ensure its permanence, and with that view erects temples, monasteries, spires, and preaching-houses, where religious exercises may be practised, and the monks may cherish their religion in peace, and be a leaven for the future. This is most excellent almsgiving.

"Another kind is when a man seeks the happiness and pleasure of all men—those he loves and those he hates, those he has a cause of revenge against, and those against whom he has none—and with that view digs canals and pools, and makes roads and bridges and salas, and plants large trees to give shade. This generally diffused charity is most excellent almsgiving.

"Another is when any show kindness to their elder relatives, parents, etc., seeking their happiness during their lives, and showing respect by merit-making and almsgiving after their deaths. This, too, is very meritorious.

"Another is when, from compassion to the poor and miserable who have none to help them, and suffer extreme misery, a man erects rest-houses and drinking-fountains, and gives them food and clothes, and necessaries and medicine for their ailments, without selecting one more than another. This is true charity, and has much fruit.

"There are four classes who make merit by almsgiving without pure compassion and piety. One class does it for show, another from greediness, another from jealousy, and another from envy.

"Those who do it for show are such as, without

any real desire to aid religion, or genuine feeling of compassion, make merit as they see others do, from a desire to display their wealth, not for future advantage. Sometimes they do not even own the gifts they pretend to bestow, and hire them for half-a-crown from some priest who owns them, and give him another half-crown to carry them away, ostentatiously piled up on a stand.

"Those who do it from greediness are such as, having much wealth, distribute it before their death, partly to prevent their heir getting it, and partly in hopes that they will be rewarded by going to heaven, and having tens of thousands of houris to minister to them.

"Another class makes merit from jealousy; as when some person of property dies, and the administrator of his estate, in order to prevent some person receiving a share, distributes the whole in alms and merit making.*

"Another class gives alms from envy, that is, when they see an enemy make merit in any way, they go and make more merit, not from piety, but from a desire to be born in their next existence in a superior condition to that their enemy will have.

"Let no one who makes merit by giving alms have such a disposition as any of these."

Ostentatious merit-making is common among all the Siamese. The kings annually, in person or by deputy, make offerings at the principal temples throughout the country, accompanied by procession of sometimes more than a hundred state barges, bands of

* It does sometimes happen that all the estate of the deceased is expended in a great entertainment and feast given at the cremation of the body.

music, and every material of display. Those who can afford it combine in similar processions on a smaller scale; even poor people will, from time to time, invite two or three monks to receive some trumpery presents at their houses, and will proclaim the fact by beating a drum for several hours. The Siamese certainly support their priests well, not only by occasional gifts of clothing, etc., but by daily gifts of food.

Much money is also spent in the other ways designated by our author, the construction of temples especially. He himself is now, and has been for years, superintending the building of one called Pratom Prachidee, near Bangkok, which will, when finished, be one of the finest and largest Buddhist temples in the world. It is built principally with funds supplied by the late king, who also built many other temples. It is unfortunate that the desire is always to build new temples rather than to repair old ones, so that there are but too many temples in a ruinous condition.

Charity of the kind which is best known in England is scarcely ever called for in Siam, where it is easy to live with but little labour, and where the respect shown to family ties and the prevalence of a mild system of slavery enable almost every one to support himself, or get supported without recourse to beggary.

It is only just to the Siamese to add, that though fond of ostentatious almsgiving, as above said, they are also privately charitable, and kind and hospitable to strangers.

From "Than" we pass to "Sin," which is defined as meaning "abstinence" from the offences specified in the Five Commandments. In common parlance, the Five Sin are the Five Commandments, which are all of a negative character, that is, are orders to abstain. The Five Commandments are :—

1st, Thou shalt abstain from destroying or causing the destruction of any living thing.

2d, Thou shalt abstain from acquiring or keeping, by fraud or violence, the property of another.

3d, Thou shalt abstain from those who are not proper objects for thy lust.

4th, Thou shalt abstain from deceiving others either by word or deed.

5th, Thou shalt abstain from intoxication.

The offence of breaking these Commandments may be greater or less according to the quality of the person injured by the act, the amount of premeditation leading to the act, the desire or passion which causes the act, and lastly, the object of the act, *i.e.*, the value of the thing stolen, the damage done by a lie, etc. We give one example of the way in which these Commandments are analysed.

"There are five essentials of Athinnathan (the 2d Commandment). 1st, Property which another sets store by. 2d, Knowledge that it is so. 3d, Intention to get possession of it. 4th, Means taken to do so personally or by agent. 5th, Obtaining said property against the owner's will."

In the same manner, for a breach of the other Commandments, there must be not only a completed act, but also intention.

Having thus defined the Commandments, our author remarks that the mere fact of not committing the offences therein named, cannot be called the practice of Sin, although it is good in that it prevents the rise of demerit.

"When the abstention arises from the impulse of the moment, without any predetermination to observe the Commandments, it cannot be called 'keeping the Commandments' (Sin); but when the abstention is caused by the reflection that these offences will be punished in future generations, and the consequent determination to guard against committing them; or when it results from the unerring purity of mind of those who have entered on the Paths of the Saints, then it is called observance of the Commandments, or Sin."

Excellent as these Commandments are, few men keep them all.

"At the present time very few men, even Buddhists, perfectly observe these Five Commandments. Some can abstain from all but lying. Others take care not to destroy large animals, but cannot restrain themselves from killing gad-flies and mosquitoes. Some can keep from actual theft, but not from getting other people's property by oppression and fraud. Some can refrain from other men's wives, but not from their daughters. Some can keep from great lies, such as bearing false witness, but will tell other lies, such as saying they have not seen or heard, when they have seen or heard, regarding these as trifling offences. As for drunkenness, some abstain from all intoxicating things, even in medicine, others take them in moderation.

"He who cannot abstain from these five offences is guilty—not because the religion of Buddha is cruel, and forbids that which men best like and cannot abstain from, or because the rules are cruel and will cause misfortune to those who believe in them—but because of his own passions.

"The observance of these Five Commandments is good at all times, and in all places. There has never been, and there never will be, a wise man who would not praise them."

Comparing these Commandments with the laws of other religions, he observes that theft, adultery, lying, and the destruction of human life (with exceptions), are regarded as sins by all people; that intoxication is only forbidden by Buddhists, Brahmins, and Mahometans, and that the destruction of life, other than human, is regarded as sin by none but Buddhists and Brahmins, believers in the Buddh Avatar. The sanctity of animal life and the use of animal food first claim attention:—

"It is to be observed that animals are agitated, tremble, feel sorrow, show jealousy and envy, and fear death, much as men do. Their existence cannot be compared with that of plants or trees. We know not whether they will after death have another existence or not. But those persons who do believe in other births in varied conditions, who believe in transmigration, must believe that it is sinful to kill any animal; whilst those who believe in a single resurrection only, or none at all—who do not believe in the theory of Kam—will not hold it as sinful. He who is merciful and compassionate, and believes in the certainty of future existences, will not venture to kill or shorten the life of any being, from compassion and fear of the consequences.

"Question.—If, then, he who has compassion will

not injure their lives, why does he support his life on their flesh ? were there no eaters, there would be no killers. Is not the eating of flesh sin ?

"Answer.—There is a Buddhist ordinance which declares that there is no sin in eating proper meat, although it is a sin to cause the death of animals. With respect to this argument, we observe that those who hold the slaughter of animals to be sinful, are few compared with those who believe that there is no harm in it. Supposing that those who are compassionate were to refuse to eat meat, others would kill and trade in it, and the animals would die. The Mahometans do not eat pork, so pigs ought to abound in their countries, but in fact there are none at all. Animals must die by the law of nature, nor will the absence of any one to eat them prevent their death. The religion of Buddha does not compel any to act against their own dispositions, it only indicates good and evil."

"If any one who is perfectly indifferent to the nature of the food he receives, accepts killed meat given to him, or buys it in the market, or takes for food an animal which has died a natural death, there is no offence, for there is not the intention which is essential to any breach of the commandments ; but when, on a present of meat being made, the receiver expresses his great pleasure, says that he has been longing for that kind of meat, and orders it to be cooked at once, and makes it clear to the giver that he wishes for more, and so incites him to go and kill more, this is unrighteous. Again, when one insists on one's servants getting some kind of meat which one knows they will not find ready killed in the market, and so forces them to have some specially killed, this is uncompassionate and wicked. If a monk knows in any way that animals are killed merely to supply him with flesh, he should abstain from that flesh; it is impure, and the laws of the priesthood forbid him to eat it."

"The Lord Buddha was asked to forbid animal food, but he would not. There are those who hold his religion, but will not accept the First Commandment, like the Chinese, who believe in transmigration as Buddhists, but assert that there is no sin in executing criminals, or in killing animals for food."

Next, as to the vice of intoxication.

"As to the sin of drinking intoxicating things, consider! It is a cause of the heart becoming excited and overcome. By nature there is already an intoxication in man caused by desire, anger, and folly; he is already inclined to excess, and not thoughtful of the impermanence, misery, and vanity of all things. If we stimulate this natural intoxication by drinking, it will become more daring; and if the natural inclination is to anger, anger will become excessive, and acts of violence and murder will result. Similarly with the other inclinations. The drunken man neither thinks of future retribution nor present punishment."

"Again, spirituous liquors cause disease, liver disease, and short life; and the use of them, when it has become a habit, cannot be dispensed with without discomfort, so that men spend all their money unprofitably in purchasing them, and when their money is spent become thieves and dacoits. The evil is both future and immediate."

"As for the argument urged by some people, that it is customary to make offerings of spirituous liquors to the Dewa angels, and that that practice tells in favour of spirit-drinking, I can only answer that we have no proof that the angels consume these offerings; and the only foundation for such a supposition is the statement of some ancient sages that the Asura angels of Indra's heavens got drunk, which, after all, only amounts to the assertion that the Dewa (or sensual) angels resemble men in their taste for liquor."

He refers to the Total Abstinence Movement and the Mahometan law thus:—

"In the present age, many Americans have declared spirit-drinking to be an evil, a cause of much immediate mischief, and of no future good. The Jews used not to consider spirit-drinking a sin, but Mahomet declared that Allah had ordered him to forbid its use, on the ground that spirit-drinkers, if they went to heaven, would smell so offensively that the angels could not endure their vicinity."

On the subject of the Third Commandment, we are told that women who are the objects of another's jealous care—that is, wives and unmarried women, who are cared for or supported by their husbands or relatives, and women who are betrothed, are all improper objects of desire; but as this is "the undisputed opinion of all except those bad men who think there is no harm in adultery unless it is discovered," the main point considered is, why, under this Commandment, men and women are put on a different footing—that is, why polygamy is allowed?

"If we say the Commandment is different for men and women, we make two commands of it; but it is not so; it is only one—an order that sensual intercourse should be suitably regulated."

"Women are not allowed to have more than one husband, because they are under the rule of man, and not superior to man. If women might have many husbands, they would not know who was the father of their children, and these children might injure their father, and even commit parricide, without knowing it. And, moreover, the dispositions of men and women differ; men, however many wives they have, and whatever their liking or dislike to any of them, have no desire to kill them; but if women had more husbands than one, they would wish to kill all but the one they liked best, for such is their nature. There are many stories in point, one of which I will relate concisely.

"There was once on a time a priest who daily blessed a great king, saying, 'May your Majesty have the firmness of a crow, the audacity of a woman, the endurance of a vulture, and the strength of an ant.' And the King, doubting his meaning, said, 'What do you mean by the endurance of a vulture?' and he replied, 'If a vulture and all kinds of other animals are caged up without food, the vulture will outlive them all.' And the king tried, and it was so. And the priest said, 'I spoke of the strength of the ant, for an ant is stronger than a man, or anything that lives. No other animal can lift a lump of iron or copper as large as itself, but an ant will carry off its own bulk of either metal, if it be only smeared with sugar. And I said 'the firmness of the crow,' for none can subdue the boldness and energy of the crow; however long you cage it, you will never tame it. And if the king would see the audacity of a woman, I beg him to send for a couple who have been married only one or two months, who are yet deeply in love with one another, and first call the husband and say, 'Go and cut off your wife's head, and bring it to me, and I will give you half my kingdom, and make you my viceroy.' And if he will not do it, then send for the woman, and say, 'Kill your husband, and bring me his head, and I will make you my chief queen, ruler of all the ladies in the palace.' And the king did so. He found a newly-married couple who had never quarrelled, and were deeply enamoured of one another, and sending for the husband, he spoke to him as the priest had suggested. And the man took the knife, and hid it in his dress, and that same night rose when his wife slept, thinking to kill her, but he could not, because he was kind-hearted, and reflected that she had done no wrong. And the next day he returned the knife to the king, saying that he could not use it against his wife. Then the king sent messengers to the wife secretly, and they brought her to him, and he flattered and enticed her with promises, as the priest had told him, and she took the knife, and as soon as her husband slept, stabbed him, and cut off his head, and took it to the king. This story shows not only that woman is more audacious than man, but also that if any one entices and pleases them, they will plot their husband's death, which is a good reason for not letting them have more than one husband."

"At the time Jesus Christ lived, and still later in Mahomet's time, there was no law of monogamy. Mahomet limited the number of wives to four, and after a time Europeans instituted monogamy by law, not from religious motives, but from conviction of its expediency, considering that plurality of wives was unfair to women, and gave rise to jealousy and murder, and constant trouble."

"The religion of Buddha highly commends a life of chastity. Buddha stated that when a man could not remain as a celibate, if he took but one wife it was yet a kind of chastity, a commendable life. Buddha also censured polygamy, as involving ignorance and lust, but he did not absolutely forbid it, because he could not say there was any actual wrong in a man having a number of wives properly acquired."

Polygamy is extensively practised in Siam, the kings setting the example. The late king's life affords an instance of both celibacy and polygamy. At the age of twenty, his Majesty, who had been already married for some years, entered the priesthood and remained a monk for twenty-seven years; he then came to the throne, and accepting the custom of polygamy as suitable for his new position, he was, within the next sixteen years, blessed with a family of seventy-nine children. The number of his wives we could not ascertain. Many noblemen have thirty or forty, or more wives. So far as our own observation goes, this polygamy, accompanied by a facility for divorcement, is not attended by very evil results. There is a great deal of domestic happiness in Siam, and suicides and husband and wife murders, so common in monogamic Europe, are rare there. Nevertheless, many of the best men we have known there were theoretical admirers of monogamy, and one practised it.

The commandments against theft and lying are not

dilated on, as "they are regarded in the same light by all people throughout the world."

Having thus treated of morality and charity, we might expect our author to discourse on the nature of meditation, which is the great Buddhistic means of self-improvement. We presume that he omits it because it is only practised by monks, whilst his book is intended for laymen. In the absence of any remarks from him, we will only observe that by meditation and self-abstraction from all human concerns and passions, Buddhists believe man can purify himself, and can attain supernatural knowledge and power, and ultimately perfection.

We now revert to the nature of future existence. Firstly, we have a sketch of the ideas of Christians, Mahometans, and Brahmins, as to a future life, heaven and hell, which we need not quote, but pass to his exposition of the Buddhist views.

"In the religion of Phra Samana Khodom we also find mention of heaven and hell, and we are taught that those who have kept the Commandments, given alms, and lived righteously, will after death go to heavenly palaces furnished with houris, more or less numerous, according to the amount of merit they have acquired. And those who have no merit, but have only acquired demeritorious Kam, will on death go to hell, and remain there until their Kam is exhausted, when they will be born again as animals or men; or if there is any merit still belonging to them, they may even go to heaven. Those whose merit has caused them to be born as angels in heaven will, when the power of their merit is exhausted, be extinguished in heaven, and reappear as men or animals, or sometimes, when a demeritorious Kam still attaches to them, they will fall to hell. There is no fixity, but continual circulation and alternation, until such time as the spirit has become perfect in 'the four ways and the four fruits,'* which extinguish all further sorrow, stay all further change, and cause eternal rest in a state of perfect happiness where there is no further birth, nor old age, nor death. Even those who do not believe in the religion of Buddha, by good actions acquire merit, and will on their death attain heaven, and by evil actions acquire demerit, and on death will pass to hell. Buddhism does not teach the necessary damnation of those who do not believe in Buddha, and in this respect I think it is more excellent than all the other religions which teach that all but their own followers will surely go to hell."

After remarking that women as well as men can enjoy the highest pleasures of heaven, and that there may be a change of sex with a change of state, he gives his own views of the common sensual idea of heaven.

"The fact of the matter is this. The Hindoos who live in countries adjoining the Mahometan countries believe that in heaven every male has tens and hundreds of thousands of female attendants, according to what their teachers of old taught them concerning the riches of heaven, and their idea is akin to that of the Mahometans. The Mahometans had held out great inducements representing the pleasures that would result from their religion; and the Hindoo teachers

* These are the four highest grades of sanctity. He who attains the first will reach Nirwana within seven existences; the fourth leads to Nirwana direct, without any existence intervening. See also Note 14.

fearing that their people might be excited by this most promising new doctrine, themselves introduced it into their own teaching. At least, this is my impression on the subject. But if we must speak out the truth as to these matters, we must say that the world of heaven is but similar to the world of man, only differing in the greater amount of happiness there enjoyed. Angels there are in high places with all the apparel and train of their dignity, and others of lower station with less surroundings. All take up that position which is due to their previous merits and demerits. Buddha censured concupiscence; Buddha never spoke in praise of heaven; he taught but one thing as worthy of praise, 'the extinction of sorrow.' All this incoherent account of heaven is but the teaching of later writers, who have preached the luxuries and rich pleasures of heaven in hopes thereby to attract men into the paths of holiness, and the attainment of sanctity. We cannot say where heaven and hell are. All religions hold that heaven is above the world and hell below it, and every one of them uses heaven to work on men's desires, and hell to frighten them with. Some hold forth more horrors than others, according to the craft of those who have designed them to constrain men by acting on their fears, and making them quake and tremble. We cannot deny the existence of heaven and hell, for as some men in this world certainly live well and others live ill, to deny the existence of heaven and hell would be to deprive men's works of their result, to make all their good deeds utterly lost to them. We must observe, that after happiness follows sorrow, after heat follows cold; they are things by nature coupled. If after death there is a succession of existence, there must be states of happiness and of sorrow, for they are necessarily coupled in the way I have explained. As for heaven being above the earth and hell below it, I leave intelligent people to come to their own conclusion; but as to future states of happiness and sorrow, I feel no doubt whatever."

He next remarks, "That both in ancient and modern times there have been instances of persons who, on recovering from a state of trance, have declared that they have visited other worlds during their trance."

As an ancient instance he gives this story:—

"An old story of this class is that a certain Chinese Emperor—named Hli Si Bin, on recovering from a three days' trance, told his courtiers that he had visited hell and undergone fearful sufferings, and had clearly seen there many whom he knew; and that when he asked the officials of hell how these men might be rescued from their misery, he was told to follow the teaching of the Holy Buddha, and make merit on their behalf; by which means they would escape. Then the Emperor sent Som Chang to seek out and learn the religion of Buddha, and he introduced it into China from Sai Thi, a city of the Brahmins, or, as some say, Ceylon."

This story seems to refer to the dream of the Emperor Ming Ti (A.D. 62), mentioned in the Rev. S. Beal's Buddhist Pilgrims, which dream is supposed to have led to the introduction of Buddhism into China.

We next quote one of his modern instances of visions seen during a state of trance.

"A young Cambodian, aged eighteen, living at the hamlet of Phrakanong, in Siam, being sick of fever, swooned for a day, and then recovered animation. On recovery he said that he had been bound and taken to a place where there were a number of seething frying-pans containing oil or water, he was not sure which, and crowds of men and women were being unceasingly hurried along and thrown into the frying-pans, but they rejected him, saying that he had been brought there by mistake, and they drove him back to his own place."

Lest the preceding remarks should mislead any readers into the "heretical opinion that any part of the actual life existing in one state, is carried on to another, or that the actual idea which constitutes the dream is that which is born again," our author carefully reminds us that "it is only the fruit of merit and demerit, the Kam which has been created by a being, that constitutes that being in the next state of existence." He does not, however, dwell on this metaphysical subtlety of Buddhism, but passes on to the question of eternal damnation, which he combats on the ground that "there is no being who has not done something good, and that to recognise the liability of any one to suffer eternally in hell, would be to deny to good works the same power of producing fruit that is ascribed to evil works."

Some observations on the disposal of the bodies of the dead appropriately follow. "This," he writes, "is not a religious question, though Christians, in preferring burial, do look to rising in their own bodies at the sound of the trumpet when God shall come to judge them; but it is a matter of custom and convenience." The Siamese practise "cremation, a rite derived by the Buddhists from the Brahmins," and he approves it, as causing less pollution of air and water than burial does. He considers, however, that cremation in air-tight iron cases would be preferable, on sanitary grounds, to the open cremation now practised.

He next refers to the Buddhist belief, that there have been successive Buddhas who have enlightened the world at various times, between which times all knowledge of true doctrine has been lost, and he asks, "What is the fate of all those who have lived in the dark ages of the world, and of those others who, living on remote islands or in uncivilised countries, have had no opportunity of learning the religion of Buddha?" He answers that "all men have ideas of right and wrong, and according to their virtues and vices, they will accumulate merit and demerit to shape their next existence." Taking this in connection with other passages, we may say that his idea of the difference between the virtuous man who follows the teaching of Buddha, and the virtuous man who does not, is that the one is in a safe road which will prevent the recurrence of all sorrowful existence; the other, though he will also be rewarded for his virtue, is liable again to pass through a course of painful existences, for he is not in the path to Nirwana.

In the latter pages of the "Kitchanukit," there are many repetitions of ideas that have been already dilated on. There are, however, two passages of much significance, which I must quote: "What is this unseen God, personified by the Theists (Këks) as God the Creator, the Divine Spirit, and the Divine Intelligence? It seems to me that this Divine Spirit (Phra Chitr) is but the actual spirit (chitr) of man, the disposition, be it good or evil. And I think that the Divine Intelligence (Phra Winyan) which is said to exist in the light and in the darkness, in all times and in all places, is the Intelligence (Winyàn) which flies forth from the six gates of the body, that is, the faculties of sight, hearing, smell, taste, touch, and knowledge, whose Intelligence exists in all places and at all times, and knows the good and evil which man does. And God the Creator (Phra phu sang) is the Holy Merit and Demerit (Phra kusala, a-kusala), the cause and shaper of all existence. Those who have not duly pondered on these matters may say that there is a God who exists in all places, waiting to give men the reward or punishment due to their good or evil deeds, or they may say that prosperity and adversity are the work of angels or devils; but to me it seems that all happiness and misery are the natural result of causation (Kam) which influences the present existence, and will determine the nature of the next existence."

"How can we assent to the doctrine of those who believe in but one resurrection—who believe in a man being received into heaven while his nature is still full of impurity, by virtue of sprinkling his head with water, or cutting off by circumcision a small piece of his skin? Will such a man be purified by the merit of the Lord Allah, or of the Great Brahma? We know not where they are. We have never seen them. But we do know, and can prove, that men can purify their own natures, and we know the laws by which that purification can be effected. Is it not better to believe in this which we can see and know, than in that which has no reality to our perceptions?"

Such are the ideas and arguments of an honest and earnest Buddhist of the present day, defending his religion against the assaults of the numerous body of missionaries, who live in comfort, and teach without molestation among his countrymen. He is indebted to them for much information, and willingly accepts it. He listens to and admires the morality of the Christian religion, until they believe him almost a Christian, and then he tells them that Buddha too taught a morality as beautiful as theirs, and a charity that extends to everything that has breath. And when they speak of faith, he answers that by the light of the knowledge they have helped him to, he can weed out his old superstitions, but that he will accept no new ones. Their cause is, as the late king said, hopeless:—

"You must not think that any of my party will ever become Christians. We will not embrace what we think is a foolish religion."

The religion of Buddha meddled not with the Beginning, which it could not fathom; avoided the action of a Deity it could not perceive; and left open to endless discussion that problem which it could not solve, the ultimate reward of the perfect. It dealt with life as it found it; it declared all good which led to its sole object, the diminution of the misery of all sentient beings; it laid down rules of conduct which have never been surpassed, and held out reasonable hopes of a future of the most perfect happiness.

Its proofs rest on the assumptions that the reason of man is his surest guide, and that the law of nature is perfect justice. To the disproof of these assumptions we recommend the attention of those missionaries who wish to convert Buddhists.

PART II.

A LIFE OF BUDDHA,

TRANSLATED FROM THE SIAMESE PATHOMMA SOMPHOTHIYAN
OR FIRST (FESTIVAL OF) OMNISCIENCE.

IN TEN CHAPTERS.

NATIVE INTRODUCTION.

The Great, the Holy Lord, the Being who was about to become a Buddha,[1] passed the first twenty-nine years of his life as a layman by the name of Prince Sidharta.[2] He then became a religious mendicant,[3] and for six years subjected himself to self-denials of a nature that other men could not endure. Thereafter he became the Lord Buddha, and gave to men and angels the draught of Immortality,[4] which is the savour of the True Law. Forty-five years after this the Lord, the Teacher, entered the Holy Nirwana,[5] passing thereto as he lay between two lofty trees in the State Gardens of the Malla Princes, near the Royal City of Kusinagara.[6]

Note.—The numbers refer to the Notes printed at the end of Part II.

A LIFE OF BUDDHA.

CHAPTER I.

THE GLORIOUS MARRIAGE.

But a short time after the death of Buddha, Adjatasatru,[7] king of Magadha, convened an assembly of the monks of the highest order of sanctity, at a monastery built by him on the Wephara[8] Hill; and having done homage to them, requested the patriarch[9] Kasyappa to teach him the doctrine which the great Buddha had preached.

Then Kasyappa answered that he was an authority only in meditative science[10] (Bhawana), and that his knowledge of the words and acts of the great master was not equal to that of Ananda,[11] who had lived with him, and attended on him. He suggested, therefore, that Ananda should be called upon to speak.

Now Ananda was not then present in the Assembly, but was meditating in a solitary place, yet by his knowledge of the thoughts of others, he became aware that Kasyappa desired his presence, and arranging his garments suitably, he entered the assembly.

And all the men and angels who saw (his miraculous approach) were astonished.

Having done reverence to the patriarch, he inquired what was desired of him, and being informed that the king desired to hear the doctrine of the Wheel of the Law[12] as Buddha had taught it, he arranged his robes so as to leave one shoulder exposed, and holding his screen[13] before him, took his place in the pulpit, and spoke as follows :—

"The Holy Wheel which the Lord taught is plenteous in twelve ways, just as water poured on a flat stone slab streams in all directions. The Holy Wheel utterly exterminates the evil dispositions of all beings, and establishes them in the four highest degrees of saintliness.[14]

"Again, this Holy Wheel may be likened to the Chakkra of Indra,[15] king of the angels, which exterminates those against whom it is hurled, and leaves no angel remaining in the heavens it is thrown to; for even so does the Holy Wheel of the Lord Buddha extirpate evil from the dispositions of men, and bring them to holy Nirwana.

"I, Ananda, have learned but one of its twelve ways. I can only speak of what I have seen and heard in the company of our Lord the Teacher.

"When the Lord fixed his desire on becoming a Buddha, he was a man named Chotiban.[16] He bore his mother on his shoulders to her house, and diligently ministered to her; and then it was that the desire arose in him to arrive at perfect wisdom.

"After he had destroyed the five elements[17] of corporeal being, he was reborn in the Brahma heavens.

"The grandfather of our Lord Buddha was King Singhanu, of the noble race of Sakyas,[18] who ruled the kingdom of Kapila.[19] He had three sons, and when the eldest, named Suddhodana,[20] reached sixteen years of age, he resigned his sovereignty to him, and sought as his queen a princess of the most kingly descent, endowed with the sixty-four marks of perfection,[21] and the five great beauties, perfect in manners, and steadfast in observing the Five Commandments[22] and the Eight Commandments. To this end he selected eight Brahmins[23] skilled in the three Vedas, learned in all arts, able to interpret the signs of the qualities of men and women; and bestowing on them a large sum of money, he ordered them to seek a princess such as he desired.

"Now in the time of the Buddha Wipassi,[24] the Princess Maia was daughter of the King of Panthumawadi, and she having offered to that Buddha a stick of precious sandal wood, had placed the remainder in a holy building, and had made a prayer. "O Lord, who excellest in the three[25] worlds, let the reward of my offering be that in an after generation I may be the mother of a Buddha like thyself!" And the Buddha Wipassi assented to her prayer. From thenceforth she devoted herself to works of piety, and passed through many transmigrations, until the time of the Buddha Kasyappa, when she was born as the daughter of King Kingkisa, and was called Sutharama. And then hearing the teaching of that Buddha, her heart took delight in his religion, and she gave immense alms to its followers, and its Lord; and thereafter she was born in the Dewa heavens, and when she left them, was re-born in the world as daughter of the King of Mathura by name Phusadi, and she married the Prince Saiyachai. When she had extinguished the five attributes of corporeal being, she was again born in the

Dewa heaven, named Tushita,[26] and thereafter was again born as daughter of Ankana,[27] King of Dewadaha. She was exquisitely lovely, her form a perfect picture, her complexion golden, her hair of surpassing fineness, and glossy as the wings of the beetle; eminent in the five beauties, and possessing all the sixty-four signs of superiority in women. And she was named Maia. And she grew in beauty and in virtue. One day when distributing rice to the poor, her bowl supplied the wants of a vast number of people, and yet remained full; again all sick persons who touched her hand were cured of their diseases.

"Nor was this all—the Chiefs of the Genii (Yak)[28] guarded her on all sides with their royal swords; and the four[29] guardians of the world unceasingly watched and protected her. And whenever she saw poor men or hermits, her desire was to help them, and the gifts she desired to present to them came miraculously to her hands. Having grown to maidenhood, she one day, attended by her train of guardians and companions, a crowd of lovely women, visited her garden, and after bathing in a shady pool, collected flowers, and weaving them into garlands, made an offering of them to the Buddhas of former times, her mind at the time being full of the desire to become the mother of a Buddha.

"At this very time, the eight Brahmins who had been sent forth by King Singhanu entered the garden where Maia was walking with her maidens. They had travelled through many countries, vainly seeking for a princess having the sixty-four signs of perfection; they had indeed found some few endowed with eighteen signs, but none with sixty-four. Hearing the sound of many pleasant voices, they entered the garden, and their venerable appearance having attracted the attention of the princess, she ordered them to be provided with seats that they might converse with her.

"After offering to supply whatever they required, she inquired the object of their visit, and they told her; and then she asked who Singhanu was. 'He,' they answered, 'is a glorious monarch, steadfast in the Five Commandments, firm in the Ten Rules of Kings,[30] and his eldest son, Prince Suddhodana, is graced with every art and accomplishment. He is of middle height; no woman sees him without loving him; his age is sixteen years, and his father desires to resign his sovereignty to him, and has sent us to discover a princess possessed of the five beauties, and the sixty-four signs of perfection, to be his queen. Hitherto we have searched in vain, but now in you we see one who would be an equal match for our prince.

"And the princess, hearing their words, was pleased and felt a passion for the Prince Suddhodana, but she concealed it as a light in a dark lantern, saying, 'O Brahmins, this is no matter for my ears—go tell it my father.'

"Having been introduced to the king, that monarch strictly examined them as to the position and qualities of Prince Suddhodana, and being perfectly satisfied, and with the approval of his counsellors, he consented to the marriage; and loading the messengers with presents for themselves, and royal presents for their king, he sent them away to announce their success.

"In the middle watch of the night King Singhanu, calmly sleeping on his royal couch, dreamt a dream. A magnificent jewelled palace sprang up from the earth—its base rested on the world of men, its roof reached to the Brahma heavens, and it embraced all the ten thousand worlds within its walls. Its first story was in the lowest angelic world (Chatu Maharachika), its second in the next higher angelic world (Dawadungsa); in each of the six Dewa heavens was one story, and its stories extended throughout the sixteen heavens of the Great Brahmas, and the (still higher) heavens of the formless. Its dazzling radiance shone throughout all worlds. And in its midst there was a jewelled throne two hundred and fifty miles in height and fifty miles in width. And on it sat a mighty lion-like man, beside a beautiful lady. Then there arose a great cloud, and rain fell in gentle showers over the whole world. Then all formed beings fell before the feet of the mighty man, and he made them learn the rules of virtue, and bestowed exceeding happiness upon them. And on the east of the palace there was a vast lake, so wide that none could see across it; and the mighty man made a ship, so that all who desired might be able to cross it.

"Next morning the king summoned his Brahmin soothsayers, and he declared the dream to mean that his messengers had been successful, that they had found a princess whose child would be a Buddha, and that they were about to return with the news. And as the Brahmin spoke, the eight messengers entered the palace, and laid their presents before the king. Having fully reported their acts, the king sent them to conduct his ambassador, Suthathiya, and three Sakya princes, as an embassy, to demand Maia in marriage for his son; and the King of Dewadaha graciously received the embassy, and assented to the marriage.

"Then King Singhanu assembled the Sakyas (the princes of his family), and made a broad road from his own country to Dewadaha. Beside it were planted sugar canes and bananas, and it was adorned with royal standards and other insignia. In the adjoining fields were halls for music, and all kinds of festivities. Over the road was spread an awning of white cloth, hung with bunches of flowers, filling the air in all directions with their rich fragrance. And all being prepared, King Singhanu, and the Prince Suddhodana, mounted on royal elephants, with gorgeous trappings, and surrounded by a large escort, with ten thousand horsemen, and a great train of chieftains and ladies, marched towards Dewadaha.

"When King Ankana learnt of their approach, he summoned his courtiers around him, and, arriving at the gardens where they were resting, he descended from his litter, and entering on foot, offered homage to King Singhanu, and then sat down on a suitable seat on one side. King Singhanu clasped his hand, and invited him to come close to him, and they conversed pleasantly together. The King of Dewadaha would then have escorted his guest into the city, but he declined, on the ground that his followers were better away from the city, where, perchance, they might make broils. And it was agreed between them that he should reside in the garden.

"Great preparations were then made for the marriage. Three palaces and a temple were erected, and in the temple was placed a lofty jewelled throne.

"And on the first day of the fourth month, the King of Dewadaha caused his royal daughter to be bathed with sixteen bowls of scented waters, and to adorn herself with rich garments, like an angel of the Tushita heavens. And King Singhanu caused his son to bathe, so that not a spot of impurity might remain on his body, then to anoint himself with scented waters, and put on the vestments of a king, with the five insignia[31] requisite at the coronations of sovereigns.

"And when the moment of good omen arrived, the King of Dewadaha brought forth his daughter in a magnificent chariot, and at that moment, Indra, king of the angels, perceiving that she who would be the mother of a Buddha was on the point of her espousals, attended by a vast number of angels and houris, descendedto Dewadaha, and there, with the angels of the earth, the angels of the trees, and the angels of the air, united in singing praises, loud sounding praises, audible even in the worlds of the highest Brahma. And Suthawat, the great Brahma, brought his great royal parasol and extended it; and Sahabodi, the great Brahma, brought in his right hand a crystal jar full of scented water, and in his left a crystal cup, and, attended by the host of Brahmas, appeared before the king; and the king joyfully exclaimed, 'Wonderful is the merit of my daughter, and worthy of all praise; the very skies are radiant with the glory of the heavenly host which comes to praise her.'

"At the moment she mounted her car, the Angel Queen Suchada anointed her head with heavenly fluid.

"Thus attended by angels and men, the Princess Maia was escorted to the temple.

"On his part, the King of Kapila escorted his son with equal pomp; and he, too, was attended by a host of angels.

"And they all entered the temple.

"And when the moment of good omen arrived, the Brahmin Chipho took the wrists of Prince Suddhodana and placed him on a jewelled throne, and the noblest lady of the harem led the Princess Maia by her wrist and placed her on the same seat. Then they made them clasp each other's hands, entwining their fingers. And the angels filled the air with music. Indra blew his loud cornch. Suthawat, the great Brahma, repeated a blessing, and poured scented water on both their heads,[32] the ceremony of assumption of royal dignity.

"Then the earth quaked; the sea heaved in great waves, and was covered with foam, and all the angels of all the infinite worlds made offerings of flowers, and gave praises with one voice.

"And all beholders were astonished, their hair stood on end, and they shouted the praises of the royal pair, saying, 'Surely this miracle betokens the vastness of their merit.'

"And their royal parents were equally astonished, and the Queen Sunantha,[33] mother of the Princess Maia, made an offering to the angels—candles, incense sticks, dried rice, and flowers, and all kinds of scents, and prayed thus: 'Hear me, all ye angels! In that I am old, and shall not live to see the child that this my daughter will bring forth to be the holy Teacher, may I after death be reborn in the heavens of the Brahmas, and thence come to listen to the Wheel of the Law, that I may escape further evils in the circle of existence.' Having made this prayer, she returned to her palace.

"The two kings and their attendant princes raised their hands in adoration to the angels, and pronounced blessings on the royal couple; and the angels offered sacrifice to them; and the eight kings of the Yakkhas offered sacrifice of the most precious sandal-wood; and a great king of angels, the Wetsuwan, brought an offering of angelic raiment, and two great kings of angels offered the most exquisite fruits of the earth; and all the angels invoked on them four blessings—'May you both live to a full age! May your glory increase, and become more lustrous than that of any of the beings on this earth! May you live in perfect happiness; and may the powers of your minds and bodies be beyond all comparison!' And having thus blessed them, the angels departed to their own places.

"Immediately after the ceremony, the King of Kapila despatched officers to build three palaces—one of seven stories, constructed entirely of sandal-wood; a second of nine stories, constructed entirely of eagle-wood; and a third of gold and jewels.

"And when news was brought of their completion, they took leave of the King of Dewadaha, and ascended a glorious chariot prepared for them by Indra, king of the angels, in order that they might return to Kapila, and they took their way escorted by the King Singhanu, and the royal tribe of Sakyas, and the four divisions of the army, and Indra and a host of angels, and King Ankana, and the four divisions of his army.

"And King Ankana sent vast presents after them to follow them to Kapila.

"Now, the road from Kapila to Dewadaha was about twenty miles; and in general when people travelled to and fro by it the dust rose in clouds, darkening the air; yet as this great procession marched along it, there was not one handful of dust, it was like one smooth slab the whole way.

"On arrival, the coronation ceremony was repeated by the Sakyas, and Prince Suddhodana governed the kingdom in place of his father. And when the King Singhanu died, Suddhodana ruled over the realm of Kapila."

END OF THE GLORIOUS MARRIAGE.

CHAPTER II.

THE DESCENT FROM THE TUSHITA HEAVENS.

THE most illustrious king, the Grand Being who was born the exalted crown of the world, the anointed head of the world, was moved by his vast compassion to endeavour to redeem all teachable beings sunk in the great ocean of ever-circling existence, and lead them to the jewelled realm of happiness, the immortal Nirwana. For this object he gave up the glories of universal [34] dominion, the pomp of state, and the possession of the seven great treasures,[35] which he was within seven days of attaining; he gave them up, regarding them as no more than a drop of spittle, or the dust upon his feet, and entered the great order of mendicants, in order that he might obtain the fruit, which is Omniscience, in the tree of perfect virtue and charity.

This had the Lord steadfastly desired for an almost infinite period of years,[36] from the time when the holy Buddha Dipangkara [37] was the Teacher of the world. He was then a hermit, named Sumetta, proficient in meditative science,[38] and perceived with his angelic sight that misery is the lot of all beings; yet did he not seek to escape from transmigrating existence, because of his vast compassion. Even though by lying down in a pool and making a bridge of his body for the great Teacher to pass over, he perfected his merits, and might have at once obtained the fruits of the highest sanctity and escaped the sorrows of life, he declined the fruit of his merits because of the charity he felt towards all beings, and the desire he had to become their future Buddha. For this he persisted in enduring toil, trouble, and pain; for this he bore the miseries of life and the pangs of death through an uncountable number of transmigrations; and no suffering ever turned his thoughts from his one great object—the Buddhahood. He cut off portions of his flesh and gave them in alms so vast a number of times, that, if collected, the mass would be greater than this world. He poured out his blood in alms, more than there is water in the great ocean. He gave his head so many times, that the heap would be higher than the mightiest of mountains, Meru. He gave his eyes, more than there are stars in the sky. Throughout the immense period that passed from the times of the Buddha Dipangkara, to the present Buddha age, he steadily practised the thirty virtues,[39] and the five great charities, and perfected himself in the power of righteousness.[40]

When he appeared in the world as the Prince Wessantara,[41] continuing his practice of the highest virtues, he caused the earth to quake seven times in acknowledgment of his seven most eminent acts of charity; and on ending that existence, he was born in the Tushita heavens, there to reign throughout five thousand angelic years, which are five hundred and eighty-six millions of the years of men.

Such has ever been the custom of Grand Beings, whose virtues are perfect; but if their virtue is not yet perfected, they do not complete their whole period of existence in the heavens, but, closing their eyes, they pray: "Now let me fulfil my time," and they immediately descend and are reborn among men according to their desire, that they may perfect their power of righteousness; and when they have perfected it, they are reborn as angels to dwell their full age in the Tushita heavens, preparatory to reappearing in their last transmigratory existence as Buddha.

When our Grand Being had ruled in the Tushita heavens to within one hundred thousand years of the end of his time, there was a portent followed in due course by four others, for such has ever been the case with Buddhas.

The first portent is, when the angels of the tempest,[42] clothed in red garments and with streaming hair, travel among the abodes of mankind crying: "Attend all ye who are near to death; repent and be not heedless![43] The end of the world approaches; but one hundred thousand years more, and it will be destroyed. Exert yourselves then, exert yourselves to acquire merit. Above all things be charitable; abstain from doing evil; meditate with love towards all beings, and listen to the teachings of holiness. For we are all in the mouth of the King of death. Strive then earnestly for meritorious fruits, and seek that which is good."

And the second portent is, when the great Brahma proclaims: "Oh let us all seek to do good, and give alms, that we may profit by it; that we may meet him whose merits are perfect. The time is near, but one hundred years distant, that the Lord of the universe will be born in this world, to teach us all, and lead us all to the glorious possession of men, the glorious possession of heaven. Be not heedless!"

And the third portent is, when the great Brahma Suthawat comes and cries in the worlds of men: "Be not intent on that which is around you. But twelve years hence, and the Lord, the Jewel, Buddha, will teach his glorious secrets, will teach that which is glorious for all beings, that they may arrive at the perfection of their desires! Be not heedless, but endeavour to acquire merit!"

And the fourth portent is, when the Dewa angels proclaim in similar manner his advent in seven years.

And the fifth portent is, when the great Brahma, in the gorgeous attire of his order, travels through the ten thousand worlds proclaiming: "Attend all ye who are in the jaws of death! one hundred thousand years hence, the omniscient Lord, the venerable Teacher of the three worlds, shall be born in this earth. If ye would meet him, ye must abstain from the five great offences,—the destruction of life, fraud, adultery, lying, and intoxication; ye must give alms, observe the rules of religion, practise thoughtful love, and seek to do meritorious acts, and be not niggardly in doing them."

Such are the five portents which invariably precede the birth of a Buddha.

The time having arrived, the Brahma and Dewa angels of the ten thousand worlds,[44] the four guardians of each world, in all forty thousand, and all the Dewas of might and influence assembled together, proceeded to the abode of the Grand Being, and having done homage, addressed him thus:—

"O Lord, perfect in merits, whose time is at hand; thou that hast coveted no earthly honour, no heavenly glory, no sovereignty of Brahmas or Dewas; that hast steadfastly set thy will on arriving at the Holy

Buddhahood, desiring to rescue all beings from the ocean of circling existence, and lead them to the Immortal Nirwana; now has the time arrived that thou shalt descend into the womb! O Lord Buddha, the creatures of the worlds have no protector. They are sunk in the vast and terrible ocean of existence, and there is none to help them. There is but thou alone to show compassion towards them. Accept, we pray thee, our supplication, and be born into the world of men. Thou art he that will become the omniscient Buddha. Enter the lustrous vessel of the true law! Incite, lead and redeem all beings from the four seas of existence; that by the power of thy mighty merits, we may all escape from misery!"

And as they spoke, there appeared to the Grand Being five signs.

First,—The flowers with which he was adorned withered.

Second,—His splendid robes appeared discoloured and soiled.

Third,—Sweat streamed from the pores of his body.

Fourth,—His beautiful golden skin became dark and discoloured.

Fifth,—He could not rest at ease on his heavenly couch.[45]

Yet, indeed, the flowers of heaven remain ever fresh throughout the life of the angel whom they adorn, and wither not until the day is near that their possessor will descend from his angelic existence. Neither until that time is at hand do the royal robes of angels lose their spotless beauty. Nor until then does sweat ever appear on their bodies, for they feel neither heat nor cold; nor are their bodies subject to any imperfection. Male angels ever appear in the full beauty of early manhood, and female angels with all the perfection of fair sixteen ; and they are subject to no change until they are about to enter on another life, when deformity comes upon them, and their lives, which till then have known no sorrow, are clouded with sadness. And simultaneously with these signs of an angel's approaching end, there are other portents ; not for all angels, but for those only whose merit is of the highest degree ; portents such as earthquakes, eclipses, and meteors, of like nature to those which are the precursors of the death of the great among men, signs full of meaning to those who have knowledge of astrology, and who alone can predict these great events.

Now while the host of angels yet invoked the Grand Being, as has been already set forth ; ere he vouchsafed to accord their prayer, he reflected on the five conditions of the appearance of a Buddha in the world.

These five conditions are,[46] the duration of human life, the continent wherein he will appear, the country where he will be born, the caste to which he will belong, the age of her who will be his mother.

He considered the duration[47] of human life, knowing that no Buddha ever appears when the duration of life is more than a hundred thousand years, or less than one hundred years, because in either case his teaching would be lost ; inasmuch as when the lives of men extend to so long a period they are unlikely to believe in the unchangeable teachings of Buddha on the three subjects—Impermanence, Misery, and Unreality ; and he will be unable to rescue them from ever circling existence : and when their lives are less than one hundred years, they will be so full of ignorance and wickedness, that even though they listen for a while to the teachings, they will relapse into wickedness as soon as their teacher has left them. The effect of the teaching will entirely disappear, just as a mark drawn on water, which is visible but for a moment and then vanishes for ever. And the Lord saw that the age of beings was now a full hundred years, and that the time was therefore suitable for his birth.

Next he considered the continent, and reflecting that all preceding Buddhas had been born in the continent of men like ourselves, Jambu Dvipa, he also selected that continent.[48]

Then reflecting on the country, he perceived that the central country[49] (Mid India) had been the birthplace of all Buddhas, of Pacheka[50] Buddhas, of the two principal disciples,[51] and the eighty[52] great disciples of Buddhas, of universal Emperors, of the most eminent[53] of the warrior caste, of the men of property, and of Brahmins, of all who have surpassing merit. On these considerations he also selected the central country as his birthplace. Having duly considered the countries, he next considered of caste[54] or family, and he perceived that all Buddhas have been born either in the Royal caste or the caste of Brahmins, whichever of the two was at the time held in most esteem by men, but never had they been born as merchants, or farmers, or in other castes. He perceived that at this time the race of kings was esteemed above all others, and therefore he decided that he would be born of the Royal race of Kapila, and that the King Suddhodana should be his father.

Finally, he reflected on her who should be his mother.

According to the custom of Buddhas, he could not be born of any ill-conducted, immoral person, but of one who had passed stainlessly through countless generations, and had never offended against the Five great Commandments; and he saw that she who would be his royal mother, the Queen Maia, would continue to live but ten months and eight days from that time, and that it was now right that he should descend into the world of men.

Then the Grand Being assented to the prayer of the host of angels, saying: "Take heed, all ye that are in the jaws of death. The time has arrived that I should descend, and be born on earth as the Holy Jewel Buddha. Depart to your abodes!"

And when the host of angels had left him according to his command, surrounded by his own train of Tushita angels, he entered the Nanthawan [55] Gardens. Beautiful are the Nanthawan Gardens! They abound in trees, covered with angelic flowers and fruits of exquisite loveliness, amid whose branches innumerable birds of the most gorgeous plumage make the air resound with their harmonious songs. Mid masses of ever-blooming flowers, there are lotus lakes wherein grow scented lilies of the choicest kinds, and shoals of fishes, large and small, disport themselves. And there are stairs leading down to the water, overlaid with gold and jewels.

Thither the Grand Being went, surrounded by his train, and seeing the suitable moment, he descended from the abodes of angels.

Then was seen a prodigy. The earth trembled—the worlds throughout the universe trembled and quaked. A brilliant light shone among all worlds.

The blind who desired to see, saw. The deaf who desired to hear, heard. The dumb recovered their speech. The cripples became straight. The prisoners were set free. The flames of hell were extinguished. The insatiable hunger and thirst of the Pretas[56] was appeased. All pain ceased. Detraction was at an end. All beings spoke kindly to one another. The elephants trumpeted their joy. The horses neighed with delight. Every instrument of music gave forth sweet sounds of itself without being touched. Even the very jewels people wore clanged together in sweet harmony. The air was filled with flowers. The winds blew mild, cool, and refreshing. The rain fell in soft showers. The birds ceased to fly through the air. The rivers stayed their current. The waters of the sea became sweet. The whole sky was dotted with the five kinds of lotuses. All flowers burst into bloom and distilled the most delicious fragrance. Lotuses sprang from every tree, and branch, and shrub, and herb, even from the very stones. On every lotus stem were seven flowers. Garlands hung suspended in the skies, and flowers rained down on all sides. And there was a mighty sound of music, spontaneously rising from the instruments of music of the angels.

Such were the prodigies which appeared when the King, the Descendant of Mighty Conquerors, the Holy Grand Man, the Highest Crown, the Perfection of Power, the Infinitely Meritorious, the Lord excelling all, descended from the Tushita heavens, and was conceived in the world of men.

CHAPTER III.

THE BIRTH IN THIS WORLD.

In the city of Kapila, on the fifteenth[57] day of the eighth month, Suddhodana the king commanded his people to celebrate the festival of the constellation Asanha. And they had great rejoicings, feasting and music, and sports of all kinds, and gave themselves up to pleasure without restraint.

For seven days before the festival, the Queen Maia, clad in her sumptuous royal robes, and perfumed with precious ointments, appeared in all the glory and pomp of her high dignity. On the morning of the seventh day, rising from her couch, she had sixteen jars of scented water poured over her, and then distributed four hundred thousand pieces of money among the sick, the crippled, and the destitute. Then she put on the robes and insignia of a queen of the highest rank, and entering her breakfast chamber, partook of the most delicious food, and then diligently performed the religious observances proper to the holy day.[58]

Having finished her duties, she entered her beautiful sleeping chamber, and falling asleep on her couch, she saw a vision.

The four kings of the world bore her away on her couch, and placed her on the top of an immense rock in the Himalayan forest. They then retired; and their queens advancing, led her to bathe in the

Anodat[59] Lake, and having caused her to wash off all human impurities, they anointed her with heavenly scents, robed her in heavenly raiment, and adorned her with heavenly flowers. Then they led her to a golden palace, standing on a silver mountain, and prayed her to rest on a couch with her face turned to the west. Thence she saw a golden mountain, whereon the Royal Being that should be Buddha marched in the form of a white elephant. The most admirable of white elephants leaving the mountain of gold, came to the foot of the mountain of silver, and passed round to its northern side. In his beautiful trunk he held a newly-expanded white lotus flower. He ascended the mountain, and having trumpeted loudly, entered the golden palace. Thrice he marched around[60] the couch, and at the end of the third circuit, he appeared to enter her right side and pass into her womb.

And at the very time that the Queen Maia had this vision, the Grand Being descended from the Tushita heavens, and was conceived in her womb.

Next morning, the Queen Maia related her vision to the king, and the king summoned sixty-four Brahmins, learned in the three Vedas, that they might show its interpretation, and tell him whether it was of good or evil import. And when they had heard it, they answered, "Be not grieved, O king! for this is a most auspicious vision. Thy queen shall bear a son, a Grand Being, of excelling glory and power, of infinite merits, and wisdom beyond estimation. If he devote himself to a worldly life, he will be a Chakkravartin Emperor, possessor of the seven treasures, and ruling over all the world. If he devote himself to religion, then will he become a Buddha."

Then the king rejoiced exceedingly, and gave orders that all care might be taken of his queen during her pregnancy; that wherever she might be, sleeping or waking, she might be surrounded by that which was pure, melodious, harmonious, refined, elegant, and simple.

And the forty thousand guardian angels of the ten thousand worlds watched around her, with perfect delicacy. Never were they seen when she desired privacy, but at all other times she saw them guarding her by day and by night, and she saw them without fear.

From this time no sensual desire ever disturbed her thoughts. She steadfastly obeyed, as she had done from her youth up, the Five great Commandments, and abstained from all impurity, as the mothers of Buddhas ever have done.

In those days, when the teachings of a Buddha were unknown, men raising their hands with reverence, held as their creed the commandments taught by the followers of the Tapas and Parivrâjaka.[61] And the Queen Maia herself had been wont to follow the rules of the ascetic Kaladewila,[62] but, from the time of her conception, she would no longer sit at the feet of others, but worshipped according to her own thoughts.

And the great kings of the earth vied with each other in bringing gifts to the great King Suddhodana, impelled thereto by the influence of the merits of the Grand Being who was in the womb of Maia.

And the Grand Being dwelt in his mother's womb, not in pain and discomfort, as is the lot of other beings, but in comfort and happiness, sitting erect like to one of those beautiful images[63] which men erect on jewelled thrones, or like to the Great Brahma sitting in a glorious palace of the heavens, plunged in deep meditation.

Beautiful in form, free from all contact with impurity, he sat in the womb enjoying the full use of his reason, and fully aware of the three circumstances of his existence, namely, his conception, his gestation, and his birth, unlike all other beings, which have no knowledge of these things.

And Maia felt no pain, nor had she the troubles of other women in her condition, nor was the elegant contour of her figure enlarged or changed. Her body became clear and brilliant, so that she and her child could see each other through it, even as the red thread can be seen through the bright pearls threaded on it.

Such were the effects of the infinite merits of the Grand Being.

When Maia had completed a period of ten months, she obtained the king's permission to visit her parents at Dewadaha. The king had the road cleared and levelled, and made gay with flags and flowers, and jars of water were placed at intervals along it. A golden litter was provided for the queen, and an escort of a thousand noble ladies attended her.

Between the cities of Kapila and Dewadaha, there was in those days a forest of the most splendid trees, named Simwaliwana. It was a lovely spot. Interlacing branches, richly covered with foliage, sheltered the traveller as if he were covered with a canopy. The sun's scorching rays could not penetrate to the delicious shade. All over the trees, from their trunks to their very tops, bunches of flowers budded, bloomed, and shed their fragrant leaves, and unceasingly budded and bloomed again. Attracted by their sweet pollen, flights of shining beetles buzzed around them, filling the air with a melodious humming like to the music of the heavens. There were pools full of lotuses of all colours, whose sweet scent was wafted around by gentle breezes, and whose fruit floated on the waters in all stages of ripeness.

When the Queen Maia entered this forest, the trees, the inanimate trees, bowed down their heads before her, as if they would say, "Enjoy yourself, O queen! among us, ere you proceed on your journey." And the queen, looking on the great trees, and the forest lovely as the gardens of the angels, ordered her litter to be stayed, that she might descend and walk.

Then, standing under one of the majestic trees, she desired to pluck a sprig from the branches, and the branches bent themselves down that she might reach the sprig that she desired; and at that moment, while she yet held the branch, her labour came upon her. Her attendants held curtains around her; the angels brought her garments of the most exquisite softness; and standing there, holding the branch, with her face turned to the east, she brought forth her son, without pain or any of the circumstances which attend that event with women in general.

Thus was he born, on Friday, the fifteenth day of the sixth month of the year of the dog, under the astronomical sign Wisakha.

The Great Brahma Sutthawat receiving the child in a golden net, held him before his mother's face, crying, "Happy art thou, O queen, whose son hath merit beyond all comparison." And at that moment there poured from heaven two streams of water, one on the queen and one upon the Grand Being.

From the hands of the Great Brahma, he was received by the four guardians of the world, from them by the archangel Indra, and from him by the host of Brahmas, and, leaving their hands, he stood erect upon the earth on his own holy feet. The Great Brahma held over him the white parasol of kings, the Dewa Suyama brought a royal fan, and other angels bore the royal sabre, gleaming with jewels, the royal golden slippers, and the jewelled crown, the five great insignia of royalty. These things were seen, but the angels who bore them were invisible.

The Holy King, the Grand Being, turning his eyes towards the east, regarded the vast host of angels, Brahmas, and Dewas, Yom[64] and Yakhas, Asuras, Gandharvas, Suparnas, Garudas, and men; and they rained flowers and offerings upon him, and bowed in adoration, praising him, and crying, "Behold the excellent Lord, to whom none can be compared, to whom there is none superior." Then, in order, he turned to the other points of the compass, and from each received the same adoration. And having thus regarded the whole circle of the heavens, he turned to the north, and, gravely marching seven paces, his voice burst forth in the glorious words, "I am the greatest being in the world, excelling in the world; there is none equal to me, there is none superior to me. This is my last generation. For me there will be no future birth into the world!"

Then the ten thousand worlds quaked. The universe was illumined with an exceeding bright light. The moon shone with heavenly radiance. The sun's heat ceased its violence, and gave out but an agreeable warmth. A refreshing shower fell upon the four continents, and all musical instruments gave out harmonious sounds of themselves; and in all places there appeared the thirty-two miraculous signs which had attended his conception in the womb.

These are the signs, and the interpretation which the learned give of them:—

The ten thousand worlds quaked; signifying that he would be omniscient.

The angels assembled; signifying that the angelic ruler would teach them the true law.

The Brahma angels first received him; signifying that he would attain the meditative science[65] of the formless Brahmas.

Men received him from the angels; signifying that he would attain the meditative science of the formed Brahmas.[65]

He at once stood firmly on his feet; signifying that he would have the four miraculous powers.[66]

He turned to the north; signifying that he would rescue all beings from false doctrines.

He took seven steps; signifying that he would have the seven constituents[67] of the highest wisdom.

The Great Brahma held over him the white parasol of kings; signifying that he would arrive at the perfection of saintly fruits of emancipation.

The angels bore after him the five insignia of royalty; signifying that he would be master of the five great principles of emancipation.[68]

He looked upon all points of the compass; signifying that he would attain the science which makes all things perfectly manifest.[69] (?)

He declared that he was the most exalted of beings; signifying that he would teach the law of the revolving wheel.

All jewels in the world shone with unwonted lustre; signifying that the earth would be enlightened by the holy jewel of the true law.

The guitars sounded of themselves; signifying that he would enjoy the meditative tranquillity of perfect freedom. (?)

The drums gave out their notes; signifying that he would possess the drum of victory, which is the true law.

All who were in torment and fetters were set free; signifying that he would cause all pain to cease.[70]

The sick were healed; signifying that he would attain the knowledge of the four pre-eminent truths.[71]

The mad became sane; signifying that he would attain the four applications of reflective power.[72]

The vessel crossed the seas and returned to its port; signifying that he would attain the four classes of distinctive knowledge.[73]

Those who had been enemies, became friends; signifying that he would attain the four virtuous inclinations.[74]

The fires of hell were extinguished; signifying that he would extinguish the eleven fires, of which lust is the fiercest.[75]

The blind saw; signifying that he would be all-seeing.

The deaf heard; for that he would be all-hearing.

The lame walked; signifying that he would lead his disciples to the attainment of miraculous powers.

Light shone through the darkest hells; signifying

that he would repress ignorance, and make manifest understanding.

The water of the ocean became sweet and pleasant to drink; signifying that he would enjoy the most excellent flavour of Nirwana.

The violent winds ceased their fury; signifying that he would make an end of the sixty-two false doctrines.[76]

The birds no longer flew hither and thither through the air, but remained still on their trees; signifying that all beings would take their stand in the Holy Triad[77] of the excellent religion of Buddha.

The moon's rays became supernaturally brilliant; for men and angels would love the Lord: and the sun's rays fell with unusual mildness; for that the Lord would bestow happiness of body and spirit on all teachable beings.

The angels stood and clapped their hands at their palace gates; signifying that he would display the divine authority of a Buddha.

The ever ravenous Pretas ceased to crave for food; signifying that he would bestow the happiness of emancipation on all his disciples.

Doors opened of themselves; signifying that he would open the royal gates, the eight-fold paths[78] of the saints, to all teachable beings.

All trees and plants burst into bloom; signifying that he would cause all who acted according to his teaching to receive the reward of their works.[79]

Lotus flowers appeared in every place; signifying that he would constrain the paths and fruits to appear for the advantage of all teachable beings.

And lastly, the appearance of flowers and flags of

victory throughout the ten thousand worlds, signified that he would bestow the monk's robe, which is the flag of victory of the saints, on all teachable beings who desired to receive ordination.

Now, when the Grand Being marched those seven paces, and the universe was filled with the portents that have been related, he, though naked, appeared to be clad in rich vestments; though but a small babe, he appeared like a youth of sixteen; though walking on the ground, he seemed to tread upon the air.

The sages tell us that at the same time that the Grand Being was born into the world, seven other things came into the world—namely, the Princess Phimpha, Ananda, Phra Luthayi (Kaludari), Channa, the horse Kanthaka, the great Bodhi or sacred Po tree, and the four great gold mines.[80]

Then all the royal Sakyas of the cities Dewadaha and Kapila made glad and rejoiced, and brought offerings to the Grand Being and his mother, sacrificial offerings of the most glorious kind; and they escorted them back to the royal city of Kapila, amid songs and rejoicing.

CHAPTER IV.

PREDICTIONS OF FUTURE GREATNESS.

On that day, the angels of the Davadungsa heavens, led by the archangel Indra, vied in joyful cries, saying—"To Suddhodana, king of Kapila, and Maia his queen, there is now a son born, who, in days to come, when he attains the full age of manhood, shall sit on the jewelled throne beneath the holy tree, and shall there arrive at the Buddhahood, and shall make manifest the law of the revolving wheel to all teachable beings who are now enveloped in ignorance. We, too, shall see the glory, and praise the beauty of the Lord Buddha, and shall hear his teachings[81] of the true law." They shouted forth their praises, and worshipped him with offerings;[82] they waved cloths and flags; male and female, they gave expression to their joy by the grandest of festive ceremonies.

In those times lived a holy man named Kaladewila, who was a member of a religious body whose doctrines differed from those of Buddha; and he was the teacher of the King Suddhodana. He was master of the five supernatural arts, and of the eight perfections of meditative abstraction, and had the power of flying through the air, etc., etc. This day he had transported himself to the Davadungsa heavens, and, sitting there, heard the rejoicings of the angels, and was told by them of the birth of King Suddhodana's son, a being who had more accumulated merit than any other in the world.

Immediately he returned to earth, and entering the palace, seated himself before the king. The king ordered the ladies in attendance to adorn the child, and bring him to do reverence to the holy man; but instead of doing reverence, he rose into the air, and placed his beautiful feet on the head of the holy man. Nor, indeed, would it have been right that the incipient Buddha, who had arrived at his last generation, and had perfected the powers of righteousness, should have shown signs of respect to any being. Had any constrained him to bow his head to the feet of Kaladewila, doubtless, at that moment, the head of Kaladewila would have split into seven pieces.

And Kaladewila was filled with astonishment, and, respectfully leaving the seat (of honour), he bowed down and did homage to him, raising his hands, and reverentially embracing the feet of the being who would be Buddha.

And the King Suddhodana, amazed at what he saw, did homage to his son for the first time. [83]

Then Kaladewila, whose supernatural powers enabled him to tell all that had happened during forty past creations of the world, and to foresee all that would happen for forty generations to come, perceiving that the body of the Grand Being was marked with all the signs of eminence, recognised that he would certainly become Buddha, and his countenance beamed with joy; but immediately reflecting as to whether he himself would live to see the day, he divined that he would not; but, dying before that time, would be reborn in the worlds of the formless Brahmas, an impassible, insensible, immovable spirit, which not all the powers of a thousand Buddhas could move to a knowledge of the ways and fruits. Overcome by the thought of his misfortune and want of merit,[84] he could not restrain his tears, but sat and wept.

And the wondering courtiers inquired the cause of his joy and sorrow so quickly succeeding one another, and when they had heard it they told the king.

But Kaladewila, as he thought sadly of these things, seeing that he himself would not hear the teaching of the Buddha, cast about to see which of his relations would be more fortunate, and he saw that his nephew Nalaka would certainly behold the Great Teacher. Quickly rising, he sought his nephew, and said to him, "Take heed, Nalaka, the son of King Suddhodana is endowed with the thirty-two signs of a Grand Being; he is an incipient Buddha, who has perfected the powers of virtue. Arriving at manhood, he will be crowned king, and afterwards, retiring from lay life, and receiving holy orders, he will obtain the Buddhahood!" Then Nalaka, who was a good man, and had accumulated merit during a hundred thousand creations, and was now born in a noble and wealthy family, reflected on his uncle's words, which he knew were ever spoken for his advantage, (and acting on them), he forthwith purchased in the market place the requisites for those who take holy orders,[85] an earthen pot, and some yellow cloth; and shaving off his beard and hair, became a member of an association of holy men; and having turned towards the holy being who would be Buddha, he offered adoration; and then slinging over his right shoulder the bag containing his pot, he proceeded to the Himalayan forest, and practised asceticism[86] and meditation,[87] until the time that the Grand Being attained the Buddhahood. Then he sought his presence, and from him received the instructions named Nalaka-patipada,[88] and when he had studied them, he took leave of the Lord and returned to the hills and forests of Himalaya, that he might practise meditation without interruption. In due course, he became the first to attain the highest degree of sanctity by means of the Nalaka instructions, and within seven months of that time, placing himself on a hill top, he entered Nirwana, at that very place.

On the fifth day after the birth, King Suddhodana held a great festival for the naming of his child. The palace was gaily decorated, the princes and chieftains assembled, and one hundred and eight Brahmins, all skilled in the Three Vedas and the Shastras, were requested to predict the prince's fortune.

Of the one hundred and eight Brahmins, there were eight more learned than their fellows; by name Rama, Lakkhana, Yaiya, Tucha, Bhocha, Sudhatta, Suyama, and Konthanya (or Kondanya). These eight Brahmins gladly responded to the king's desire, saying—

"Angelic king, thy son has the soles of his feet full fleshed and perfectly flat, like unto golden sandals. They move, not alternately, like the feet of ordinary men, but they both touch the ground at the same time, and leave it at the same time. Nor does one end of the foot touch the ground before the other, but the whole sole touches the ground at the same moment. This is a very great sign of a Grand Being."[89]

Then was the question asked,[90] "How came it that he who should be Buddha had this remarkable peculiarity? Was it on account of merit amassed in his previous existence?" And the master, who knew the truth of these matters, answered, "The Grand Being was distinguished by the thirty-two principal characteristic marks of a Grand Being, and the eighty minor ones by virtue of the infinite amount of merit he had accumulated by the practise of duty and charity. He himself taught, saying, The Tathagata [91] had these distinctions, because, throughout an infinite number of creations of worlds, he had steadfastly and without wavering practised all kinds of meritorious works; had followed the law of truth in act, speech, and thought; had constantly made merit by the most bountiful charities; had ever taken delight in observing the abnegations ordered by the Five Commandments and the Eight Commandments; [92] had continually exercised himself in charitable meditations; [93] had ever shewn respect to the aged of his own rank; and had always acted for the benefit of his parents. Such were the merits to which those signs were due, and even had he been born in the heavens instead of on the earth, he must necessarily, as the result of those merits, have had ten advantages over other angels. He must have excelled them in certainty of life, in beauty, in advantages of comfort and possessions, in power, in form, in voice, in odour, in taste, in sensibility (touch), and in strength of body and mind. Being born on earth, by virtue of these merits, he could not fail to be either an universal Emperor or an omniscient Buddha."

The Brahmins continued their discourse on the signs, as follows:—

On each of his feet [94] is a figure of the beautiful wheel Chakkra, with its thousand rays or spokes, all richly adorned as if it were a wheel of emeralds. Its outline is shewn by elegantly drawn circles, and its centre is filled with exquisite devices, which gleam in beauty like the jewelled chakkra of the angels. Around the chakkra are one hundred and eight other figures, namely, the crystal spear, a female figure with ornaments, the flower Phutson, a chain and neck jewel, a baisi standard, a wicker seat, two fishes, a palace, the royal elephant goad, a stand for torches or candles, a royal sword, a palm leaf fan, a peacock's tail fan, a royal white parasol, a crown, a monk's food pan, a bunch of Mali flowers, the green (? blue) Utpala lotus, the white Utpala lotus, a chakkra, a royal chowrie (fly flap), the royal lotus (nymphœa), a full water jar, a tray full of water, the great ocean, the mountains which form the walls of the world, the Himalayan forest, Mount Meru, the moon, the sun, the constellations, the four great continents, the two thousand lesser continents, a figure of the Lord of the Chakkra (Vishnu ?), a chank shell, with reversed spiral; the seven great rivers or seas, the seven chains of mountains that encircle those seas, the seven great lakes, the elephant Chatthan, a crocodile, the flags Chai and Patat, the monk's fan (chani), Mount Krailasa, the king of lions, the king of royal tigers, the king of yellow tigers; Walahaka, the king of horses; the elephant Uposatha, the kings of Garudas, Nagas, Burmese geese, and jungle fowl; the ox Usupharat, the elephant Erawan, the dragon Mangkara, a golden beetle, a crystal throne, a golden tortoise, a golden ship, a cow and calf, a kinnara, a kinnari; the birds karawek, peacock, karien, chakphrak, and krachip; an angel, the angels in the six Dewa heavens, and the Brahmas of the sixteen Brahma heavens of the formed. Such are the hundred and eight subordinate figures which appear as a guard of honour around that most excellent sign, the holy and glorious Chakkra."

The Lord, after He became Buddha, taught that He bore this most excellent sign, because, throughout innumerable previous existences, He had ever sought the welfare of all other beings with the same zeal with which He had sought His own.

The Brahmins continued: "The heel of the Prince is not like that of other men, but long (and projecting). The sole of his foot is divided into four parts—the heel, the neck, and the two fore-portions. His heel is smooth and round as a ball of thread, and excels in beauty the heel of any other being. His toes are all of equal length, perfectly straight, long, and tapering." This peculiarity was due to the Lord having ever abstained from causing death.

The Brahmins continued: "This extraordinary length of heel is one of the signs of a Grand Being. The length and beauty of his fingers and toes is another sign of a grand being. The palms of his hands and the soles of his feet are softer than floss cotton [95] carded one hundred times; they are exquisitely marked, and the fingers are set so close [96] that no drop of water can pass between them. His feet are high, shapely, and not flat and spreading like the feet of ordinary persons. They are not jointed to the ankle in the usual manner, but the ankle rises from the centre of the foot, and is so formed that, without the trouble of moving his feet, he can turn his whole body [97] in any direction he pleases. His knees are round, [98] full, and fleshy, with the bone in the centre. His arms are so long that, without stooping, he can touch his knees with his hands. That which should be secret is concealed.[99] His skin is of the tint of the purest gold,[100] or gold rubbed with vermilion. His skin is perfect, pure, delicate, without spot, and of such a nature that no impurity can adhere to it. His glossy blue-black hairs grow one by one, regular, and curling upwards, as if they were each endeavouring to look upon his face. His body is without deformity, straight and beautiful as that of the great Brahma, or the golden candlestick of the Davadungsa heavens. His voice is endowed with the eight qualities, it is melodious, soft, resonant, and full of modulation, it is indeed sweeter and more agreeable than the voice of Brahma ; this is one of the most eminent of the marks of a Grand Being. His body is rounded and full in the seven places ; his hands and feet are round as the back of the great golden tortoise ; between his shoulders there is no depression, and his arms are as round, smooth, and free from irregularities or veins, as a well made candle or a golden image. He has the bold front of the king of lions ; and the front of the lion is perfect in its outline and proportions, each part being long or short, or full or scant, as best suits its place ; the hind part of the lion cannot be said to be so admirably shaped. His back is full and fleshy, it has no channel or depression down its centre, but is flat as a golden plank. His body is like the banyan-tree, a perfect circle of beauty, (*i.e.*, perfectly proportioned). His neck is not long and curved like that of a peacock or a stork, but is like a well-made golden tube. He has about seven thousand nerves of taste converging at the entrance of his throat, by means of which, the moment that food has passed the end of his tongue, he has the sensation of taste all over his body. His jaw is like that of a lion. He has forty teeth, closely set together, without any space between them; forty below, forty above, even and perfect as a row of polished gems set in a golden plate. He has four canine teeth (or tusks), white and gleaming like planets. His tongue is soft and flexible, and long enough to reach to his forehead. His eyes flash forth rays of every colour, and are beautiful as the gems of heaven. His eyelashes and eyes are perfect orbs, round and beautiful as a precious pearl. On his forehead, between his eyebrows, is clearly to be seen a spiral tuft of long, soft, brilliant white hairs turning to the right. On his head there is a sirorot[101] (or glory), like to a glorious angelic crown, in imitation of which all the kings of the world have made crowns a sign of royal dignity. Such are the thirty-two signs of a Grand Being."

Now, if it be asked, How did the Brahmins know of these signs? the reply is, that the great Brahma Suthawat, knowing the approaching advent of a Buddha, and desiring that men should know the means of identifying him, came upon earth in the form of a superior Brahmin, and taught the three Vedas and the Shastras. After the Lord entered Nirwana, the original treatises of the science of the Shastras were lost, and now no one truly knows them.

Of the eight superior Brahmins who recited the above-stated signs, there was one more learned than all the others, and he was the youngest, by name Kondanya. He remained silent whilst the seven prophesied thus: "This prince, endowed with the thirty-two signs of a Grand Being, has two careers before him; either he will remain a layman, and will become an emperor of the world, possessor of the seven jewels, ruling over the four continents, and their two thousand dependencies, father of a thousand mighty sons who will overcome all his foes; or he will relinquish lay occupations, will become an ordained religious mendicant, and will attain omniscience, and become the Lord Buddha."

So spake the seven; but Kondanya, the youngest and most learned of all, the first of all Buddhists who arrived at the highest degree of sanctity, reflecting on the marks on the feet, was assured that they denoted a being no longer subject to circling existence. He therefore did not hold up two fingers as did the other Brahmins, but he held up one finger only; and when they had ceased, he added: "O king! thy son will not take delight in the pleasures of the world, or remain a layman to become an universal emperor, but after twenty-nine years, he will enter holy orders, and will become an omniscient Buddha of the world."

CHAPTER V.

THE FOUR VISIONS.

THE King, Súddhodana, inquired of the Brahmins who had interpreted the signs: "By what vision will my son be induced to adopt a religious life?" And they answered: "He will see four visions—an old man, a sick man, a dead man, and a man in holy orders; these will cause him to adopt a religious life."

Then the King, desiring that his son might become the emperor of the world, determined to prevent his seeing those signs which might lead him to adopt a religious life; and to that end, stationed officers all round the city, to watch that none of those four objects should come under the Prince's notice.

And the Brahmins named the Prince, Angkhirasa,[102] because of the brilliant rays which streamed from his royal head, and they also named him Sidharta,[103] because of the perfection of his prosperity. And each of his relatives brought one son to follow him through life whichever of the two careers he might adopt.

On the seventh day after the birth of the Being that should be Buddha, his mother, the Queen Maia, died and was re-born in the Tushita heavens; and her younger sister, Pachâpati,[104] giving her own son, Nanda, to be reared by wet-nurses, became the prince's foster-mother. And the King appointed sixty high officers to guard the Prince, and numerous nurses, free from all bodily defects,[105] to be his constant attendants.

When the time came for the festival[106] of the commencement of sowing-time, the city of Kapila was gaily adorned; and the King, and Brahmins, and noblemen marched out to the appointed place for sowing the first seeds, and commenced to break the earth with seven hundred and ninety-nine ploughs, richly gilt and decked with flowers.

The young Prince was carried thither, and laid asleep on a couch, surrounded with curtains, and shaded by a tree whose thick foliage let no ray of sunshine pass through it. His nurses, seeing that he slept, left him one by one that they might watch the ceremonies, and he was left alone. After a while he woke, and leaving the curtains, gazed for a time at the splendid festivities. Then he re-entered his curtains, and, sitting in a cross-legged position, became absorbed in spiritual meditation. And as he so sat, the hours passed away, the sun passed across the skies, and the shadow of the trees all around fell on another side of them to that it had fallen on during the earlier part of the day. But, wonderful to relate, the shadow of the tree beneath which he sat did not change its position in the least; and when his nurses and attendants returned to him, they found him still perfectly shaded from the sun's rays, even as they had left him; and they told the King, and the King having seen the miracle with his own eyes, again for the second time did homage to his son.

When the Grand Being reached his seventh year, the King ordered a lotus-pool to be dug for his amusement. At that moment, Indra, king of the angels, felt uncomfortable[107] on his couch; and perceiving the cause, the thousand-eyed one summoned the angel Wetsukam, and commanded him without delay to make, by his miraculous powers, and present to the Prince, a pool such as the King desired for him.

Immediately the angel descended from the heavens and did his bidding. He made a pool with a hundred sloping banks, a hundred pleasant shallows; its bed shone with the seven kinds of precious stones, and its sides were lined with brick, and ornamented with crystal and jewels. Growing amid its clear cool waters were abundance of lotuses of the five kinds; and floating about on them were a hundred golden bowls filled with ever-blooming blue lotuses; and there were boats of gold, and silver, and crystal, and one with a beautiful throne, and golden and jewelled parasols. This pool, which the angel Wetsukam made for the Grand Being, was beautiful as the lotus-lake of heaven, which is called Nantabokkharani.

Having completed his task, the angel returned to the heavens; and next morning, when the people assembled to dig the pool, lo! it was there.

And the young Prince took pleasure in His lotus-garden, and walked there attended by a crowd of children, numerous as the retinue of a king of angels.

And when he reached his sixteenth year, his father ordered his skilled workmen to build him a palace with three residences, one for each season.[108] For the cold season the palace was nine stories high, with close-fitting doors and windows, so that no draught could enter. For the hot season the building was in five stories, and with doors and windows admitting the breeze. And for the wet season, the building was in seven stories, with close-fitting doors and windows. When the builders had finished their work, the artists decorated them with beautiful paintings, and they were fitted with the most costly hangings and furniture. Then they raised four Maradops,[109] one on each side of the seven-storied building; one of these was named Chanthalokaya, referring to its being a place wherefrom (or wherein) the Prince might take delight in the perfection of the moon and the planets. High above it were raised columns firmly bound together, to which were hung bells which gave out sweet music whenever there was motion in the air. And round about the buildings were lotus-pools, and on a lofty flagstaff, a flag towered over everything else. And round about the palace were seven walls.

And when the palace was finished, the King announced his intention of raising his son to the sovereignty, and called upon the Sakya Princes to offer their daughters as his wives. But they answered, "O King! thy son is of proper birth, and his appearance is admirable; but so far as we know he has never learned anything, and has no knowledge or accomplishments. Therefore we hesitate to offer our daughters to him!"

Then the King told his son what the Princes had said, and he answered, "My father, I have all these accomplishments without having studied them. Proclaim, then, throughout the kingdom, an assembly of all the people, and on the day appointed, I will show my skill."

On the day appointed, in the midst of the Brahmins and the Princes and the people, he showed his skill in the twelve arts;[110] he strung the bow which required a thousand ordinary men to string it, and firing an arrow from it, pierced a hair, hung so far from him that no other man's eye could see it at that distance.

Then the Sakya Princes acknowledged his wondrous skill, and presented their daughters to be his wives, and he was invested with the royal dignity,[111] and the beautiful Yasodara[112] became his Queen. He passed his days in honour, luxury, and comfort; no cares assailed him, and his beautiful Queen, and the lovely daughters[113] of the Sakyas, unceasingly strove to promote his happiness.

One day the Grand Being felt a desire to visit his flower-garden, and ordered his chariot to be made ready. They brought him the royal chariot, inlaid with the seven kinds of precious stones, and carpeted with lion and tiger skins, furnished with all kinds of military weapons, and drawn by magnificent horses, of the colour of the red lotus, like to the glorious car of the conquering Indra. Mounting his chariot, he rode towards the garden, and on his way he saw the first of the four visions.

He saw an old man, blear-eyed, toothless, deaf, hollow-cheeked, bald, bent, and with shrivelled skin hanging loosely on his bones, endeavouring to support his tottering trembling body with a crutch.

And he was deeply moved at the sad sight.

Again, another day, riding towards his garden, he saw the second vision.

Rolling in agony on the ground, weeping and groaning without ceasing, was a wretched sick man, his whole body foul with humours oozing from his sores, and incessantly tormented by swarms of flies.

And his heart grew more and more sorrowful.

Again, a third time, riding towards his garden, he saw a corpse. A horrible smell rose from it, swarms of maggots crept in and out of the nine portals, and crows, and vultures, and dogs, feasted upon its entrails. His heart fell within him. What is this? he asked of his charioteer; and the charioteer answered, "This is a dead man, a body from which the breath has passed; this is the certain lot of every man, whoever he be."

Then the Prince was overcome by sadness, and no longer taking any pleasure in his garden, he returned to his palace.

And his father, the King Suddhodana, heard of his seeing these three visions, and increased the strictness of his watch that the Prince might not see the fourth.

Nevertheless when the Prince again rode towards his garden, a messenger from the heavens,[114] assuming the form and dress of one who had taken holy orders, appeared before him.

The Prince saw the stranger, charming in manner and appearance, and inquired of his charioteer, "Who is this man, who dresses so differently to all other men?" And the angel inspiring the charioteer, he answered, "Most excellent Lord, this is a man in holy orders, a man of the highest merit,"

Then the Grand Being, reflecting on what he saw and heard, said to himself, "No being that is born can escape age, sickness, and death; happiest by far is the lot of a monk, who lives free from all entanglements or concern with wives or children."

Rejoicing in such thoughts, he passed on to his garden, and wandered happily amid the lovely flowers, and the harmonious birds. He bathed in the delicious lotus-pool, and then sitting on a marble throne, he conceived a desire to put on his state robes; but as his attendants bore them to him on golden trays the archangel Indra felt a sensation of warmth, and knowing the cause, sent one of his angels in the form of a barber to adorn him with the glorious robes of a king of angels.

So he sat until the setting sun showed the approach of night, and then remounting his chariot, he rode homewards.

On his way he met a messenger from his father, bringing the news that his wife, the royal Yasodara, had brought forth a son, and at first he showed every sign of delight, but immediately after he sadly exclaimed, "This child is a snare and a fetter to hold and bind me to a life of transmigrations."

And thenceforth the child was called Rahula.[115]

As the Prince, the Grand Being that should be Buddha, re-entered his palace, the beautiful lady Kisagotami looked out on him from one of the upper stories, and sang his praises, saying, "Happy the parents of the Prince Sidharta, for he will keep all sorrow from them. Happy the wife of the Prince Sidharta, for he will make her heart glad, and keep all sorrow from her!"

And the Grand Being heard her song, and thought, "How shall I extinguish the sorrows of my parents and my wife? What is the means by which sorrow can be destroyed? If I could destroy concupiscence, or pleasure in love, anger, or the desire to injure others, and folly which causes men to err—if I could destroy the sources of evil, such as arrogance and falsehood, then I might be called the extinguisher of the misery of my parents, and of all living beings. For this end must I now seek the way of Nirwana, that misery may be destroyed. I must relinquish this royal pomp, and devote myself to religion."

Having thus thought, he sent to the lady Kisagotami a string of pearls of immense value; and she received it with delight, regarding it as a token of love.

Thus had the Grand Being lived as a layman for twenty-nine years, when his Queen, Yasodara, bore him a son.

CHAPTER VI.

THE COMMENCEMENT OF A RELIGIOUS CAREER.

THE Grand Being entered his magnificent palace, redolent with fragrant perfumes, brilliantly illuminated with innumerable candles, and gay with wreaths of flowers—a palace splendid as the abode of Indra—and sat down upon his royal couch. A bevy of the most lovely and fascinating girls surrounded him, striving by dancing, music, and songs to attract his thoughts to pleasure ; but all their enticements were vain. He no longer found any satisfaction in such things, and, heeding them not, he fell asleep.

When they saw that their lord slept, they, retiring to a short distance, lay down on the floor, and also fell asleep. Then a lord of the angels, exerting miraculous powers, caused those ladies to sleep in a most unseemly manner, quite different to that usual with ladies of high birth and good education. Some of them snored loudly or painfully, others lay with their mouths wide open, others gnashed their teeth, others rolled about in ungraceful attitudes, and let their clothes fall off their bodies. And when the Grand Being awoke from his sleep, and looked around, his heart sank within him. He conceived a disgust for a worldly life, and regarded his royal palace, full of lovely women, as if it were but a cemetery full of horrid corpses. The more he looked, the more sorrowful he became—the more his heart quaked for the miseries of circling existence.

"Take heed, Sidharta," he said to himself, "be not vain! Transmigratory existence must be attended by destruction. Ignorance leads all beings astray, and makes them think that to be good which is really evil; it hinders them appreciating the truth that life is an evil, and it prevents their becoming disgusted, and relinquishing their cleaving to circling existence."

Moved by such sights and thoughts, he determined to adopt a religious life without delay. That very day he would become a mendicant.

Rising from his throne, he inquired who was on guard at the door. It was Channa. To him the Grand Being gave orders immediately to prepare his horse.

His horse was the splendid Kanthaka, thirty feet in length—his coat white and lustrous as a well-polished conch-shell, his head black as the black sapphire, his mane soft and delicate, his power enormous—a horse fit to be the bearer [117] of a sovereign of the world. And Kanthaka knew wherefore he was required, and neighed loudly with delight; yet was not his neighing heard, for an angel prevented the noise spreading (lest it might awaken the guards, and so prevent the Prince leaving).

And while Channa was preparing the horse, the Prince, reflecting on the uncertainty of his return, determined to have one look at his son before setting out.

He stood at the door of the Queen's chamber, and lovingly gazed at her sleeping, with her child in her arms. He, too, longed to embrace his son, yet refrained, from the fear that the mother might wake, and prevent him carrying out his purpose of stealing away from the palace. He stood at the door, and longingly, lovingly continued to look at his child, until his thoughts showed him his error. "How can I continue to live thus," he reflected; "how can I live, loving my wife and child, and at the same time escape the evils of circling existence? It is impossible! If I remain with them I shall never attain omniscience. I will away at once; and when I have attained all knowledge I can return to visit my relations." And, so thinking, he turned away.

Then he addressed his horse, "Help me, O Kanthaka! to enter the class of mendicants this very night!" and the horse was delighted. He mounted the horse, Channa held on to its tail, and the four guardians of the world held lotus flowers, one under each of the horse's feet.

Now the King, thinking to prevent his son's flight, had caused the gates of the palace to be covered with iron-plates, studded with mushroom-headed nails, and they were of immense weight, so that they could only be opened by the united efforts of many men. Yet these heavy gates would not have stayed him. Had it been necessary he would have jumped over them; but it was not necessary, for the guardian angels of the gate[118] opened it.

Then the King of the Maras,[119] the Evil One, trembled as he thought of the Prince passing those gates, for he knew that if he entered the religious profession, he would rise beyond his power, and he determined to prevent him. Descending, therefore, from his abode in the highest of the Dewa heavens, and floating in the air, he cried—

"Lord, that art capable of such vast endurance, go not

forth to adopt a religious life, but return to thy kingdom, and in seven days thou shalt become an emperor of the world, ruling over the four great continents."

He that should become Buddha heard the voice. "Who art thou?" he cried; and the voice answered, "I am Wasawadi, the King of the Maras."

"Take heed, O Mara!" replied the Grand Being; "I also know that in seven days I might gain universal empire, but I have no desire for such possessions. I know that the pursuit of religion is better than the empire of the world. See how the world is moved, and quakes with praise of this my entry on a religious life! I shall attain the glorious omniscience, and shall teach the wheel of the law, that all teachable beings may free themselves from transmigratory existence. You, thinking only of the lusts of the flesh, would force me to leave all beings to wander without guide into your power. Avaunt! Get thee away far from me."

Deeply vexed was the King of the Maras as he listened to these words. "Vain will be my efforts," he reflected, "if Sidharta perseveres. Yet, perchance, he will not be able to free himself from the lusts of the flesh—hatred and envy—and then my opportunity will come!" So he withdrew to a short distance, and watched without ceasing, that he might seize the first occasion that presented itself.

The Grand Being left his palace on the middle day of the sixth month.[120] The lovely full moon shone without a speck; and the earth, flooded with its rays, appeared like a sea of gleaming white milk. The angels of the ten thousand worlds illuminated the spheres with the bright lights of heaven.

As he rode along, he thought of the city he had left, and desired once more to see it. Then the earth, which has neither life nor intelligence, appeared endowed with both; and turning round, as does a potter's wheel, it brought the city directly in front of him. Gazing on the city of Kapila, he invoked its guardian angels, saying: "Angels of yon glorious city, listen to my vow! Never will I return hither while I have not achieved omniscience, and my heart is yet subject to lust, passion, and folly.[121] But when I have attained the mastery of the most excellent law—when I am surrounded by the crowd of saints, then will I return!"

The place where this occurred became famous, and a spire was erected there by the name of Kanthaka niwatana Chedi.

The Lord rode onwards, intent on his purpose of entering the noble body of mendicants, and no regret assailed him for the glory, the power, and the family that he had left behind.

A vast train of angels attended him; the skies rained flowers, and delicious odours pervaded the air. In this splendid state he, in one night, passed through the three kingdoms—Kapila, Sawatthi,[122] and Wesali,[123] and reached the river Anoma,[124] a distance of thirty yojana (about two hundred miles).

Just before daybreak he arrived at the river Anoma, and the great train of angels, having done obeisance, returned to their heavenly abodes. "Excellent is the augury to be drawn from the name of this river," exclaimed the Lord, "for it refers to the success of my entry into holy orders."[125]

He crossed the river, dismounted from his horse,

and, standing on the sandy bank, took off his royal ornaments, and, having made a parcel of them, handed them to Channa, that he might take them back to Kapila.

Next, he reflected that his long hair did not become the character of a poor ascetic,[126] and he determined to have it cut off; but as no one was worthy to touch his head, he cut it off with his own sword, praying: "May my hair, thus cut, be neat and even!" and by the force of his prayer, the hair parted evenly, leaving each hair about an inch and a half in length, and they curled in right-handed spirals, and never grew more to the last day of his life.[128]

Then, desiring to know if he would truly become the Buddha, he prayed again: "If I shall indeed attain to holy omniscience, may this roll of long hair, which I shall now throw upwards, remain suspended in the sky; but if not, let it straightway fall to the ground;" and by the force of his prayer it remained suspended ten miles above the earth, until the angels carried it to the Davadungsa heavens, where it is adored to this day.

Next, he desired to change his dress for the garb suitable to an ascetic, and at that moment the great Brahma angel Khatikara, who had been an intimate friend of the Grand Being when they were both living on earth in the time of the Buddha Kasyappa, and had since passed his time in the Brahma heavens, knowing his desire, brought him the eight articles requisite for a monk—the food-pan, the three robes, the razor, the needle-case, the girdle, and the filtering-cloth, which grow on the tree called Karaphrük. And the Lord received them from the hands of the Great Brahma,[130] and putting on the yellow dress, which is the flag of victory of the saints, he appeared as a well-conditioned professor of religion.

Then again praying, as he had done when he cut off his long hair, he threw upwards the royal vestments he had taken off, and they were taken by the great Brahma Khatikara, and placed in a great relic temple in the Brahma heavens as an object of adoration for all the Brahma angels.

CHAPTER VII.

THE PRACTICE OF ASCETICISM.

THEN the most excellent Grand Being, turning to Channa, said: "Channa, that hast been my friend, helping me to enter the noble order of mendicants, now take these my ornaments to my royal parents, and tell them from me, that they should not grieve nor feel anxiety on my account. Tell them that I have entered the order of mendicants, not from want of gratitude towards them, nor from any feeling of spite or annoyance, nor because any desire of mine has not been gratified; but because I have pondered on the miseries which are caused by transmigrating life, on age, sickness, and death. Tell them that I have embraced a religious life from the earnest desire to redeem and save all beings who are now whirled vaguely and helplessly in the continuous channel of the sea of transmigrating existence—from the desire to conduct them across that sea to the farther bank, which is the holy immortal Nirwana. It will be no long time ere I attain the meditative knowledge of all things—the realisation of my desire for the Buddhahood.[131] Then will I return to my father, and will wipe away the tears of my family with the most excellent of kerchiefs—the teaching of the true law. Go then, quickly go, and deliver this message to my father!"

When Channa heard these words, he fell at his master's feet and implored him to let him also enter into the religious order, that he might stay with him and serve him, and not leave him alone in those desolate jungles; but the Lord would not, but answered him, saying: "If Channa remained here, my father, my aunt, and wife, and my sister, would remain in painful doubt, and would give way to unendurable grief; their hearts would break, and their years be diminished. If they were gone, who would take care of my son, Rahula? who would preserve him? Go, then, and watch over the well-being of those my relatives, and you will do that which is most profitable."

Channa, fearing to displease his master, urged his wish no more. Respectfully taking leave of him, he withdrew to a short distance from where he sat, and, holding his hands before him in an attitude of adoration, he walked thrice round him from left to right, thinking of the journey he was about to make.

Now, when the horse Kanthaka heard the conversation between his master and Channa, he reflected: "Why should my master send me back? What is the use of my going? Channa alone can carry back the ornaments, and he can tell the King of what has occurred; but I am a mere animal, I can tell nothing; it would be better that I should remain here." Tears streamed from his eyes and fell on the holy foot of the Grand Being. Then the Lord laid his hand on the back of his charger, and spoke to him, saying: "Kanthaka, you have done me good service, you have been my bearer to the noble order of mendicants; be not sad and sorrowful, but return joyfully."

Then Channa led the horse away; and when they had gone a short distance, Kanthaka turned to look again at his master; but his heart could no longer contain itself; he staggered along the road overcome with grief, until he lost sight of his master, then he shuddered and fell dead; and by virtue of his fidelity to his master, he was immediately re-born in the Davadungsa heavens as the angel Kanthaka, to live in a golden palace with a thousand lovely houris to attend on him.

Channa fell weeping on the horse, and presently recovering himself, he took off his trappings, and, gathering some flowers in the woods, made of them an offering to the remains of the horse. This done, he pursued his journey to Kapila, and in due course arriving there, went straighway into the palace, refusing to give any information to the towns-people, who pressed him with their inquiries. He laid the ornaments and the trappings of the horse before the King; but before he could utter a word, the Princess Yasodara, and the aunt and half-sister of the missing Prince, rushed into the audience-chamber with loud lamentations, bewailing[132] the fate they supposed to have befallen their beloved. After some time, they listened to Channa's story; and the King recalling the prediction of Kaladewila and the Brahmin Kondanya, their grief abated.

The Grand Being, when Channa had left him, remained alone, full of compassionate thoughts for all beings subject to circling existence—to an existence inseparable from liability to death and incessant change. He reflected—"When I left the royal city of Kapila, a vast host of angels, with one accord, escorted me to the bank of this river Anoma. Then they left me, with Channa and my horse Kanthaka. Channa and Kanthaka left me, and now I am alone, alone without a companion. How changeable, how sad, is the law of this existence!"

In that region there was a forest of mango-trees called Anupia. There the Grand Being remained seven days, without ever taking food, satiated with the joy which he felt in his religious profession.

On the eighth day, alone and on foot—walking on those beautiful feet adorned with the Chakkra, eminently distinguished by the thirty-two signs of a Grand Being, and by the eighty minor signs, radiant with a moon-like glory—alone, like the solitary lion of the Himalayas—without a companion, yet attracting the loving admiration of all the beasts of the forest—in one day he marched two hundred miles, and crossing a river near the city of Rajagriha,[133] he entered the city, and visited each house he came to, that he might receive alms.

Astounded at his beauty, the people crowded round him, wondering who it might be. Some said, "Surely it is the moon fleeing from the ravenous Asura Rahu,[134] how else can we account for his radiant glory?" Others made other guesses, and they could come to no conclusion. So they went and told the King—Bimbisara, King of Rajagriha—that there was a being in the city whose beauty made them doubt whether he were not an angel. Then the King, looking from a window of the palace, saw him, and, filled with astonishment, gave orders to ascertain who he might be, saying, "Follow him! If he is not a human being, when he leaves the city he will disappear; if he is an angel, he will fly through the air; if a snake-king,[135] he will sink into the earth; but if a man, he will remain and eat his food."

The Grand Being, that was approaching the Buddhaship, calmly continued his walk, regarding but the small span of earth close[136] around him; and having collected sufficient food, he left the city by the same gate he had entered it.

He passed on to the Banthawa Hills,[137] and sitting down on the summit of a lofty rock, he looked at the food collected in his pan.

He—who had ever been accustomed to the most dainty meats, the most refined delicacies—looked at the mixed mess in his pot, and loathed it; he could scarcely swallow it. Yet even this caused no wish to return to his city and his palace. He reflected on the foulness of his own body, and ate without further aversion. He finished his meal, rinsed his mouth, washed his pan, and replaced it in his wallet, and seated himself in a position of contemplation[138] on the rocky cliff.

Then the officers who had been set to watch him returned, and told King Bimbisara that he was certainly a man; and the King, desiring to converse with him, called for his royal palankeen, and attended by a great train of noblemen and soldiers, went forth to seek him at the Banthawa Hills.

Sitting on a rocky slab, the King gazed with delight at the Grand Being, and observed the grace of his manner, and thus addressed him:

"Man of beauty, whence comest thou?"

"Most excellent lord, I come from the country of the Sakyas."

"From what Sakya country?"

"From the royal city Kapila."

The King continued to question him as to his caste, family, and name, and was informed, in answer, that he was of the royal race (caste) of the Sakyas, the son of King Suddhodana, and named Sidharta.

Now King Bimbisara and the Prince Sidharta were on most friendly terms. Though they had never met, and did not know each other by sight, they were in the constant habit of exchanging presents as tokens of good-will; and when the Grand Being announced his name, the King was assured beyond all doubt, by his admirable manners and language, that it was none other than his friend.

He reflected that perhaps the Prince had fled from his country on account of some family quarrel, and, under that impression, he invited him to share his power—to rule over half the great country of Magadha. Then the Grand Being told him the reasons, the object for which he had resigned the empire of the world. He told him of the four sights which had influenced his thoughts, and of his determination to achieve the omniscient Buddhahood. And the King, having obtained from him a promise that after the attainment of omniscience he would first teach in Rajagriha, did homage, and returned to his city.

Travelling on through the country, collecting alms, the Grand Being came to the dwellings of the hermits Alara and Kuddhaka,[139] and staying with them, learned the whole course of their instructions—the end of their knowledge. By their aid he acquired the science of Dhyana meditation[140] from its first degree (in which the mind, in an ecstatic state, fixes itself on one object, and perfectly comprehends it) to the seventh degree (wherein the mind, attaining the idea of nothingness, is in the tranquil state of an ethereal, formless Brahma of the heaven next to the highest). But when he asked them to instruct him in the eighth Dhyana, the perfect quietude of the highest Brahmas, they could not do it.

The Lord, seeing that those seven Dhyana did not constitute Nirwana, and that the teaching of those hermits was unsatisfactory, left them and proceeded to the country of Uruwela.[141]

In the Uruwela forest there was a quiet spot suitable as an abode for those who desired to lead an ascetic life. Rich verdure, noble trees, and lovely flowers were suggestive of enlightened thoughts. There was abundance of cool water in pools close at hand, and not far off was the river Nairanjana, in whose clear waters thousands of fish and tortoises might be seen disporting. The advantages of the situation were completed by its being sufficiently near to a village for convenience in seeking alms, and yet not so near as to be disturbed by its proximity.

This place he selected to practise a course of the severest asceticism[142] or mortification; and thither came to him Kondanya the Brahmin who had prophesied at his birth, and four others, who were the sons of all the Brahmins who had taken part in that prediction. These five had adopted the religious profession, waiting for the Grand Being, and from that were called the five Wakkhi.[144] They wandered from place to place seeking for the Lord, and having found him, remained with him to minister to his wants.

The Grand Being applied himself to practise asceticism of the extremest nature. To this end he devoted himself incessantly to the meditation called Bhawana, and in order that his meditation might not be interrupted, he gradually reduced his daily allowance of food until a grain of sesame sufficed for his nourishment. Still he considered that the duty of seeking food occupied too much time; time he required for his religious observances, and thenceforth he ceased to seek alms. He sat under a tree and ate the fruits that fell within his reach, but never rose to seek any. Even this he regarded as an interruption, and thenceforth ceased to eat. Then the angels, observing it, preserved his life, by insinuating food through the pores of his skin; nevertheless his body became extremely attenuated, his blood and his flesh dried up, his ribs protruded, and he had nought left of him but skin and bones. The thirty-two marks of a Grand Being, and the eighty minor signs, entirely disappeared, and his body became like a withered leaf.

For six years he endured this extremity of mortification without ever wishing to discontinue it; and never did it occur to him to say, "Long as I have practised asceticism, I have not arrived at the Buddhahood. It is useless to continue. I will, therefore, return to my father."

Such a thought never entered his mind; but steadfastly pursuing the self-achieved[144] omniscience of a Buddha, he never wavered in the object of his desires.

At last, one day, when attempting to move, his whole body was racked with the most violent pain, and he fainted senseless on the ground.

A certain lady of heaven, seeing him lying senseless and motionless, hastened to the King Suddhodana, and told him that his son was dead; but the monarch would not believe, saying, "My son cannot die ere he has become Buddha."

When the Grand Being recovered consciousness, he changed his seat, and a few days afterwards, dissatisfied with the result of his previous mortifications, he reflected that the asceticism which did not remove the necessity of respiration was but a coarse unrefined method, and he therefore determined to restrain his breath, as the most exquisite of all acts of endurance. He held his breath, and the air, unable to pass through his nostrils, turned upwards into his head, and made it suffer exceeding pain; and then, unable to escape through the head, it again passed down, and entering his belly, caused intense agonies. Yet with all this suffering, he was perfectly firm and constant, and never thought of relinquishing this extremity of mortification.

Then it was that the royal Mara sought occasion to induce the Grand Being to cease his exercises. Craftily pretending to be influenced by motives of compassion, he offered his advice, saying, "Beware, O Grand Being! Your state is pitiable to look on; you are attenuated beyond measure, and your skin, that was of the colour of gold, is dark and discoloured. You are practising this mortification in vain. I can see that you will not live through it. You, who are a Grand Being, had better give up this course, for, be assured, you will derive much more advantage from sacrifices of fire and flowers."

Him the Grand Being indignantly answered: "Hearken, thou vile and wicked Mara! thy words suit not the time. Think not to deceive me, for I heed thee not. Thou mayest mislead those who have no understanding, but I, who have virtue, endurance, and intelligence, who know what is good, and what is evil, cannot be so misled. Thou, O Mara! hast eight generals.[145] Thy first is delight in the five lusts of the flesh, which are the pleasures of appearance, sound, scent, flavour, and touch. Thy second general is wrath, who takes the form of vexation, indignation, and desire to injure. Thy third is concupiscence. Thy fourth is desire. Thy fifth is impudence. Thy sixth is arrogance. Thy seventh is doubt. And thine eighth is ingratitude. These are thy generals, who cannot be escaped by those whose hearts are set on honour and wealth. But I know that he who can contend with these thy generals shall escape beyond all sorrow, and enjoy the most glorious happiness. Therefore I have not ceased to practise mortification (*i.e.*, the subjugation of these generals of Mara), knowing that even were I to die whilst thus engaged, it would be a most excellent thing."

Then Mara, unable to answer his severe reproach, fled in confusion.

After he had departed, the Grand Being reflected as to why even this extreme course of mortification failed to bring him into the path leading to the omniscience of the Bo-tree. Then the archangel Indra brought a three-stringed guitar, and sounded it at a short distance. One string, too tightly strained, gave a harsh and unpleasant sound; the second, not strained enough, had no resonance; the third, moderately stretched, gave forth the sweetest music. Having thus done, the thousand-eyed angel returned to his abode, and the Grand Being, having pondered on the meaning of the vision, determined to draw a lesson from the string moderately stretched, and in future to practise asceticism with moderation. He resolved to resume his former practice of sitting contemplatively under a tree, thereby hoping to attain the Buddhahood.

In order that he might have sufficient bodily strength to effect his purpose, he again collected alms and ate sufficient for his absolute needs, and thus after a few days he regained his pristine strength, his flesh, his blood, his beauty, and his significant marks.

And when the five Brahmins who had till that time attended him saw this, they were offended, saying to one another: "How shall he who has ceased to practise mortification attain to the Buddhaship?"

And they left him and went to a distance of one hundred and twenty miles, to the Isipatana deer-forest (near Benares).

CHAPTER VIII.

THE FINAL EFFORT.

IN the village Sanekka of Uruwela, there lived a maiden named Suchada, the daughter of a rich man. She had made a vow to the angel established in a great banyan-tree, that if she married a worthy husband, and if her first-born proved to be a son, she would yearly make an immense offering in honour of the angel of the tree.[146] The objects of her vow having been accomplished, she prepared her offering for the fifteenth day of the sixth month. She selected a thousand cows, fed in the richest pastures; with their milk she fed five hundred others; with theirs, two hundred and fifty; and so on until the number was reduced to eight cows, from whose udders the most luscious milk flowed without pressure into the vessels placed to receive it.

With this rich milk she prepared her offering, and lo! when the vessel was set on the fire, bubbles rose from it in waves curling to the right, yet not one single drop was spilt, neither did any smoke rise from the fire, for these things were controlled by the power of the merits of the Grand Being, now about to become Buddha. The angels also brought ambrosial flavours, and placed them in the savoury rice.

And Suchada wondered at these miracles, exclaiming, "Often as I have made offerings, the angels have never before shown their satisfaction as they have this day;" and she sent her servant Bun without delay to sweep the ground around the banyan-tree, that it might be perfectly clean and neat.

Now in the last watch of the preceding night, the Grand Being, sleeping soundly, saw five visions.

Firstly, He dreamt that the world was his couch, the Himalaya mountains his cushion, and his outstretched hands reached to the eastern and western oceans.

Secondly, He dreamt that a shoot of the grass named Kha sprouted from his navel, and growing, growing, growing, reached the skies, more than ten thousand miles above him.

Thirdly, He dreamt that all kinds of birds, of the most varied plumage, flew towards him from all directions, and falling at his feet, became perfectly white.

Fourthly, He dreamt that four kinds of grubs, with white bodies and black heads, crawled from his toes to his knees, quite covering his feet.

Fifthly, He dreamt that he walked on a heap of filth twenty miles in height, yet not the least particle soiled his feet, which remained clean as though he had been walking on a stone slab.

When he awoke, he pondered on these visions, making the reflection, "Had I still been in my former royal state, I should have sent for the soothsayers to expound these dreams; but as it is, I must use my own meditative science to explain them." And by his meditative science he perceived clearly that the first dream meant that he would become the lord of all law and of all knowledge. The second dream meant that he would relinquish desire, wrath, and folly, and would bestow (the knowledge of) the eight paths to salvation on all angels and men. The third dream signified that beings would flock in from all quarters to hear his teaching, and would alter their nature, till then given up to desire, wrath, and folly. The fourth dream showed that he would bestow the rite of monasticism and the adoration of the Triad upon all men. The fifth dream was a sure token that abounding in (a knowledge of) the four causes of misery, he would (no longer) be detained by them.

When he had interpreted the visions, he washed his face and hands, took his food-pan, and went and sat under the shade of the great banyan-tree (where Bun, the slave of Suchada, had just finished sweeping), and she saw him radiant with a glory, and ran and told her mistress. Great was the joy of Suchada. "You are no longer my slave, but my daughter," she exclaimed; and she gave her suitable attire and ornaments. Then elegantly dressed, followed by her attendant, she went to the tree, bearing on her head her savory rice, in a golden bowl which had cost a hundred thousand pieces of silver, covered with a second golden bowl, and with a clean white cloth over all.

As she entered beneath the spreading branches of the great banyan-tree, she saw the Grand Being, and filled with angelic happiness, she respectfully approached him, and placing her bowl on the ground, took from her attendant a golden scent-vase, and offered it to the Lord.

Now, at this very moment, the bowl which the great Brahma Khathikara had presented to him, disappeared, and the Grand Being stretched forth his right hand to receive the bowl of Suchada.

Suchada first poured perfume on his hand, and then offered her golden bowl, offered it joyfully and freely, gave it as if she prized it no more than an old cracked clay pot.

And the Lord accepted it, saying, "Your desire shall be accomplished." And she offered homage, and went away joyfully, singing, "My desire will be accomplished." She thought she had seen the angel (of the tree).

Then, following the precedent of all the Buddhas, the Grand Being rose, and carried the bowl thrice round the banyan-tree, and then proceeding to the Nairanjana river, placed his golden bowl on the spot where previous Buddhas had placed their bowls, bathed, resumed the monk's dress, sat for a time meditating, with his face turned towards the east, and ate forty-nine portions of his savory rice, each portion the size of an egg.

Having finished his meal, he cried, "If I shall indeed become a Buddha, let this golden bowl float upwards against the stream;" and setting his bowl adrift upon the river, it became, as it were, endowed with life and intelligence, and floated against the stream, swift as a racehorse. It travelled about eighty cubits, and then, sinking into the realms of Kala, the Naga King,[148] it clashed loudly against the three bowls which had been similarly set afloat by former[149] Buddhas, and placed itself beneath them.

Kala, the King of Nagas, was awoke by the loud resounding clash, and, starting from his resting-place, exclaimed, "It was but yesterday that a royal Buddha assumed his dignity; to-day there is another. I never have time for a comfortable sleep." Then he went forth and offered sacrifice, and sang a vast number of songs of praise.

The Grand Being that should be Buddha saw the miracle (of the bowl), and was filled with joy; for he knew that he should now certainly attain the Buddhahood.

He sat all day by the river side, in a spot perfumed with the fragrant flowers of the forest-trees; and in the evening, when the flowers were falling from the trees, he marched thence to a copse of the flower-abounding forest. Royally he marched, with the bold bearing of the king of lions of the Himalayan forests, his thoughts intent on a single object, the Buddhahood.

In the direction to which he turned, there was a grand Bo-tree, perfect in the beauty of its trunk and branches and brilliant dark-green foliage. To it the angels made a road, five hundred cubits wide, for him to pass by.

Then the whole host of Indra angels of the thousand worlds approached with sacrificial offerings. The great Brahma, Sahabodi, held over him the white umbrella[150] of royalty. The angels of the Tushita and Yama heavens brought a chowrie, six thousand fathoms in length, and waved it, fanning the Grand Being. The thousand-eyed Indra marched before him, blowing his great conch-shell, two thousand fathoms long. Thus the Grand Being pursued his way, escorted by the angelic host. And he met a certain Brahmin, named Sotiya, and from him accepted eight handfuls of long grass. Arriving at the tree, he placed the grass on the south side. Then the very earth itself, as if it knew, showed that that was not the proper place for the jewelled throne; and the Lord, reflecting on it, took up the grass, and proceeding to the east side, spread it there, exclaiming, "If I shall indeed be master of the omniscience of the tree, may these eight bundles of grass become a jewelled throne for me to sit on." And it became a beautiful jewelled throne, fourteen cubits in height.

The Lord took his seat on the throne, and with upright figure and well-steadied mind, he plunged his whole thought, in perfect purity, to attain the omniscience of the Buddhahood, by virtue of his charity and avoidance of sin throughout a countless number of existences of the world.

"Never will I rise from this seat," he exclaimed, "until I have attained the Buddhahood."

Thus the royal Holy Being of the order of Buddhas, now in his last state of transmigrating existence, seeking to insure the happiness of men and angels, unequalled in intelligence, in patient endurance, and in bodily strength, sat on the jewelled throne, and exerted that persistence by which the Buddhahood was to be attained.

And the host of angels of the ten thousand worlds gathered round him with offerings of precious perfumes, and raised a heavenly concert, the strains of which resounded even in the most distant universe.

CHAPTER IX.

THE CONTEST WITH THE EVIL SPIRIT.

THE great King Mara, who ruled over all the Mara angels, he whose nature is sinful and filthy, had throughout these six years been vainly seeking an occasion against the Grand Being. He heard the rejoicings of the angels, and knew their cause, and determined that he must at once destroy the man who was about to pass beyond his power.

For this purpose he sent his three daughters, Raka, Aradi, and Tanha.[151]

Beautifully bedecked, and escorted by five hundred maidens, they approached the throne of the Grand Being, and Raka first addressed him, "Lord! fearest thou not death?"[152]

Having inquired her name, he further demanded the object of her visit; and being answered that she came because it was her wont to chain all beings in the fetters of concupiscence, he drove her away, with the words, "All this course of mortification have I endured, that I might purge myself of concupiscence."

With similar words he drove away Aradi, whose wont it was to bind all beings in the fetters of angry temper, and Tanha, whose fetters were those of desire or delight in voluptuous sensations.

The Grand Being drove them from him in confusion, for the daughters of Mara could suggest no pleasure to him, and had no charm of sufficient power to entice him.

Then the royal Mara, in fury, assembled his generals, saying, "Listen, ye Maras, that know not sorrow! Now shall I make war on the Prince Sidharta, that man without an equal. I dare not attack him in face, but I will circumvent him by approaching on the north side. Assume, then, all manner of shapes, and use your mightiest powers, that he may flee in terror." And they, obedient to their King, assumed the most horrible and fearful forms, and raised an awful sound, as of a hundred thousand thunders.

King Mara himself, assuming an immense size, and with a thousand arms brandishing all kinds of martial weapons, riding on his elephant Girimaga, a thousand miles in height, led on his army. The van stretched two hundred and fifty miles before him, and the rear-guard extended to the very walls of the world.

"Advance, my soldiers!" he shouted; "seize and bind the Prince Sidharta, and bring him to me, that I may cut off his feet and cast them across the great ocean."

Terrible in appearance, they advanced. Yet did none of them dare enter beneath the shade of the great Bo-tree. Vainly their King shouted to them to enter and seize him, for none could pass the precincts of the tree.

Nevertheless, the angels who, till then, had watched around him, when they heard the tumult, and saw the horrible army coming from the north, fled in terror. They fled and left him—left him alone, sitting on his glorious throne, like the Great Brahma in his heavenly palace.

The Grand Being, deserted by the angels, looked towards the north, and saw the army of Mara advancing, as if by the feet alone of its innumerable hosts it would trample the great Bo-tree into impalpable dust. Then he reflected: "Long have I now devoted myself to a life of mortification, and now I am alone, without a friend to aid me in this contest. Yet may I escape the Maras, for the virtue of my transcendent merits will be my army!" "Help me," he cried, "ye thirty Barami![153] ye powers of accumulated merit, ye powers of Almsgiving, Morality, Relinquishment, Wisdom, Fortitude, Patience, Truth, Determination, Charity, and Equanimity, help me in my fight with Mara!"

Yet the approach of Mara's army caused in him no fear, nor did he move in the least from his perfectly calm position of meditation on the jewelled throne.

Loudly King Mara shouted to his army to advance and seize him, to slay him, and cut out his heart. Vainly King Mara, his eyes darting flames, urged on his army to the attack; vainly they brandished their weapons and assumed the most hideous forms. As elephants, horses, and stags, lions, tigers, and panthers, they crowded round about him; with long wild hair they floated around and above him, shaking their spears, and trying to strike terror with huge pestles and mortars; but they could neither hurt him nor inspire him with fear.

Then King Mara caused a rain of all kinds of missiles to pour from the skies. He made his own form huger and huger every moment; he became five miles in height—ten miles—twenty—and even thirty. He caused a violent gale to blow from the east, of exceeding force, such that the mountain peaks fell before it, and the earth shook and cracked beneath its rage. He caused a rain of burning ashes to fall, so that the Grand Being might be destroyed; yet, by the virtue of his merits, the burning ashes were changed into wreaths of flowers—into an offering of sweet-scented flowers.

"Come down from my throne," shouted the evil-formed one; "come down, or I will cut thine heart into atoms!"

Then the Grand Being spoke:

"This jewelled throne was created by the power of my merits, for I am he who will teach all men the remedy for death, who will be Buddha, and will redeem all beings, and set them free from the sorrows of circling existence."

Fierce was the rage of Mara when he heard these words. He dismounted from his elephant, and armed with the most exquisite of weapons, the splendid Chakkra,[164] he approached the Grand Being and again addressed him:

"Why, O Sidharta! wilt thou not rise and leave that throne, which should be mine alone, for thou becomest it not? My intelligence is higher than thine, my power greater than thine; and it was by the virtue of my merits that this throne was created."

And the Lord answered, "Are these words true?" And Mara asserting that they were indeed true, the Grand Being again declared, "This throne, O Mara! has been created by the virtue of merits accumulated by me in previous existences."

Still did Mara shout to him to leave the throne, and assert that it had been created by his merits, for he trusted to the numbers of his host, that they would offer themselves as witnesses of all that he asserted. Then the Lord, putting forth the majesty of his power, spoke: "O Mara! thou knowest not the force of my Chakkra, or the might of my army. Thou knowest not that my intellect is a piercing weapon against which no enemy can contend."

And Mara, hearing these words, reflected: "Indeed (it seems that) this Prince Sidharta has no equal among men or angels in keeping to the truth, and every word he speaks is spoken with due care. But I must further inquire into this matter." So he asked: "Now I know, O Prince Sidharta! that thou art a liar; sitting alone, thou yet declarest that thou hast a large army. If it exists, why cannot we see it?"

"Mara! I cannot lie. Through a countless number of successive existences, I have persistently accumulated the Barami, the virtue of transcendent merit, of thirty kinds. They are my forces. They will accomplish my desires."

"What," demanded Mara, "are these forces thou hast so long maintained?"

"Hearken, O Mara! I have given my wealth, my garments, my children in charity. I have given my wife in charity. I have given my flesh, my blood, my head, my heart in charity. Such are my forces. By the thirty virtues of transcendent merits, and the five great alms, I have obtained this throne. Thou, in saying that this throne was created by thy merits, tellest an untruth, for indeed this is no throne for a sinful, horrible being such as thou art."

Angered beyond endurance, King Mara now put forth his highest powers. He hurled the awful Chakkra, and it clove the mountains in its course, but it could not touch the Grand Being, nor pass the miraculous canopy of flowers outspread to protect his head. Vainly did Mara seize the rocks and mountains, and hurl them forth to crush him; for by the virtue of the Grand Being they were changed into fragrant flowers, and fell as offerings at his feet.

And the angels, who had fled to the walls of the world, and thence watched the combat, saw him, sitting like a noble lion surrounded by deer, calm and unmoved by the army of Mara.

Then the Grand Being called to King Mara, and said, "Where are the witnesses of those acts of merit by the performance of which thou sayest thou hast caused the creation of this throne?" And King Mara, pointing to his generals, answered, "Behold my witnesses!" and with one accord they shouted that they could bear him witness. "Tell me now," he continued, "where is the man that can bear witness for thee?"

The Grand Being reflected. "Truly here is no man to bear me witness; but I will call on the earth itself, though it has neither spirit[155] nor understanding, and it shall be my witness. Stretching forth his hand, he thus invoked the earth: "O holy earth! I who have attained the thirty powers of virtue, and performed the five great alms, each time that I have performed a great act have not failed to pour[156] water upon thee. Now that I have no other witness, I call upon thee to give thy testimony. If this throne was created by my merits, let the earth quake and show it; and if not, let the earth be still!"

And the angel of the earth, unable to resist his invocation, sprang from the earth in the shape of a lovely woman with long flowing hair, and standing before him, answered:

"O Being more excellent than angels or men! it is true that when you performed your great works you ever poured water on my hair." And with these words she wrung her long hair, and a stream, a flood of waters gushed forth from it.

Onwards against the host of Mara the mighty torrent rushed. His generals were overturned, his elephant swept away by the waters, his royal insignia destroyed, and his whole army fled in utter confusion, amid the roarings of a terrific earthquake, and peals of thunder crashing through the skies.

Thus the Grand Being conquered King Mara and his army; and forthwith the whole world was filled with the sound of the rejoicings of the angels, singing songs of praise.

And King Mara and his generals feared and trembled, and a strong feeling of compassionate sorrow affected them, and they cried, "Oh! truly is made manifest the reward of acts of charity which will fulfil the desire of Prince Sidharta." Then joy filled the heart of the King of the Maras; and throwing away his weapons, he raised his thousand arms above his head, and did reverence, saying, "Homage to the Lord who has subdued his body, even as a charioteer breaks his horses to his use! Homage to the Lord, more excellent than men, or angels, or Brahmas. The Lord will become the omniscient Buddha, the Teacher of angels and Brahmas, Yakkhas, and men. He will confound all the Maras, and will rescue men from the whirl of transmigration!"

Thus did King Mara praise the Lord ere he returned to his abode.

Then the host of angels shouted praises, saying, "Worthy is he of the offerings of men and angels, for there is none that can overcome or equal him!"

CHAPTER X.

THE ATTAINMENT OF THE BUDDHAHOOD.

THE Lord, the Teacher,[158] not having yet attained omniscience, continued to sit on his throne shaded by the holy jewel the Bo-tree, where he had routed King Mara and all his host.

His victory had been completed in the evening near about nightfall.

And in the first watch of the night, the Lord entered into that state of meditation which gave him the power of remembering[159] his former existences to a number beyond count. He remembered the time and place and nature of each existence, his form, his colour, his good and evil fortune, and the condition to which he transmigrated on death. All this the Lord saw clearly, as if it had been a world illumined by a hundred or a thousand suns of exceeding brightness.

And on entering the middle watch, the Lord entered into that state of meditation which confers angelic sight and hearing,[160] the power of seeing and hearing what is desired, irrespective of distance, or of intervening obstacles.

And at the beginning of the third watch of the night, the Lord applied himself to the consideration of the Laws of Cause and Effect, the sequence of existence.[161]

Then he saw that life, or the state of transmigrating

existence, was but one condition of a series of twelve, of which the first was ignorance, and the last sorrow, decrepitude, and death; a series of which each condition was an effect of that which preceded it, and a cause of that which followed it.

He saw that the first condition was IGNORANCE, which, during some preceding state of existence, had prevented the recognition of the vanity of all things, and had led to acts of merit and demerit, instead of to perfect rest. It might therefore be justly regarded as the cause of merit and demerit, which, in the form of PREDISPOSITION, or active tendency to arrangement, was the second condition. This predisposition was the disposer of the fruits of merit and demerit; indeed, was that which caused the fruits to be just and consistent with their origin.

In order that effect might be given to the predisposition, there was need of an appreciating power (of which it might be regarded as the cause,) and that power was INTELLIGENCE, the third condition.

This intelligence at once led to a fourth condition that of DISTINCTION, and the EXPRESSION of distinction, or form and name, that is, the elements of objects and their qualities.

From the existence of these naturally arose that which was necessary for their manifestation, that is to say, the fifth condition, the six SEATS OF THE SENSES.

And in order that they might develop themselves, they caused a sixth condition to arise, and unite them with the feelings it was their object to express; this condition was CONTACT, uniting ideas with their sensations. The seventh condition, which followed on contact, and was caused by it, was the SENSATION itself, agreeable or disagreeable, as it might be.

And this sensation was naturally followed by the eighth condition, that of DESIRE for, pleasure in, or inclination towards something which would promote its continuance.

Desire gave rise to a ninth condition, that of firm ATTACHMENT to the object of desire, a cleaving and adherence to it.

This cleaving to its object gave rise to a tenth condition, that of EXISTENCE in general, the state of devil, man, and angel, or, in fine, the worlds.

The eleventh condition, dependent on general existence, was the existence of a being in the conditions of transmigration, or the LIFE of the individual.

The twelfth and last condition, the invariable sequence of life, was DECREPITUDE and DEATH. Such were the twelve conditions of the sequence of existence which the Lord considered of as He sat on the jewelled throne shaded by the great tree of wisdom.

And he saw clearly their perfect connection, unbroken as a stream of water. He saw that decrepitude, death, and sorrow were but the consequences of individual life; that individual life depended on general existence; that general existence sprang from attachment to that which was desired, and that from desire. He saw that desire could not arise without sensation; that sensation could not arise without contact; and that contact was impossible without the six seats of the senses. He saw that the seats of the senses were a result of the pre-existence of distinction and its expression, and that these existed because an intelligent influence gave rise to them; that that intelligence was caused by a predisposition to action, and the predisposition by ignorance of the four great truths.

And he saw that by extinguishing ignorance, predisposition to action would be extinguished also; and that by the extinction of predisposition, each of the other conditions would in turn be done away with, and sorrow would be destroyed.

The Grand Being sat on the jewelled throne raised above the plain of virtue, holding in the hand of truth the sword of thorough investigation,[162] sharpened on the whetstone of contemplation,[163] with which to cut off the circulation of transmigrating existence.

With patient perseverance in good deeds[164] for his strength, he wielded the sword of thorough investigation.

Then did he see that all the twelve conditions were but unstable, painful, and illusive.[165]

Earnestly persisting in his meditation, he progressed to a knowledge of the paths which lead to salvation.

Meditation on all things in due sequence,[166] and that meditation which reveals Nirwana to the mind,[167] were the steps that brought him to the first path.[168]

Reaching the first path, he destroyed belief in the existence of self and of possession. He destroyed doubt, and destroyed false doctrine.

Earnestly persisting in meditation, he arrived at the second path, and annihilated the coarser evils, lust, avarice, and anger.

Still persisting in meditation, the Lord arrived at the third path, and annihilated the more refined passions still remaining in him.

And further persisting in meditation with yet increased force, the Lord arrived at the fourth path, and utterly annihilated all contamination,[169] all evil that remained in him.

Thus did the Lord arrive at the Samma-samphotthiyan,[170] the omniscient Buddhahood, perfected by self-confidence[171] in his knowledge, his goodness, his just appreciation of difficulties, and the completeness of the law he would teach.

Thus did the Lord become the Buddha worthy of the adoration of all beings—Angels and Asuras, Gandharvas, Suparnas, and Nagas.

Then there were signs and portents and earthquakes throughout all the ten thousand worlds, the same great wonders as had attended his birth.

SIAMESE CONCLUSION.

The Lord Buddha having obtained omniscience, yet remained seated on the jewelled throne beneath the great holy Bo-tree for a space of seven days, full of satisfaction and happiness, arising from the fruition of his holiness.

And at the end of seven days, rising from his throne, and proceeding to a short distance from it, he stood on its east and on its north in due order, and thus reflected—

"Vast has been the kindness and the service which this great holy Bo-tree has rendered to me. Trusting to its protecting shade have I attained to omniscience. Yet have I nothing here by which to express my gratitude. I have but my eyes with which to make my offering, in place of flowers, or lights, or incense."

Thus thinking, the holy Lord of compassion stood with unclosed eyes for seven days, as an offering to the holy Bo-tree. He kept open the azure lotuses, his eyes, and offered them instead of scents and flowers.

And that place became famous by the name of the Anila Chaitya.

Then many of the angels wondered and doubted, saying: "Is this all that happens on the attainment of the Buddhahood? Does the Buddha merely venerate the great Bo-tree with unclosed eyes? or will he perform some other work?"

And the Lord, the conqueror, knowing their thoughts, relieved them by a great miracle, causing the miraculous appearance of a crystal portico for himself to walk in, a crystal portico with ten thousand golden columns.

NOTE.—The story of Buddha's Life is continued in Note 173.

NOTES TO THE LIFE OF BUDDHA.

1.

In this note I will endeavour to explain the words Buddha, Bodhi, Bodhisatva, and Phra.

Buddha, in Siamese, *Phut* and *Phutha,* 'The Wise,' is the principal title of every Buddha, of whom it is supposed there have been infinite numbers, who have enlightened the world successively at distant intervals. The word comes from the Sanscrit "Budha," which is derived from "budh"—to fathom, penetrate, understand.

Bodhi, a Sanscrit word, in Siamese, *Phothi*, has in both languages the same meanings—(1.) wisdom; (2.) the sacred fig-tree, pipul, ficus religiosa, or Bo-tree—the tree under which Buddha sat during the meditation which raised him to omniscience, and which is to be found in the grounds of almost every temple in Siam.

M. Burnouf remarked of the word *Bodhi*, that he preferred not to translate it, as although it could be translated as "intelligence," its meaning would be incompletely conveyed by that word, and it in fact implied the "condition of a Buddha."

In Siamese it is most commonly found in compound words, such as—

Phothisat (Sanscrit, *Bodhisatva*), a being who is passing through transmigrations on the way to become a Buddha. At the beginning of the Siamese story of Buddha are mentioned some of these pre-existences of the Phothisat, the term applied to him up to the very time he achieves the Buddhahood.

Phothiyan is another compound of frequent occurrence. It is a contraction for Somphothiyan (Sanscrit, sãm, bodhi, jnâna), the omniscience of a Buddha.

Phra is a Siamese word applied to all that is worthy of the highest respect, that is, everything connected with religion and royalty. It may be translated as "holy." The Siamese letters p-h-r commonly represent the Sanscrit v-r. I therefore presume this word to be derived from the Sanscrit "vri—to choose or be chosen," and "vara—better, best, excellent," the root of ἄριστος. I also find a Sanscrit word, varh, or barh, to be pre-eminent.

In Burmah the words Parâ and Bhurâ are used in a similar way to the Siamese Phra.

2.

Sidharta, a Sanscrit word meaning "one who has attained his aim;" the name of Buddha Gotama during his youth, and until he attained the Buddhahood. See also Note 103.

3.

Religious mendicant.—The whole narrative assumes that, previous to Gotama Buddha, there were numerous sects of religious mendicants, apparently all Brahmins, who wore a special dress. The same presumption is found in the stories supposed to have been related by Buddha, recounting his various lives in former states of transmigration, in which the Brahmins are continually referred to as persons deserving high respect. The idea of the religious mendicant, of the man who believes that he does a good action in devoting himself to the salvation of his own soul, while he leaves others to work to maintain his body, is undoubtedly a very ancient one.

4.

The draught of immortality.—The word I have thus translated is Amrita, a Sanscrit word meaning immortal, the elixir of life, the beverage of the gods.

5.

Kusinagara, the scene of Buddha's Nirwana, is identified by General Cunningham with Kasia, about 110 miles N.N.E. of Benares. He believes that the very spot, marked in ancient times by a reclining figure, representing Buddha in the attitude in which he died, may be recognised in a heap of ruins, whose name he translates as "The Fort of the Dead Prince."

6.

Nirwana, by Siamese called Nipphan or Niruphan. A fierce fight is ever waged as to the exact nature of Nirwana, and Buddhists themselves have differed as to whether it is annihilation or not. Whichever it be, it is certainly exemption from all future anxiety and sorrow, from all the chances of transmigrating life, in fact, rest or peace.

The Siamese always refer to it as something existing, as in the phrases, "Nirwana is a place of comfort, where there is no care; lovely is the glorious realm of Nirwana!" which I take from the story of "Buddha's Nirwana." In the second chapter of this work (The Life), it will be found described as the "Jewelled realm of happiness, the immortal Nirwana."

Max Müller, in his introduction to the Dhammapada, gives an interesting disquisition on Nirwana, to which I may refer my readers. He comes to the conclusion that though the word etymologically means extinction, or literally blowing away, and though the third part of the Buddhist Canon (the Abhidharma) teaches it as annihilation, it was not so taught by Buddha. I quote the following passage (page xlv.):—"What Bishop Bigandet and others represent as the popular view of Nirvâna, in contradistinction to that of the Buddhist divines, was, in my opinion, the conception of Buddha and his disciples. It represented the entrance of the soul into rest, a subduing of all wishes and desires, indifference to joy and pain, to good and evil, an absorption of the soul in itself, and a freedom from the circle of existences from birth to death, and from death to a new birth. This is still the meaning which educated people attach to it, whilst to the minds of the larger masses Nirvâna suggests rather the idea of a Mohammedan paradise or of blissful Elysian fields."

I cannot profess any certainty of opinion as to what Buddha taught on the subject. His teaching, as the modern Buddhist tells us, did not profess to explain the beginning, and it seems to me that it did not explain the end. It dealt with material existence, ever-circling existence; it considered it an evil, and suggested its annihilation as desirable. Nirwana was the annihilation of that existence.

7.

Adjata-sattru and the first Buddhist Council.—Adjatasattru, the son of Bimbisara, the great supporter of Buddha, was King of Magadha, in Central India, his capital being Rajagriha (about 150 miles E. by S. of Benares). He gained the throne by murdering his father, seven years previous to Buddha's death; and at first opposed the great teacher, but afterwards became strongly attached to him and his religion. He enlarged his dominions by subjugating the neighbouring states of Kapila (Buddha's own country), Kosali, and Wesali; in the latter case, effecting his purpose by using means which the legends tell us were suggested by Buddha.

The assembly convened by him, immediately after Buddha's death, is known as the first Buddhist Council, and is said to have consisted of five hundred monks, who had all attained to the Rahatship, or highest degree of sanctity, which confers miraculous powers, and immediately precedes the reception of Nirwana. The council was presided over by Kasyappa, under whose direction the whole canon of Buddha's teachings was recited. These teachings are divided into three parts, known as the three baskets (Trai Pidok, or Pitaka).

The first, called Winya, in Siamese, Phra-Winai, "discipline," consisting of the series of instructions for the monks, was recited by Upali, now eminent among monks, but formerly following the despised profession of a barber.

The second part, called Sutras, in Siamese, Phra-Sut, "things strung together," or sermons addressed to all, was recited by Buddha's personal attendant, Ananda.

The third part, called Abhidharmma, in Siamese, Phra-Baramat, the "superior truths," or metaphysics, was repeated by Kasyappa himself.

These three parts, carefully remembered by the auditors, are supposed to have been orally transmitted for some hundreds of years, though some say that they were at once written in the Sanscrit language.

Such is the tradition of this first council; but with respect to the third part of the canon, called Abhidharmma, the northern Buddhists teach that it was not among the oral traditions of early Buddhists, but was first taught by Nagarjuna (about the Christian era), who learnt it from the superhuman Nagas, who had heard Buddha teach it. European scholars do not allow that books differing so much as the Sutras and the Abhidharmmas can have had a simultaneous origin.

8.

Wephara Hill.—The council is said to have been held in the Sattapani cave, on the Wephara or Webharo mountain, which Cunningham shows to be Mount Baibhâr, one of the five hills around the city of Rajagriha (150 miles E. by S. of Benares).

9.

Kasyappa, generally called the Great Kasyappa, is said to have been a great teacher previous to his conversion to Buddhism; and when, after a contest, he acknowledged the superiority of Buddha's teaching, and became a convert, he was followed by five hundred, who had previously been his own disciples. His conversion took place in the first year of Buddha's teaching.

His succession to the patriarchate or primacy of Buddhists is attributed to Buddha's own designation, and is associated with a story that Buddha either exchanged robes with him, or said that he would wear his mantle.

10.

Bhâwana (Siamese, Phâwana) is meditation. The Sanscrit word Bhâvana has the meanings mental perception and meditation.

The monks of Buddhism have converted this practice of meditation into a formal rite, with an elaborate ritual, which is well described by Spence Hardy in his "Eastern Monachism," chapter xx.

There are five chief sections of Bhâwana, named respectively the meditations of Charity (Maitri), of Pity (Karuna), of Joy (Mudita), of Sorrow (Asubha), and of Indifference (Upeksha). Those most frequently mentioned among the Siamese are the first and last, called by them Meta and Ubekkha.

To practise the first it is necessary, as a preliminary, to abstain from doing evil, and then seeking a solitary place, to reflect on charity, or universal love, repeating a number of texts appropriate to the occasion, and calculated to remove from the heart every feeling opposed to universal charity.

To practise Upeksha Bhâwana, it is requisite to cultivate such reflections and repeat such texts as will lead the mind to regard all beings with perfect equanimity, neither loving nor hating one more than another.

The fact that Phawana is for the most part a repetition of set forms or texts, has caused it to be translated as "prayer." The Siamese expression Suet mon, which means "to repeat mantras or texts," is also translated "to pray;" but I object to the translation in both cases, bearing in mind the saying of the "Modern Buddhist," that the Buddhists are Samanyang, *i.e.*, do not believe that there is any one to pray to. My ideas on Buddhist prayer are stated in the Preface.

11.

Ananda, the cousin of Buddha, must not be confounded with Nanda, Buddha's half-brother.

Ananda, born on the same day as Buddha, is throughout his career represented as a man of a peculiarly sweet disposition, and a great favourite of his Teacher. He was converted in the first year of Buddha's teaching, and in the twentieth season was appointed his personal attendant, and remained in that capacity until Buddha's Nirwana. Nevertheless, he is represented as somewhat deficient in intelligence, and outstripped in the race of sanctity by many who had less advantages. There was a question as to whether he could be admitted to the first council of five hundred, owing to his not having attained the requisite degree in the priesthood. The objection was overruled, and at the same time, by a night of intense meditation, he attained the sanctity required, and with it the miraculous powers of knowing the thoughts of other men and of flying through the air, which are referred to in the text.

But for the direct assertion in chapter iii. that Ananda was born at the same time as Buddha, everything in the stories of Buddha that I have read seems to assume Ananda as younger than his master.

12.

Wheel of the law (Phra thamma chak).—In this passage the Siamese author speaks of the wheel as if it was the quoit-like weapon (chakra) the emblem of power of Indra, King of the Angels, and of Emperors of the World; a very few lines farther on the allusion seems to be to the circle of cause and effect, by which, in chapter x., Buddha is said to account for continued existence in transmigration. The twelve causes and effects (nidanas), are called the twelve constituent parts of the wheel.

The ancient sculptures of Sanchi, which I refer to in the account of the Footprint, give several examples of the mystic wheel, as drawn by Buddhists, probably a short time before the Christian era. In them the wheel is not a weapon, but a true wheel with spokes.

Practically the favourite Buddhist expression "turning the wheel" means simply teaching the law. I suggest an explanation of this in my account of the Chakra on the Footprint.—See Part III., chap. iii.

One of the most curious forms of wheel superstition is the praying-wheel of Northern Buddhists, a box full of texts, the turning of which is supposed to be as efficacious as repeating the text. This is praying by machinery, and is perhaps an improvement on the not uncommon practice of praying by rote.

The word I have translated "law," is the Siamese Tham or Thamma (Sanscrit, Dharma—"right"), meaning right, truth, the eternal principle followed by nature, the law of nature.

13.

The word I have translated "screen" (Phat chani) is generally rendered priest's fan. It is not a fan, but a spoon-shaped screen to assist the monk in keeping from his sight objects which might distract his thoughts. The rules of his order forbid him to look about when he walks, enjoining him to keep his eyes fixed on the ground within a plough-length of his feet.

One of these screens is figured on the Footprint, No. 48.

14.

The four highest degrees of saintship.—The reference is to what are called "the four paths and the four fruits," or otherwise "the eight paths." The four degrees are in Siamese called Soda, Sakkitha, Anakha, and Arahatta, each degree being divided into the path Mak or Makkha, in Sanscrit, Mârga, and the fruit (or perception of the path), Phon—Sanscrit, Phala. The four Siamese terms given above will be easily referred to the Sanscrit in the following list:—

1st degree.—Srota âpatti—"the state of entering into the stream of wisdom." The saint who has attained this cannot have more than seven births among men and angels before he enters Nirwana.

2nd degree.—Sakridâgâmin—"he who must come back once." After attaining this degree there will be only one birth among men or angels before reaching Nirwana.

3rd degree.—Anâgâmin—"he who will not come back." There will be another birth, but not in the worlds of sensuality. From the heavens of the Brahmas Nirwana will be attained.

4th degree.—Arhat—"the venerable." This is the perfect saint who will pass to Nirwana without further birth.

15.

Indra, King of Angels.—I must request my readers to bear in mind the system of sensual or Dewa heavens, and spiritual or Brahma heavens, described on page 13. Indra (Phra In) is King of the lower Dewa heavens; his palace, Wechaiyanta, is in the second tier of heavens, reckoning from the earth, called Dawadungsa. There the thousand-eyed Lord, as he is called, is attended by thousands of houris. His charger is the three-headed elephant, Erawan, and his great weapon the disc, Chakra, with which he drives from heaven the fallen angels, Asura. Among other treasures, he has for a trumpet a huge chankshell, of the kind still held precious by Eastern kings.

No Hindoo deity, unless it be the great Brahma himself, is so frequently introduced in Siamese legends as is Indra, to whose inspiration they attribute the Lak Inthapat, one of their oldest books on the principles of law.

16.

Chotiban (Pali Jotipalo) was Buddha's name in the days when Kasyappa, the Buddha next preceding himself, taught among men. At that time Chotiban was a Brahmin of wondrous piety and learning, and his ultimate succession or accession to the Buddhahood was predicted by Kasyappa. It is not, however, in accordance with the legends to say, as our text does, that he then commenced his approach to the Buddhahood; for the legend is, that he commenced in the days of Dipangkara, a much earlier Buddha. The general idea conveyed is, that almost an infinite time elapsed between the day on which he fixed his desire, and the time when he attained the object of his desire; throughout which period, in innumerable transmigrations, he steadily persevered in amassing merit. Many stories of what occurred in these transmigrations are supposed to have been told by Buddha, in illustration of his teachings. Those who would read some of them can do so in Captain Rogers' translation of Buddhaghosha's Parables.

17.

The five elements of corporeal being; Siamese, Khan; Pali, Khandha; Sanscrit, Skandha.—Bigandet calls them the five aggregates constituting a living being. Hardy explains them as the elements of sentient existence. The Siamese say of them that they are utterly destroyed at death, and a fresh series of them created by the merit and demerit which, under the influence of Kam (Karma), causes re-birth. They are—

1. Rup (Rûpa), form or materiality.
2. Wethana (Vêdanâ), sensation of pleasure, pain, &c., &c.
3. Sanya (Samdjñâ), perception, enabling us to distinguish things.
4. Sangkhan (Samskâra), translated by Hardy "discrimination;" by Bigandet, "consciousness;" and defined by Siamese as "arrangement," or perhaps "tendency to arrange." In chapter x. I have translated it as "predisposition," or active tendency to arrangement. As one of the Khan (Skandhas), it is said to be a general term embracing fifty ideas; for example, touch, thought, attention, effort, shame, fear, &c., &c. The

Ceylonese and Siamese have a list of fifty-two classes of ideas, of which this term includes fifty, and the other two are Wethana and Sanya, sensation and perception.

5. Winyan (Vidjñâna), intelligence.

The term in the text, "destroyed the five elements," means simply "died."

18.

Sakyas.—An interesting account of the Sakya race is to be found in Turnour's "Introduction to the Mahawanso." Its founders, princes who had been defrauded of their own birthrights, established a sovereignty for themselves in forests they found uninhabited; and in the absence of any other princesses of sufficiently illustrious descent to be fit mates for them, took their sisters as their wives or queens, and were thence called Sakya, or "self-potential."

19.

Kapila, or *Kapilavastu.*—General Cunningham identifies this town as Nagar, near the river Ghaghra, about a hundred miles north of Benares. Those who wish to study the geography carefully should procure his "Ancient Geography of India." For my part, I only roughly indicate the positions by reference to bearing and distance from Benares.

20.

Suddhodana; in Siamese, Si Suthot.—In the second chapter of the Mahawanso is an account of the genealogy of Suddhodana, and his descent from the first king of the world, Maha Sammato, "the great elect," who is said to have been a preexistence of Buddha. Suddhodana is called a king, but would be more correctly described as the rajah of a petty state.

21.

The sixty-four perfections and five beauties of women.—Literally, "the sixty-four female (Itthi) characteristics (laksana), and the five beauties of woman in the five places." The last part of the description seems analogous to an expression in the description of the thirty-two personal characteristics of a great man, viz., "he is rounded in the seven places," which are the hands, feet, arms, and back.

The Lalita Vistâra states that the mother of Buddha had thirty-two perfections, and her family sixty-four distinctions. The family distinctions are, being well-descended, wise, brave, virtuous, rich, pious, &c., &c. The personal distinctions are: "She is well-known, well-respected, dutiful, of an excellent family, of excellent maternal descent, of ripe beauty; she has an excellent name, and a graceful figure; she has never borne a child; her morals are perfect; she is self-denying; she has a smiling countenance and kind manner; she is wise, submissive, free from timidity, experienced, learned, straightforward, without guile, and free from anger, envy, jealousy, rudeness, and levity; she is not given to vain talking; she is patient, truthful, modest, and chaste; she yields neither to passion nor dislike; folly finds but little place in her; she is free from the defects of women, and devoted to her husband."

22.

The five and the eight commandments; Siamese, Sin (spelt sil); Sanscrit, çil—to practise, to worship.—It would perhaps be proper to call these observances rather than commandments.

The five observances are:—

(1.) Abstinence from taking life.
(2.) Abstinence from theft.
(3.) Abstinence from fornication.
(4.) Abstinence from lying.
(5.) Abstinence from intoxication.

These five which are dilated on in the "Modern Buddhist," are obligatory on all persons. They are increased to eight by the addition of—

(6.) Abstinence from food after midday until next sunrise.

(7.) Abstinence from feasting, theatrical spectacles, songs, dances, &c.

(8.) Abstinence from adorning the body with flowers, and the use of perfumes and unguents.

These eight are obligatory on all who have entered holy orders, and are also observed by pious laymen at times, for such periods as they may determine on; that is to say, they observe "sin" for a day, or two days, or any longer period, just as some Christians appoint fasts for themselves.

The eight commandments are increased to ten by the addition of the following two, which are binding on all who have entered holy orders, though the last is commonly disregarded:—

(9.) Abstinence from the use of high couches.

(10.) Abstinence from receiving gold and silver.

23.

Brahmins skilled in the Vedas.—In ancient Vedic times the Indian monarchs used to have attached to their establishments a Purohita, or Brahmin priest, to attend to their sacrifices, &c., and act as family astrologer. Even to this day the Kings of Siam maintain a body of Brahmin astrologers or soothsayers (Hon) to inform them of the days and hours of good omen, and to superintend state ceremonies.

In Siamese religious and historical works there are frequent references to, and (supposed) quotations from, the three Vedas (Trai Phet), and the Shastras (Sat), to which sources they attribute many of their superstitions—such as the idea of the thirty-two signs of a great man, &c., &c. They believe that the Vedas, as they now exist, are spurious, and that the true Vedas, now lost, were taught by the angel Maha Brahma, who descended from heaven in the form of a Brahmin for that purpose. This is but a variation of the Hindu tradition that they were revealed by the god Brahma.

When a reference is made in Siamese writings to the Vedas,

they are always called the Three Vedas (Trai Phet). They reject the Atharva Veda, as does also the most ancient Indian Code, the Laws of Manu, in the words: "The divisions of the Rig, the several branches of the Yajur, and the manifold strains of the Sâman, must be considered as forming the triple Veda; he knows the Veda who knows them collectively."

Whether texts of these Vedas exist among the Siamese in an imperfect state I cannot say. I have never heard of such books, though I have met with many passages purporting to be extracts from them.

There is much information anent the Siamese Brahmins and their books in Dr Bastian's "Reisen in Siam." From his notes I learn that the race of Brahmins now in Siam came from Ligor, and succeeded to the positions of an older race, now extinct, which flourished at Phitsanulok, in Upper Siam, before the Siamese had moved their capital to Lower Siam. His informant told him that the three Vedas were the Veda of Prayer, the Veda of Medicine, and the Veda of Astronomy.

24.

The Buddha Wipassi.—The number of former Buddhas is countless, and though some classics mention differences between them, both in appearance and in the trees under which they became Buddhas, they are supposed to have all lived and taught in exactly the same manner. There is a history of the last twenty-four Buddhas preceding our Gotama Buddha, supposed to have been related by him. An abstract may be found in Turnour's "Pali Annals." Twenty-one of the number appeared in eleven previous creations of this world, which, it must be remembered, is periodically destroyed and re-created by the influence of merit and demerit. In some of these eleven creations only one Buddha appeared; in others two, three, or four. The present creation is highly fortunate, as it will number five. Of these, three, by name Kakusandha (Kukuson), Konagamana (Konagon), and Kasyappa, preceded our Buddha, and Maitri Buddha will follow him after his doctrine has been forgotten. Dipangkara is the earliest and first of the above-mentioned list, and Wipassi (mentioned in the text) is the nineteenth. Since his time the world has been twice destroyed and re-created.

The passage simply means, that she who was to be the mother of a Buddha had lived virtuously through countless transmigrations.

25.

The three worlds are the worlds of men, the heavens of the sensual Dewa angels, and the heavens of the intellectual Brahma angels.

26.

Tushita heavens; in Siamese, Dusit.—This, "the joyful heaven," is the fourth Dewa heaven above the earth, and is that in which is laid the scene of the second chapter of this volume. The name is derived from the Sanscrit Tush—to be content; and is explained by the Siamese as meaning, "that in which all desires are satisfied!"

It is the heaven in which the almost perfect beings, about to become Buddhas, pass their last angelic life before being born on earth to assume the Buddhahood. If any ask, Why does this being occupy a low, sensual heaven, instead of the highest heaven of the Brahmas? the answer given by Buddhists is, that as each heaven has a term of life allotted to it, and the allowance to the Brahmas is vast beyond imagination, the delay would be too great. We shall, in the course of this narrative, find Kaladewila bewailing his misfortune in having attained so high a degree of virtue and meditative knowledge, that he will, perforce, be re-born in the formless Brahma worlds before he has heard Buddha preach, and so will lose the opportunity of, by his aid, staying for ever the course of transmigration.

27.

Ankana, King of Dewadaha.—I have here made the parentage of Maia agree with that stated in other legends of Buddha; but the Siamese, both in this and other popular works, describe her father as Chanathiba, King of Ceylon. The error seems to have arisen from confounding Dewadaha with Dewa Langka (Ceylon). In my manuscript, the writer corrects himself, after using Dewa Langka for several pages, by using the correct term, Dewadaha.

This Dewadaha or Koli is a town or village, only a few miles distant from Kapila, and was ruled over by a family kindred to that of which Buddha was a member.

28.

Genii Yak, or Yakkhas.—A kind of demon, represented in Siamese temples as enormous and horrible, though somewhat human in form. They are not absolutely evil, for Buddha himself passed through the state of Yak, whilst on his transmigrating journey towards perfection. They are often associated with the angels, but are more often represented as of evil than of good disposition.

29.

The four guardians of the world.—In Siamese, called Chatu Maharachik Thewada, or Thao Lokaban. These are four angels named Thatarot, Wirulahok, Wirupak, and Wetsuwan, whose palaces are in the Yukunthon mountains (the circular range next to Mount Meru), and who, respectively, rule over the east, south, west, and north divisions of the system, and have under their jurisdiction the Khonthan angels (Gandharvas), the Kumphan angels or Yaks, the Nagas or serpents of supernatural power, and the local angels, &c.

30.

Ten rules of kings; in Siamese, Thosaphit Rachatham.—These are stated to be—(1.) Almsgiving; (2.) Observance of the commandments; (3.) Liberality; (4.) Justice; (5.) Kindliness; (6.) Endurance; (7.) Freedom from anger; (8.) Absence of envy (?); (9.) Restraint of heart; (10.) Care not to give offence by language.

31.

The five principal insignia of kings are—the white umbrella, or rather umbrella in stages (figured on the Footprint); the sword; the royal fan; the golden slippers; and the jewelled crown.

The Ceylonese list, given by Spence Hardy, differs from the Siamese, specifying them as golden sword, slippers, and frontlet, umbrella, and chamara (fly-flap.)

32.

The ceremony of pouring water on Maia and Suddhodana, reminds me of the coronation of the King of Siam, which it was my privilege to witness. The King, robed in white, placed himself in a gold bath, under a canopy from which a shower of water (collected, I was told, from all parts of the kingdom), fell upon him; and for about fifteen minutes afterwards His Majesty sat shivering, whilst the chief Brahmin and the highest princes and ladies poured over him each a bowl of water. This ceremony was conducted in an inner court of the palace, in presence of a very small and select audience, and no foreigner had been permitted to witness it until this occasion, when the courtesy of His Grace the Regent, breaking through customary prejudice, procured the honour for a few. After the bath, the King changed his dress for one more gorgeous, and proceeded to a hall, where, in presence of a larger, but still select audience, he sat on an octagonal throne, and changing his seat eight times, to face the eight points of the compass, repeated each time the formula called the coronation oath. He then marched along the centre of the hall, and, taking his seat at the end opposite to that where the octagonal throne was placed, he was invested with the crown, sword, and other insignia of royalty. A variety of warlike weapons were then presented to His Majesty, each one of which, having been touched by him, was returned to its place.

His Majesty then received a bowl full of small gold and silver flowers to distribute as a token of his royal desire to rain prosperity on the recipients. The reader of the "Life of Buddha" will connect this custom with the angelic habit of raining flowers on great occasions.

His Majesty first handed some of these flowers to the leading princes and ministers, and then turned to give some to the foreigners present. The Consul-General, who headed the foreign representatives, stepped forward; but on this occasion diplomatic precedence was ignored, and the good-will felt towards my country was shown by the Regent and King calling for Alaba (the name by which I am familiarly known among the rulers of Siam), to come forward and receive the first handful of golden flowers. The other foreigners were then presented with the tokens of royal good-will, and what remained were scattered among the audience.

After this ceremony the King rested for a short time, and then, in one of the great audience-halls of the palace, gave audience to the whole body of nobles. Then each leading chief, each head of a department, in turn or order of rank, resigned into the new King's hands the rank and power conferred on him by the King who had passed away, and the new King, in a few short graceful words, re-conferred all upon him. To this audience the Siamese admitted many foreigners, who, for want of space, had been debarred from the honour and pleasure of participating in the preceding ceremonies. The whole was managed by the Regent, who took care that the foreigners attending should be well provided with refreshment, and who, with that remarkable energy which characterises him, in the midst of the ceremonies found time to discuss and settle with me two important questions, about which I had had six weeks' vain discussion with the Foreign Minister and his subordinates. The stoical endurance and calmness of the young King (then an invalid) was wonderful, and eminently characteristic of a high-bred oriental.

33.

Sunantha.—The Queen of King Ankana and mother of Maia, is in other accounts named Yasodhara.

34.

Universal dominion.—Although this chapter is headed "Tushita Heavens," it commences with a part of the story which will be related more fully in a subsequent chapter. The story is that Prince Sidharta, had he not stolen away from his kingdom to become a mendicant ascetic, would have become Emperor of the whole world just seven days later than the night in which he fled. He is therefore said to have resigned the empire of the world in order to become a Buddha.

The Universal Emperor (Chakkravartin) rules over not only this earth, but the other three kindred earths or continents described in the cosmography (page 13). He can fly through the air, and convey his armies with him. He is especially fortunate in possessing the seven treasures mentioned in the next note.

35.

The seven great treasures of the Universal Emperor (Sat ratana) are—(1.) the disc Chakkra; (2.) the elephant; (3.) the horse; (4.) the jewel; (5.) the Queen; (6.) the retinue of attendants; (7.) the prince or general.

In the Thibetan version of the Lalita Vistâra, we find that No. 1 is not regarded as Southern Buddhists regard it, that is, as a quoit-like weapon; but is described as analogous to the Wheel of the Law, a glorious wheel, which, being set in motion by the Emperor, rolls before him as he visits and establishes the law in his wide dominions. In the same list, No. 3 is the flying horse (Valâhaka); No. 4 is described as a jewel which, on the darkest night, will emit a radiance that will enable the Emperor to review and perfectly see all his troops within a space of seven miles; No. 6 is a careful vizier, who has the power of discovering hidden treasures for his master's benefit.

36.

Almost an infinite period of years. The literal translation is, "four asongkhai and one hundred thousand great kalpas." A great kalpa, which is the interval of time between two creations of the universe, is divided into four ordinary kalpas; and an ordinary kalpa is so vast a length of time as to defy computation. An asongkhai is, I believe, a million raised to its twenty-eighth power.

37.

Dipangkara, or Thibangkara (Pali, Dipankaro), was the earliest of the last twenty-four Buddhas preceding our Buddha, whose histories are presumed to be known (see Note 24). Since his days, the world has been twelve times destroyed and reproduced. The story of Sumetta, indicated in the text, is to be found in other books. Its gist is, that Sumetta, a very holy and accomplished hermit, hearing that the Buddha Dipangkara was about to make a journey, solicited the task of smoothing part of the road for him. His work was incomplete when Dipangkara arrived. There was yet a gully to fill up, and he filled it with his own body, making himself a bridge. The act was so meritorious, that he might at once have become a saint of the highest degree, and might have entered Nirwana, had he not voluntarily declined it, that he might live to be a blessing to men in future ages, by becoming a Buddha.

38.

Meditative science.—Literally, "the five Aphinya Yan,

and the eight Samabatti,"—that is, "the five supernatural powers, and the eight accomplishments or perfections."

Samabatti (Sanscrit, Samâpatti) refers, I believe, to the perfect accomplishment of the state of meditative absorption or trance called Dhyâna. The Dhyânas I treat of in a separate note, No. 65, the perusal of which will show their division into four meditations of the material contemplatives, and four meditations of the formless or spiritual contemplatives; or, in other words, four meditations on subjects which are of a limited nature, and four on subjects whose nature is infinite. The attainment of each one of these eight degrees of meditation results in the Samâpatti, connected with it,—that is, a state of absorption or trance, in which the meditative saint is removed from all worldly influence, so that he neither sees, hears, nor feels. In one of the stories illustrating this, a saint thus absorbed is found in a jungle that has been burnt, and is supposed to be dead. The persons who set the jungle on fire, fearing to be held responsible for the death, make a pyre, and endeavour to burn the body, so as to remove all traces of it; but the state of Samâpatti prevents the fire having any effect, and the saint recovers from his trance.

Those who have achieved the first four degrees of meditative science (Dhyâna), acquire, by virtue of their intellectuality, the five miraculous powers, Aphinya Yan; in Sanscrit, Abhi-djñâ, which are—

1. Power over their own bodies, such that they can change their form, fly through the air, become invisible, &c., &c.

2. Power to see what they desire to see, even though obstacles intervene.

3. Power to hear in a similar manner.

4. Knowledge of the thoughts of others.

5. Remembrance of their previous existences.

These five powers are possessed in different degrees, according to the sanctity of the possessor.

39.

The thirty transcendent virtues (Samadungsa Barami) would be more properly described as the ten transcendent virtues. The Siamese enumerate them as follows:—Almsgiving (than), morality (sin), relinquishment of the world and worldly possessions (nekka); wisdom (panya), energy or fortitude (wirya), patience under opposition (khanti), truth (sattha), firm purpose or determination (athithan), charity (meta), indifference or equanimity (ubekkha). These correspond with the Sanscrit words, dâna, çîla, niskrama, pradjñâ, vîrya, kchânti, satya, adhichthâna, maitrî, upekshâ.

These ten Barami (Sanscrit, Pâramitâ) are made into thirty by dividing each into the grades—the ordinary, the superior, and the most excellent.

Burnouf tells us that Pâramitâ, which the Southern Buddhists translate as "that which attains to the other shore" (*i.e.*, Nirwana), is derived from Pâram, "to the other shore," and itâ, "the act of being gone.

40.

Power of righteousness, literally "the completion of the Barami," or virtues described in the previous note. I use the word "power," because these Barami exercise a very great influence, or power, in shaping the Karma, or destiny.

41.

The charities of Prince Wetsandon or Wessantara.—According to the legend, Wetsandon (the last human existence of Gotama Buddha previous to that in which he attained the Buddhahood), was the son of Sanda, a king of Central India. His great delight was the performance of works of abnegation and charity. He was blessed with a very loving wife and two children, and, among other treasures, owned a white elephant, which had a wonderful power of causing rain to fall.

In a neighbouring country, drought led to famine; but on some Brahmins coming to ask for his rain-causing elephant, he gave it with delight for the benefit of the sufferers.

This act caused much dissatisfaction among his father's subjects, to appease which he was ordered into banishment. Before leaving, he gave in charity seven hundred slaves, seven hundred elephants, horses, chariots, buffaloes, and treasures of all kinds.

His affectionate wife accompanied him, taking her children.

On his journey he first gave away his chariot, and then his horses, to Brahmins.

His next alms caused him some pain; for he gave his two children to be slaves to a Brahmin. Finally, he gave his wife to a Brahmin who came and asked for her; but the Brahmin was, indeed, the angel Indra, who, to prevent her being really given away, disguised himself as a Brahmin; and having had her presented to him, left her with the Prince, saying, "I leave her with you; but as you have given her to me, you cannot give her to any other."

Spence Hardy has given a translation of this Jataka, or legend of Buddha, in his Manual.

42.

Angels of the tempest.—This I suppose to be the translation of the Siamese Loka Phayu, but I am not certain. Turnour, translating an account of this same portent, says they were Kamawachara angels, that is, angels of any of the sensual heavens. Phayu seems to be the same as the Vedic Vâyu—god of the wind; and this mention of the Phayu angels clothed in red garments seems to have been suggested by a hymn of the Rig Veda, quoted in Manning's "Ancient and Mediæval India" from Muir's translation:—

"I celebrate the glory of Vâta's (*i.e.*, Vayu's) chariot; its noise comes rending and resounding. Touching the sky, he moves onward, making all things ruddy." I must add another verse, it is so beautiful:—"Soul of the gods, source of the universe, this deity moves as he lists. His sounds have been heard, but his form is not! This Vâta let us worship."

43.

Be not heedless.—The Siamese term is Pramat, which in in its ordinary acceptation means oppressive, overbearing, and insolent. I believe it to come from the Sanscrit Pramâda (mad, &c.), which admits of the interpretation I have given to it. It is, I presume, the opposite of Apramâda—which Max Müller translates by "reflection," "earnestness," "the absence of that giddiness which characterises the state of mind of worldly people."

44.

Ten thousand worlds refers to the ten thousand systems of worlds (each complete in itself), which are nearest to this system of worlds; all of which quake on the conception of a Buddha in this world. The term "four guardians of the world" has been explained in a previous note. As each system of worlds is alike, each has its four guardians.

45.

The inability to rest at ease, or becoming warm, as the Siamese term it, is the expression generally used to denote that an angel is in any way excited. Thus, whenever Indra's interposition on earth is desirable, he is represented as becoming aware of the fact by becoming warm.

46.

The five conditions; in Siamese, Pancha maha Pawilokana. —Perhaps "considerations" would be a better rendering. It is evidently derived from the Sanscrit Vilokana—"seeing," regarding.

47.

The average term of human life gradually reduces itself, owing to men's wickedness, from the immense number of years called Asongkai, to the term of ten years, when a man of five years old is full grown. The average then increases until it reaches its former length.

48.

Jambu dvipa (Siamese, Chom-phu Thawip), that one of the four great continents which we inhabit. See page 13.

49.

Central country (Siamese, Machima).—I omit the imperfect description which the Siamese author gives of its frontiers. It corresponds to that part of India now known as Oude, South Behar, Agra, and Delhi, and may be called the Buddhist's Holy Land.

50.

Pacheka Buddhas (Sanscrit, Pratyeka Buddha), called by the Singhalese Pase Buddhas, are beings who attain to the same personal wisdom and perfection as true Buddhas, but have none of that compassion which leads true Buddhas to be teachers of mankind. They only appear in the world when there is no true Buddha living.

51.

The two principal disciples; in Siamese, Akkha Sawok. Akkha being equivalent to the Sanscrit agra, eka, or aika, "one, chief;" and Sawok to Çrâvaka, "one who attends," a term applied to the disciples of Buddha.

Every Buddha is supposed to have his two principal disciples, and the list of the last twenty-four Buddhas referred to in Note 24 gives, with the record of each Buddha, the names of his principal disciples.

Gotama Buddha's two disciples "of the right and left hand" were named Moggalana and Sariputra. Both died before their master. In Siamese temples their statues may be seen standing in an attitude of adoration before images of Buddha, one on the right hand, the other on the left.

The expression "right and left," applied to dignities, is still used in Siam, where there are two Prime Ministers, one of the left, the other of the right; and where, when the King has two principal Queens (which is not now the case) they bear the titles of Queens of the left and right. The dignity of the left is the more honourable.

52.

The eighty chief disciples; in Siamese, Phra siti maha sawok; Siti is for asiti, eighty.—I have not been able to ascertain who these were; I only find that they are mentioned in the ancient Pali Commentaries as saints possessed of miraculous powers. I quote a passage referring to them in a subsequent note (159).

53.

The most eminent of the warrior caste, &c.—In Siamese the words are Khatiya, Kahabodi, Phrahmana, Maha-Sal. The three first words are clear enough. Khatiya (Sanscrit, Kchattriya), and Phrahmana (Sanscrit, Brâhmana) are the two highest castes, and Kahabodi (Sanscrit, Griha-pati) means householder. The fourth term is doubtless also Sanscrit, and occurs without variation in the Thibetan and Singhalese versions. Literally it means "the great Sala-tree," but this does not make sense. Foucaux believes it to designate a fourth class; but this will not suit the Singhalese and the Siamese texts, in which it is made not a distinct term, but one qualifying each of the three preceding terms. I have translated it as if it was an erroneous reading for Mahâ-sâra, "the great essence, or most important part of anything." Spence Hardy does not attempt to explain it.

54.

The institution of caste does not exist in Siam, but it exists in Ceylon with Buddhism, or, I should say, in despite of Buddhism. In this book we are reading of events supposed to have occurred in India, the stronghold of caste; and the object of the writer in introducing the subject is to explain why Buddha sprang, not from the Brahmin caste, generally supposed to be the highest, but from the Kchattriya caste, "the warriors," called in the text the royal caste. He tells us that this caste (now of less importance) was in those days the most respected.

55.

Nanthawan gardens.—When the term of angels' lives are ended, they enter certain heavenly gardens, and there suddenly quit their state (chut), and descend into another form. They do not die, but simply transmigrate.

56.

Preta or Pret.—One of the most miserable forms of being. Some are condemned to a weary life in regions beyond the walls of the world, where no light ever penetrates. Others rove about on earth, incessantly in motion. Though twelve miles in height, they are so thin as to be invisible. They particularly suffer from hunger and thirst, being extremely voracious, and yet, from the very small size of their mouths, unable ever to satisfy their cravings.

57.

The fifteenth day of the eighth month is the day on which Buddhist Lent or Wasa commences. It is held as a great festival, and especially devoted to making offerings to the monks, who, for the three ensuing months, are debarred from travelling, and bound to sleep in the dormitories of the monasteries of which they are members.

58.

Holy day; Siamese, Ubosot; Sanscrit, Upôsatha.—Burnouf states it to be "a term applied to the confession of offences, made by Buddhist monks on the days of the new and full moon." Siamese also apply it to the temple building commonly called "bot," in which the confession has to be made. Only monks are present at the ceremony, which I believe is a mere formality. The 227 precepts contained in the book Patimokkha are supposed to be read through, and any monk who has offended against them is bound to declare his offence, and request his superior to appoint a penance.

The term is also applied to the Upôsatha elephant, one of the elephants of the Himalayan fairyland.

59.

Anodat lake.—One of the seven lakes of the Himalayan forest or mountains; supposed by some to be the source of rain (see the "Modern Buddhist"). I use the term Himalaya in accordance with precedent, but it is not correct; for even though the Himalayan mountains first suggested the idea of the Himawonta, or, in Siamese, Himaphan forests and mountains, the word now simply means fairyland.

60.

Thrice he marched around.—This is the mystic ceremony of Thaksina, still observed by Buddhists, who, especially the women, may be seen on festival days marching thrice around some holy spire, with their hands raised in adoration, or bearing lighted scent-sticks. European residents in Siam may have noticed it on the day when they are in the habit of resorting to Paknam, near the river's mouth, to look at the vast number of pretty Siamese and Peguan girls who, on that day, devote themselves first to religious duties, and then to boat-races and other sports. A variety of this form of worship is described under the heading Baisee, in the account of the Phrabat. The word Thaksina is derived from the Sanscrit "Dakshina," meaning "right," as opposed to left; and the ceremony of showing reverence by walking round a person or thing, keeping the right hand towards them, is also Brahminical.

Professor Ferguson, in his "Tree and Serpent Worship," calls attention to the gallery round the ancient Topés or relic mounds, evidently intended to be used for this ceremony.

61.

Tapas and Parivrâjaka, Sanscrit for the Siamese Tapasa and Pariphachok.

Tapas is defined in Benfey's Sanscrit Dictionary as "penance or mortification," "an ascetic." As an example is mentioned the Pancha-tapas, or "five (fire) ascetic," who sits between four fires, exposed at the same time to the sun.

Parivrâjaka is defined as a wandering ascetic who lives on alms.

62.

Kaladewila.—As an account of this sage is to be found at the beginning of the fourth chapter of this work, it is unnecessary to give the story here.

63.

The reference is to ordinary idols of Buddha, which are always placed on pedestals euphuistically called jewelled thrones.

64.

Yom, Yak, Asura, Gandharva, Suparna, and Garuda.

Yom, ministers of the judge of hell, the Yama of the Hindoos.

Yak or Yakkhas form the subject of Note 28.

Asura, fallen angels. The same word is found in Indian mythology with a similar meaning, the opposite of Sura, "a god." The Siamese, who do not seem to have the word Sura with the meaning of "god or angel," derive Asura from Surâ,

" spirituous liquor," defining the a-sura as " no-liquor angels," angels who have suffered so much through drunkenness that they have now foresworn liquor.

The story is that they were formerly angels residing in the heaven of Indra, from which Indra expelled them in a drunken state, and drove them to a region underneath Meru, from which they make continual sallies, vainly attempting to regain their former abodes. Some of them are very powerful; as, for instance, the Asura Rahu, the great dragon, whose attempts to swallow the sun and moon are the cause of eclipses.

Gandharva, a Sanscrit word, the Siamese being Khonthan, derived from gandha, (Sanscr.) " fragrance." Described in the Traiphoom as angels of scent, born in fragrant places. In Indian mythology they are the musicians of Indra's heaven. They are also regarded as musicians in Buddhist mythology, but are removed from the heaven wherein Indra dwells to the heaven below it, and are made subject to the rule of the angel Thatarot, one of the four guardians of the world. See Note 29.

Suparna and Garuda (Siamese, Suban and Khrut) are also Sanscrit terms, denoting a race or races of enormous birds, whose chief occupation seems to be watching for and pouncing on the weaker Naga serpents. Their power is not equal to that of the superior Nagas. I give other particulars in my description of the Footprint, on which one is figured.

65.

Meditative science of the formed and formless Brahmas; Siamese, Chan; Sanscrit, Dhyâna.—The Dhyânas are a series of states of abstract meditation, or, it may be said, ecstatic trance, the attainment of which is the highest accomplishment of a Buddhist saint. I have already referred to them in Note 38; but in that note I treat rather of the result of the Dhyâna than of the Dhyâna itself. They are generally classed as four Dhyânas of the formed Brahmas, and four of the formless Brahmas, the idea being that a necessary result of the accomplishment of Dhyâna will be a re-birth in that intellectual or Brahma heaven which, by a scale I shall presently mention, they conceive to correspond to it. They consider that the soul which has attained to even the lowest of these intellectual states is too superior to enter any of the lower or sensual heavens, but must enter a Brahma or meditative heaven. It will be remembered that there are sixteen heavens of the formed Brahmas, and above them four of the formless Brahmas. The three lowest Brahma heavens are inhabited by those who have attained the first Dhyâna, in which the mind, absorbed in careful investigation, perfectly comprehends the object it is fixed on, attains the first degree of tranquillity, and frees itself from all desire, except that for Nirwana.

The next three heavens are the abode of those who have attained the second Dhyâna, which is a state of joy undisturbed by the exercise of the reasoning powers.

The next three heavens are the abode of those whose meditation has risen above the idea of joy or sorrow, comfort or discomfort, which constitutes the third Dhyâna.

The next two heavens are the abode of those who have attained the fourth Dhyâna, a meditation of such perfect calmness or indifference that it raises those who have mastered it above subjection to the laws which bind those who have not so freed their minds. While yet men, before transmigrating to the heavens, they will, by virtue of this meditative force, be gifted with more or less of the magic powers described in Note 38. They will have supernatural vision and hearing; they will know the thoughts of others; they will remember some of their past existences, and will be able to fly through the air, pass through the earth, &c. Some are represented as visiting the heavens by virtue of this power.

In reference to this Dhyâna, Barthélemy St Hilaire, in his very readable but unsympathetic book "Le Bouddha," observes, that it is a flagrant contradiction to represent impassibility and magic powers as existing together. I fail to see the accuracy of his argument. They may exist together, although not simultaneously exercised. The impassive state is only transient, but denotes such an intellectual power that he who possesses it can, in other phases of his meditation, exercise supernatural powers.

With this list of four Dhyânas, which may be called the Dhyânas proper, there are associated only eleven of the sixteen heavens of the formed Brahmas. The remaining five heavens are tenanted by those saints who have entered what some incorrectly call the fifth Dhyâna, that is, the lowest of the four paths or conditions of sanctity which lead to Nirwana. See Note 14.

The four heavens of formless Brahmas are inhabited by those who have attained the Dhyânas of the formless. These are, I believe :—

1. A condition above all limitation by form, &c.; that is, realisation of the idea of infinity in respect to space.
2. Realisation of the idea of infinity in respect to mind.
3. Realising the idea of nothingness (as regards space, matter, &c.)
4. A state in which there is neither idea nor absence of idea, or perhaps a state which realises the nothingness of mind.

Bishop Bigandet, translating the Burmese version of a Siamese book, states that the five degrees of meditation are perception, reflection, satisfaction, happiness, and fixity. His system of translation is such that one can never tell whether we are reading the text of the native author, or the comments of the Catholic scholar, but, wherever the fault lies, the statement is incorrect. The steps requisite to attain the Dhyânas are confounded with the Dhyânas themselves. The following abstract of a part of the Siamese Traiphoom will explain the mistake, which I take notice of because it once misled me, and may mislead others :—

"Only those who have practised Dhyâna can enter the Brahma worlds. The Brahmas are all males, need no food, and are satisfied with a constant blessedness. They have no sense of taste, nor scent, nor touch, but have six spiritual faculties—viz., (1.) Witok, or Witaka (consideration), which, like the wings of a bird, raises the mind to contemplation. (2.) Wichara (reflection), which is the contemplation itself. (3.) Piti, which is the satisfaction which fills the body. (4.) Suk, which is the thorough happiness following on the satisfaction, and which gives rise to Samâthi, or Dhyâna, which is thorough abstraction. (5.) Ekkhata, which is fixedness of the mind on a single object. (6.) Ubekkha, which is perfect indifference to everything."

Dhyâna is a Sanscrit word meaning "meditation," derived (Benfey's Dic.) from Dhyai, "to think or meditate on." The Siamese word Chan is evidently a corruption of it, and the statement in the "Bangkok Calendar" that "Chan is a Pali word meaning 'sin-burning'"—a statement attributed to an eminent Siamese authority on Pali—is, I presume, incorrect.

66.

Four miraculous powers (Siamese, Itthibat).—Literally, the four steps to, or effective means of obtaining, the miraculous powers. These means are—firm determination, earnest meditation, persevering exertion, and close investigation. The resulting powers are ten in number, but may be summed up as—power to reproduce forms like one's self, to change one's form, to disappear, to fly, to escape all dangers, and to cause to appear anything that one desires. The word Itthibat is compounded of Itthi; in Pali, "Irdhi;" in Sanscrit, "Riddhi" (superior power); and Bat; Sanscrit, Pâda, "a foot."

The Sanscrit "Riddhi" is much more exactly reproduced in the colloquial Siamese word "Rit" (superior power), than in the Pali form of the religious books. I mention this as an example of the occurrence in the Siamese language of Sanscrit words, apparently not derived through the Pali, but in some more direct way. There are many such words.

67.

The seven constituents of the highest wisdom—in Siamese, Photchangkha; in Sanscrit, Bodhyañga (for Saṁbôdhyagga)—are Memory (Sati), Confidence (Pasathi), Energy (Virya), Joy (Piti), Self-collection or quietude (Samathi), Research into law (Thammavisai), and Indifference (Ubekkha).

There is some discrepancy between various lists. Thus Hardy gives them as—ascertainment of truth by mental exertion, investigation of causes, persevering exertion, joy, tranquillity, tranquillity in a higher degree, and equanimity.

68.

The five great principles of emancipation (Wimuti) differ little from the four pre-eminent truths (Note 71). Burnouf gives them as the idea of progress, of passage, of the sorrow in the passage, of infinity in the sorrow, of abandonment, or relinquishment.

The Sanscrit word is Vimukti, "separation or liberation."

69.

The science which makes all things perfectly manifest.—The word is Anawara Yan, or Anawarana Yan. I take it to be the negative of the Sanscrit Âwarana, "covering," but I have some doubt as to the correctness of my rendering.

70.

Would cause all pain to cease.—The Siamese reads, "that he would cut off the Asa mi man of all living things." I do not know the word Asamiman, and my translation of it is very probably incorrect.

71.

The four pre-eminent truths, or truths of the saints (Siamese, Chaturariasat; Sanscrit, Ârya Satyâni, or Âryâni Satyâni).

1. That sorrow ever attends (transmigratory) existence.
2. That the cause of sorrow lies in the passions, or desire.
3. That cessation of sorrow can be procured by the extinction of desire.
4. That desire can be extinguished by holiness (literally, by entry into the paths).

Buddhists seem to have rather a hazy idea as to the sense in which the last term, "the paths," is to be understood.

One explanation is, that the paths are the "four ways and four fruits," the degrees of saintliness described in Note 14.

Another explanation is, that the eight paths are—right doctrine, right intention, right speech, and right conduct, right life, right application, right memory, and right meditation.

A third explanation is to be found in chapter x. of this volume, where Prince Sidharta is represented as attaining the Buddhahood by first acquiring a knowledge of the circle of causes of continued existence in transmigration, and then passing through the four paths. In this account, the first path is that which destroys belief in the existence of self, and of anything belonging to self. This evidently corresponds with the "right doctrine" of the preceding list. The second path destroys the coarser passions. The third path destroys the more refined passions. The fourth path brings perfect purity.

72.

The four applications of reflective power or memory (Siamese, Satipatthan; Sanscrit, Smrityupasthana).—Burnouf defines them as:—

1. The act of keeping one's self mindful of one's body.
2. The act of keeping one's self mindful of one's thought.
3. The act of keeping one's self mindful of one's sensations.
4. The act of keeping one's self mindful of the law.

Spence Hardy terms them the "four subjects of fixed attention," and thus enumerates them:—

1. The consideration that the body is composed of thirty-two impurities.

2. The consideration that the three modes of sensation are connected with sorrow.
3. The consideration that mental faculties are impermanent.
4. The consideration that the five elements of existence (Skandhas) are unreal and not the truth.

73.

Four classes of distinctive knowledge (Pali, Samphitha Yan).—These are evidently the four (Sanscrit) Pratisamvid mentioned in Appendix xvii. to Burnouf's "Lotus," which are—

(1.) Distinct knowledge of meaning; that is, of all which proceeds from a cause, &c.
(2.) Distinct knowledge of the law.
(3.) Distinct knowledge of the true explanation of everything.
(4.) Distinct knowledge of the transitoriness, misery, and illusion of all things.

Spence Hardy gives them as knowledge of—(1.) the meaning of any matter in its separate divisions; (2.) the doctrines of Buddha; (3.) the power of the Buddhas to perceive truth intuitively; (4.) the power of saints to know the roots and properties of things.

74.

The four virtuous inclinations, Phrommawihan.—The Siamese define them as—

(1.) Seeking for others the happiness one desires for one's self.
(2.) Compassionate interest in the welfare of all beings.
(3.) Love for, and pleasure in all beings.
(4.) Impartiality, preventing preference or prejudice.

75.

The eleven fires.—I have not been able to find a list of the passions or vices thus designated. There are lists of eight vices and ten vices. Perhaps the number eleven is made up of the eight generals and the three daughters of Mara, the Evil One, which would involve some repetition. The list would then be—sensuality, anger, concupiscence, desire, disrespect, arrogance, doubt, ingratitude, love, wrath, and lust.

76.

The sixty-two false doctrines.—An account of the sixty-two false doctrines was translated by Gogerly from the Brahma Gâla Sûtra, and an abstract of his translation appears in Spence Hardy's Manual. The Sûtra, I believe, defines them as "all the different modes of belief then in existence or that could exist." I do not think the distinctions worth recapitulating, but as an example of them give the following:—

"There are sixteen sects who hold a future state of conscious existence, and that it is either material, immaterial, a mixed state, or neither material nor immaterial; that it is either finite, indefinitely extended, a mixture of both states, or neither the one nor the other; or that its perceptions are either simple, discursive, limited, unlimited, happy, miserable, mixed, or insensible."

77.

The Holy Triad consists of Buddha, the law or teachings of Buddha, and the church or assembly of ordained Buddhists. The expression in the Siamese is Phra Trai Saranakhom, which is a Pali formulary or creed, in which the Buddhists thrice repeat the words, "I take refuge in Buddha, his law, and the church." I do not quote the Pali, as it would be waste of space. It may be found in Hardy's "Monachism," p. 23.

The three jewels is another form of the same expression (Siamese, Phra Ratanatrai; Sanscrit, Tri Ratna).

78.

The eightfold path (Siamese, Atthang khika mak; Sanscrit, Ashtaka Mârga, or perhaps Ashtangika Mârga)—consists of—

(1.) Correct religious idea, or orthodoxy.
(2.) Correct thought ending all doubt.
(3.) Correct speaking, or exactitude in words.
(4.) Correct works or conduct.
(5.) Correct life, free from sin and ambition.
(6.) Correct application, or energy in the search for Nirwana.
(7.) Correct memory.
(8.) Correct meditation in perfect tranquillity.

79.

Reward of their works.—I doubt the correctness of my translation here. The Siamese words are, Samanya phon; Sanscrit, Sâmânya phâla. Phon means fruits or effects, and Samanya means common, ordinary, general, and also "in common." One of the meanings of the Sanscrit word is "in common," and another, "common property." It may, therefore, refer to the Buddhist principle of sharing merit, or bestowing on others (by declaration, at the moment of the act, as when giving alms, &c.) a share of the merit which would otherwise all pass to the merit-maker's own credit.

80.

Seven other things came into the world at the same time as Buddha:—

(1.) Phimpha or Yasodhara became his wife.
(2.) Ananda, his attendant and favourite disciple.
(3.) Luthayi or Kaludari was his playmate, and after he became Buddha, was bearer of a message to induce him to visit his father.
(4.) Channamat or Channa was the nobleman who accompanied and assisted him in his flight when he left his palace to become a hermit.
(5.) Kanthaka or Kanthat was his horse on which he fled.

(6.) The great Bodhi or Bo-tree was the tree under whose shade he became Buddha.

(7.) The four great mines were supposed to be immense gold mines in the vicinity of Kapila, which enriched his father.

81.

We, too, shall hear his teachings.—This probably refers to Buddha's supposed ascent to the Davadungsa heaven, seven years after his attainment of the Buddhahood, to preach to the angels, and particularly to his mother, who resorted thither from the Tushita heaven to hear him. The Davadungsa heaven is the second tier above the earth, in which dwells Indra. The Tushita heaven is the fourth tier.

82.

Worshipped him with offerings (Siamese, Sakara bucha).—Bucha is evidently the Sanscrit Puja, meaning worship. Sakara I have not been able to identify, unless it be the same as Kriya, performance, religious ceremony, &c., and Sa Kriya, observant of religious duties.

The offerings made in the performance of Bucha must be distinguished from those called Than or Dana, which are given to priests, beggars, &c. The Bucha offerings are principally flowers, scent-sticks, &c., which are offered before idols and in other holy places; also to the remains of deceased persons, and to the angels of trees, &c.

83.

Did homage to his son for the first time.—In Eastern countries, intense respect is paid by children to their parents. The child, whatever his rank, renders menial services to his father. The chronicler, therefore, calls special attention to the reversal of custom shown in this passage.

84.

Want of merit.—It may seem extraordinary that Buddhist

doctors should have admitted this story of Kaladewila, who, by virtue of his high perfections in meditative science (Note 38), would be, by entering for an immense period the impassive state of the formless Brahmas, deprived of the opportunity of at once learning the way to Nirwana. The explanation is, that no one existence is the summation of the merits and demerits which govern what I must call the soul. I may perhaps say, that Kaladewila was on the crest of a great wave of preponderating merit, but not yet in the state in which, from the absence of demerit, he could pass into the calm of Nirwana.

The story is probably introduced owing to the Buddhist leaders finding it impossible to refuse to recognise the high character and attainments of some of those who did not agree with them, and yet being unwilling, like all other priests, to acknowledge that there was any way to heaven but that they were the teachers of.

In the " Lalita Vistâra," a similar story is told, but the names are different,—Kaladewila being represented by the hermit Asita, and Nalaka by Naradatta.

85.

The requisites for those who take holy orders (in Siamese, called the eight Borikhan; in Pali, the Pirikara; which words perhaps represent the Sanscrit "Parigraha," "possession")—These eight requisites and lawful possessions of a monk are—(1.–3.) three robes (Traichiwon or Chiwara), all worn at the same time; (4.) a pan (Batr) in which to collect food; (5.) a razor to shave the head, eyebrows, &c.; (6.) a case of needles for mending clothes; (7.) a girdle; (8.) a filtering-cloth.

Some schools of Buddhists object to a girdle, and I find Bishop Bigandet, in his list, substitutes a hatchet for a girdle.

The Siamese monks by no means limit their possessions to these eight articles. According to strict rule they should present, for the common use of their monastery, all gifts they receive beyond their food and these eight requisites; but this rule is a dead letter.

Instead of three patched yellow robes, they commonly wear seven articles of dress; and in some of the wealthier monasteries the priests may be seen adorned with embroidered silk scarves.

I cannot state with any certainty the reason yellow robes were adopted by Buddhists. There is a story that thieves wore yellow dresses, and that the poor ascetics, in the depth of their humility, imitated the thieves. It is far more probable that the people of the lowest caste, or outcastes, were compelled to wear yellow, and that Buddhists, voluntarily making themselves outcastes, proudly adopted the colour which marked their act. We find them boasting of their yellow robe (Kasawaphat; in Sanscrit, Kashâya), as the flag of victory of the saints. In the early days of Buddhism the monks wore whatever they could get. Some picked up and patched together the rags strewn about cemeteries; whilst others are mentioned as magnificently attired in glittering royal vestments, and in the precious dresses procured by kings for the ladies of their harems, which these ladies piously gave away.

86.

Practised asceticism (in Siamese, Samanatham; Sanscrit, Sramana dharma).—Samanatham would mean the system or practice of the Samanas, which now means Buddhist monks, and which word (Sramana) is said by the Buddhists to mean "one who tames the senses, or has quieted the evil in him." This explanation is commonly given in European works on Buddhism, but, like other efforts of Buddhist scholarship, as, for example, the Siamese explanation of Dhyâna, in Note 65, it is wrong. I quote a note from Max Müller's "Dhammapada:"—"This etymology (of the writer of the "Dhammapada") is curious, because it shows that at the time when this verse was written, the original meaning of 'sramana' had been forgotten. Sramana meant, originally, in the language of the

Brahmins, a man who performed hard penance, from sram, to work hard, &c. When it became the name of the Buddhist ascetics, the language had changed, and sramana was pronounced samana. Now, there is another Sanscrit root, 'sam,' to quiet, which in Pali becomes likewise 'sam,' and from this root, 'sam,' to quiet, and not from 'sram,' to tire, did the popular etymology of the day, and the writer of our verse, derive the title of the Buddhist priests." I should add, that Max Müller refers the date of the verses he speaks of (the "Dhammapada") to, probably as early as 246 B.C.

87.

Kammathan (Pali, Kammatthana), is one of the modes of Buddhist meditation, and may be called analytical meditation. He who exercises it fixes his mind on any one element, and reflects on it in all its conditions and changes, until, so far as that element is concerned, he sees that it is only unstable, grievous, and illusory. To aid this kind of meditation there are formulas; some people incorrectly call them prayers, in which a list of the elements is repeated; and the ordinary exercise of Kammathan is probably a mere mumbling of these formulas. One of these is a list of the thirty-two constituents of the body—a string of thirty-two Pali words, translated as, "hair of the head, hair of the body, nails, teeth, skin, flesh, muscles, bones," &c., &c. I do not know whether the term is used in Sanscrit; it does not occur in my dictionary. I presume that it is a compound of Karman, "action, the cause of life," and sthâna, "fixed position;" but I do not feel at all certain.

88.

Nalaka Patipada.—Patipada is the life of holiness of those walking in the right paths (Mak, or Megga). I cannot say what book is referred to as the Nalaka Patipada.

89.

The thirty-two signs of a great being are dealt with in the

Phrabat, and in a special Appendix; so it is unnecessary to explain them here.

90.

Then was the question asked.—This sudden interruption in the narrative will be understood by those who remember that the whole story is presumably told by Ananda, questioned by the patriarch at the first council (see chap. i.)

91.

Tathâgata (Siamese, Tathakhot,) a great name of Buddha, used in the Sutras (discourses) when he speaks of himself. It is said to signify " he who has come in the same manner as his predecessors," that is, " he who has passed, like previous Buddhas, through innumerable states of transmigration, acquiring the vast merit which will result in the Buddhahood."

92.

The five commandments and eight commandments have been set forth in Note 22. The Siamese text here is " the twenty-five eightfold observances " (Yi sib hâ assadâng khika sin); but I presume that the error arises from the copyist not knowing the meaning of Assadâng khika.

93.

Charitable meditations (Siamese, Meta Phawana; Pali, Maitri Bhâwana, the meditation of kindness).—I give an account of the five Bhâwanas or meditations of kindness, pity, joy, sorrow, and indifference, in Note 10.

94.

For an account of the meaning of the marks on the Footprint, see the part of this work called Phrabat.

95.

Softness of hands, &c.—I have omitted in the text a few

remarks of an interruptory character. With this clause it is observed that the softness of hands and feet remained throughout his life.

96.

Fingers close set.—It is added that this peculiarity arose from "his having steadily established himself in the four elements of benevolence, Sangkhriha watthu." These are the Sanscrit Saggraha vastuni, defined as almsgiving, agreeable speaking, kind acts, unity in that which is for the general good.

97.

He can turn his whole body, &c.—It is added that this was the result of observance of the Suphasit or rules which teach that which is convenient and agreeable, *i.e.*, good manners. The only works called Suphasit that I know of are translations of Chinese Confucian teachings.

98.

His knees round, &c.—This is because he had truly taught morality (Silapasat), free from greed (Matchiriya). I am not quite certain that my translation of these two words is correct.

99.

Literally, "Id quod celandum est celatur, instar bovis Brahminensis scrotum, vel calyx nymphææ qui nondum sese pandit."

100.

The golden tint resulted from the merit of abstention from anger and unkindliness, &c., and from forbearance and almsgiving. Some people hint that men first gilded their statues, and subsequently regarded a yellow complexion as beautiful. I remember that when the late King obtained the daughter of a Malay Sultan as a wife, I was told she was "very lovely, her skin quite yellow."

101.

Crowns made in imitation of the sirorot or sirotama. The Siamese crown is a tall, pointed crown, like the curious pyramidal cranium given to idols of Buddha, of which an account will be found in the Appendix on the "Thirty-two Signs of a Grand Being." The expression Sirotama occurs twice in this book, each time followed by Kesa (Sanscrit, Keça, hair), the hair of the head; the whole expression meaning the hair on the pointed skull. The Sirotama is sometimes written Sirorot in Siamese, and in this form I think it may be recognised as derived either from the Sanscrit words Çiroruh, head-growth or hair, or else from Çiras, "the head," and Ruch, "light, splendour, to shine" (the latter being the same as the Siamese word Rot, "resplendent"). If this latter derivation were correct, it would justify the term glory by which Sirorot is sometimes translated.

If taken as glory, it is to be remembered that the Siamese regard the glory as not spreading round the head, but rising up from it to a height of six cubits, flame-like as I may say. Hence the shape of their crown coincides with their idea of the form of the glory. Moreover, we Westerns, who differ from the Siamese in painting our saints with glories encircling their heads, instead of rising over them, also differ from them in the essential part of our crowns being the circlet round the head, and not the point above it.

102.

Angkhirasa.—I do not find this name given in any other Life of Buddha.

The name Ângirasa is mentioned by Csoma de Körös (translating from the Thibetan) as one of the descendants of Mahasammato, the first king of the world, and may perhaps be the Bhagiraso of the Pali Mahawanso. We also find the name Ângiras as that of one of the authors or custodian families of the Vedic hymns. The name may perhaps have crept in here by mistake. In accounting for it by connecting it with the brilliant glory or rays streaming from his head, the Siamese probably derive it from their word "rasami" (Sanscrit, Raçmi), effulgence.

103.

Sidharta (in Siamese, Sri that tha or Sithat).—In Note 2 I have given the usual interpretation of this name, which differs little from the "perfection of prosperity" given in the text. In Turnour's translation from the Pali of Buddhaghosa's Commentary, we find, "those who were conferrers of a name, as he was destined to be the establisher (of the faith) throughout the world, gave him the name of Siddhatto, the establisher."

104.

Pachâpati (in Siamese, Pachabodikhot; in Pali—*vide* Roger's "Buddhaghosha's Parables" for account of the family—Pagâpatigotami).—She was sister of Maia, and a joint-Queen of Suddhodana. She had two children—a son, Nanda, and a daughter, Ganapadakalyâni. She ultimately became a nun. Although among the respectable middle classes of Siam it is not considered proper to marry a living wife's sister, such is not uncustomary among the higher classes, and does not seem to lead to any special inconvenience. There were several sisters in the harem of the late King, and two wives of the present Regent who are best known to and most esteemed by foreigners are also sisters.

105.

Nurses free from all bodily defects.—The text is, neither too tall nor too squat, too fair nor too dark, &c., &c. Almost exactly the same words occur in the "Lalita Vistâra" in the description of Queen Maia herself.

106.

Festival of commencement of sowing-time.—This festival, by name Rekna, is one of the great annual Brahminical ceremonies of the Siamese. The King does not himself attend it, but is represented by the Minister of Agriculture, who for the day is regarded as King, and whose powers until the last reign extended even to seizing for himself the goods of any shopkeeper who dared open his shop on that day. The day is fixed by the royal Brahmin astrologers, and is usually early in May. The Minister proceeds to a field in or near the city, and superintends the ploughing. Several elderly ladies from the King's harem follow him scattering seed, and the ceremony ends by setting free the oxen who have drawn the plough, and observing which kind of seed, of several placed before them, they eat the most of. Whichever they eat most of will, it is said, be scarce during the year.

107.

Indra felt uncomfortable on his couch.—The expression is a not unusual one, and the attention of angels to matters where their interposition is required, is generally preceded by their feeling hot or uncomfortable on their seats. The thousand-eyed is a common epithet of Indra.

108.

The three seasons.—In tropical regions the year is divided into three seasons—the cold, the hot, and the wet. In Siam, for instance, the cold season lasts from November to February, being the time that the sun is in the south; this comparatively cold season has an average temperature of about 79° F., that is, warmer than an English summer. As the sun advances from the south, the heat of the hot season becomes terrible, until the middle or end of May, when rain falls and slightly reduces the temperature.

The three palaces built for Prince Sidharta, according to native ideas of what suits the seasons, were all of the same height; hence the five stories of the hot-season palace, gave him loftier rooms.

109.

Maradop or Manradop (Sanscrit, Mandapa).—The

Maradop of the present day are sacred buildings of a square form with pointed roofs. They commonly cover shrines, such as the Phrabat Footprint.

This passage about the Maradop seems to me to be extracted from some Brahmin book.

110.

The twelve arts (in Siamese, Silapasatr—that is, in Sanscrit, the Çâstras, treatises, of the Çilpa, arts).—This is another example of a Sanscrit word used by the Siamese, not derived through the Pali, which is Sippa.

I have no list of the twelve arts specially distinguished. In the "Lalita Vistâra" account of the Prince's trial, he is said to have excelled in writing, mathematics, gymnastics, swimming, running, wrestling, archery, riding, driving, poetry, painting, music, dancing, magic, astrology, logic, and almost every conceivable accomplishment.

In a Siamese historical novel, treating of the Kings of Pegu, I found a list of twenty-four arts which Princes should be conversant with. According to a note I made when I read the book, they are divided into four crafts, five arts, eight merits, and seven manners of action. The four crafts are—warlike tactics, omens, skill in dealing with men according to their characters, and the art of judiciously acquiring wealth. The five arts are—knowledge of all mechanical arts, soothsaying, history, law, and natural history. The eight merits are—truthfulness, just treatment of all people, kindliness, courage, good manners, knowledge of medicine, freedom from covetousness, and forethought. The seven manners are—noble daring when it is required, calm and even government, considerateness for the people, merciful adaptation of government according to circumstances, punishment of the wicked, and watchfulness for their detection, and just apportionment of punishments to offences without any display of malice. One of these last I have omitted, probably from not being able to understand the recondite words used in it. I should add that this list is evidently extracted from some older work, either Pali or Sanscrit.

111.

Invested with royal dignity.—This seems rather to be a ceremony of making him Crown Prince than actual King.

112.

Yasodara (in Siamese, generally called Nang Phimpha).—She was cousin of Prince Sidharta, being daughter of Suddhodana's sister Amita, married to Prince Supprabuddha.

In the "Lalita Vistâra" (Foucaux's translation) her name is given as Gopa.

113.

Polygamy.—It is noticeable that his promotion to royal dignity, and his provision with a large harem, are simultaneous. This book must throughout be regarded as conveying an ancient story moulded on general Eastern, and especially Siamese ideas, which are not very modern. Royal polygamy in Siam must be regarded not as mere sensuality, but as a state engine for binding all the leading families (whose daughters are in the harem) to the King's interests; and also probably for enlightening the King as to the secrets of those families. Of course it cuts both ways, and the wives sometimes spy in the interests of their families rather than of the King.

114.

Messenger from the heavens (Siamese, Thewathut).—The four motives to pious thoughts described in these visions—that is, age, disease, death, and religious life—are known to Siamese as the four Thewathut.

115.

Rahula.—I am unable to explain the connection between the name Rahula and the remark which, according to the text, occasioned it. There is a curious note in Burnouf's "Lotus," p. 397, respecting Rahula, but it does not much help me. He mentions that some derive the name from Rahu, the demon that causes eclipses. Benfey derives Rahu from the Sanscrit root Rah, which has the sense of "abandonment;" and perhaps this may be the root of Rahula, "the abandoned."

116.

Sources of evil or impurity (in Siamese, Upathi Kilet, equivalent to the Sanscrit Upâdhi Kleça).—Spence Hardy gives Kilet, in its Pali form, Kilesa, as meaning evil desire, cleaving to existence. In Siamese I think it refers to impurity and evil in general. Burnouf, quoting Judson, gives the following list of the ten Kilesa:—

Desire or cupidity, anger, folly, arrogance, false doctrine, doubt, impudence, rudeness, immodesty, hard-heartedness.

117.

Bearer (in Siamese, Phanana).—Evidently the same as the Sanscrit, Vahana, the term applied in Hindu mythology to the animal devoted to the use of a god as his bearer. Thus the bird Garuda is the bearer of Vishnu, who is commonly represented in pictures as being borne along by that bird. Siva, if I remember correctly, is borne by an ox; Indra by a three or thirty-three headed elephant, &c., &c.

118.

Guardian angels of the gate.—The mythological system of the Siamese admits not only the Brahma and Dewa angels of the various tiers of heavens, but also numerous Dewa angels of the earth, trees, gates, lakes, and ponds, &c., &c. Formerly, in Siam, when a new city gate was being erected, it was customary for a number of officers to lie in wait near the spot, and seize the first four or eight persons who happened to pass by, and who were then buried alive under the gate posts, to serve as guardian angels. The governess at the Siamese court declares this was done when a new gate was added to the palace a few years ago, but her book is, to my knowledge, so untrustworthy that I may decline to believe this story, the more so as it is quite inconsistent with the humane character of the late King.

119.

Mara, or *Man* (Sanscrit, Mâra, death, god of love; by some authors translated "illusion," as if it came from the Sanscrit Mâya).—The angels of evil desire, of love, death, &c. Though King Mara plays the part of our Satan the tempter, he and his host formerly were great givers of alms, which led to their being born in the highest of the Dewa heavens, called Paranimit Wasawatti, there to live more than nine thousand million years, surrounded by all the luxuries of sensuality. From this heaven the filthy one, as the Siamese describe him, descends to the earth to tempt and excite to evil. In the ninth chapter will be found an account of Mara, his daughters, his troops, his elephant, and his weapons.

120.

The middle day of the sixth month, which generally corresponds with some early day in May, is in Siam held as the festival of the anniversary of the birth, inspiration, and death of Buddha.

121.

Lust, passion, and folly.—These are the words Lopho, Thoso, Moho, on which the "Modern Buddhist" dwells so forcibly.

122.

Sawathi (the Siamese for Srâvasti).—In General Cunningham's "Ancient Geography of India" there is an interesting chapter on the identification and history of Srâvasti. He makes it out to be Oudh, north of the Ghagra, and identifies the ruined city Sahet Mahet as the city itself. In the time of Buddha, Srâvasti was the capital of Prasenajit, a convert and protector of Buddha. In Srâvasti (also known among the Southern Buddhists as Sewet) was the Jetawana monastery, where Buddha, according to the received histories, passed many years, and performed many miracles.

Taking, as I have done before, Benares as a known point, Sawatthi lies about a hundred and ten miles north of it.

123.

Wesali, or *Vaisâli*, Cunningham identifies as Besarh, lying, roughly speaking, about a hundred and forty miles east of Benares. Buddha is supposed to have frequently resided there.

124.

River Anoma.—Cunningham identifies this as probably the river Aumi, about forty miles from Kapila. This identification cannot, however, be made to tally with our story; and it is to be remembered that that learned archæologist draws his conclusions mainly from the works of the Chinese pilgrims who visited the Buddhist Holy Land a thousand to twelve hundred years after the date assigned to the commencement of Buddha's teaching. I, regarding the history of Buddha as a fiction, embracing only a few historical truths, and mainly important as showing what is now believed by Buddhists, do not look upon the question of the exact identification of sites as one of much importance in this place. Assuming, however, Cunningham's sites of Kapila, Srâvasti, and Vaisâli as correct, and that Prince Sidharta passed through these places to some river Anoma lying beyond Vaisâli, then we can make up our distance of two hundred miles, or, as I should have translated it, two hundred and ten miles. The literal translation is thirty yot or yojanas. I have taken the yojana at seven miles, on the authority of

General Cunningham. A Siamese reading the story would probably believe it to be the same as his own yot, which is nearly ten miles.

125.

Augury from name of river Anoma.—For an explanation of this I am indebted to General Cunningham's work. He suggests that the original name may have been Auma, or "inferior;" and that the Prince's remark was, "My ordination shall be an-auma, that is, "not inferior," or "superior." He doubts whether the name Anoma or Anauma was not a corruption or false reading for its opposite, Auma. Supposing that Auma, inferior, was the true name, then the crossing to the other side of the river, the passing over inferiority, has its signification in connection with this play upon words.

126.

Ascetic.—The word used is Samana, which is explained in Note 86. In Siam, it designates a monk; while its diminutive, Samanera, Samanen, or vulgarly Nen, is the designation of a novice.

127.

Touching the head.—The Siamese regard touching the head, or rather tuft of hair, as a very great insult; and the higher the rank of the person, the more sacred his head becomes.

128.

The head of Buddha.—In some Siamese idols the skull rises in a conical form, and is covered with small spikes, representing the short hairs. Foreigners often speak of this as if it were a crown; and, indeed, in some cases it is unmistakably figured as a crown by native idol manufacturers, who seem to have lost all idea of the origin of what they represent. See Note 101.

129.

Karaphruk-tree, also called *Kamaphruk*, and *Kapphruksa* (in Sanscrit, Kalpa-vriksha, the tree of Indra's paradise, which gratifies all desires).—According to the Siamese Traiphoom, this tree grows in the Tushita heavens—the heavens of the joyous—and produces as its fruit everything that can be desired by the angels—gold and silver, precious raiment, and jewels, and all that is beautiful and useful.

At all important cremation ceremonies in Siam, it is customary to hang on a framework representing this tree, a large number of limes or nut-shells, containing money and tickets, exchangeable against the articles mentioned in them—such as boats, mats, scarves, &c.—purchased with the money of the deceased. These limes are scattered, to be scrambled for by the crowd; and it is believed that the merit of this charity will be advantageous to the deceased in his next state of transmigration. On the same occasions great presents of yellow robes, screens, boats, &c., &c., are made to the monks, and these are also considered to be Karaphruk fruits.

Another curious custom, presumably connected with the same idea, is that of hanging gifts for the monks on the trees in the monastery garden at night, and then awakening the monks to get up and seek them.

130.

In the "Lalita Vistâra," Buddha is said to have obtained his yellow dress by exchanging clothes with a hunter, who, it is added, was really an angel, who had taken mortal form for this very purpose.

131.

Realisation of desire for the Buddhahood.—The word I have rendered "desire for the Buddhahood," is Manophanithan; Pali, Manopranidhâna; probably a compound of the Sanscrit words, Manas, "mind, purpose," and Pranidhâna, "attendance to, prayer." Spence Hardy gives it as the era of resolution, or of the desire, "May I become a Buddha." I have already referred to the immense period supposed to intervene between the day the soul of a Buddha first fixes its determination, and the day it achieves its aim.

132.

Loud lamentations.—In the Siamese, about two pages are filled with their exclamations; but, as any one can conceive what women would say under the circumstances, I have not thought it worth translating.

133.

Rajagriha, about a hundred and twenty miles east of Benares, and forty miles south by east of Patna. The story says, crossing a river, he arrived at Rajagriha. This river is, I suppose, the Ganges, which he must have crossed to make this journey; or it may refer to the Nairanjana, or to the Panchana, which is close to Rajagriha. As I before observed, the geography of the story will not bear too close an examination. Rajagriha was the capital city of Bimbisara, King of Magadha, the great protector of Buddha. See Note 7.

In the neighbourhood of Rajagriha are five hills, of which the Wephara hill (see Note 8) is famous as the place where the first Buddhist council was held. Another famous spot close to Rajagriha is the Weluwana, or Weloowoon monastery, a garden presented by King Bimbisara to Buddha in the first year of his teaching, and thenceforward a favourite residence.

134.

Asura Rahu.—The story is, that in a former state of transmigration, the sun (Athit), the moon (Chan, or Chandra), and the Asura Rahu, were brothers. They gave alms to the priesthood, instituted by some former Buddha—the first in a golden vase, the second in a silver vase, and the third in a black pot. Their almsgiving led to their being all born as angels: the first, the angel of the sun; the second, the angel of the moon; the third, the angel Rahu. Rahu, who had been on bad terms with his brothers, and was a wicked angel, became one of the Asuras who were expelled from heaven by Indra (see Note 64). He continually visits the heavens for the purpose of swallowing his brothers in their palaces; and his seizures of their palaces are the cause of eclipses. The rapid motion of those palaces makes it impossible for him to hold them for any time. At great Siamese festivals, one may commonly see an enormous serpent (made of lines of lamps, ingeniously jointed together, and borne about by a number of men), representing Rahu chasing the moon.

135.

Snake King, or *Royal Naga.*—The Siamese define the Nagas as hooded, and commonly seven-headed, serpents of supernatural power, who reside in subterranean kingdoms and palaces beneath this and other earths. Those of this world are ruled over by Waruna. They are also subjected to Thao Wiruphak, one of the four angelic guardians of the world. Among their miraculous powers are those of passing through the earth instantaneously, of assuming the form of men and angels, and of making themselves invisible. Their breath is deadly. They are mostly well inclined, and one reads continually of their beneficent appearance to help the pious. A common representation of Buddha is one in which the seven-headed King of Nagas shields the teacher during a storm, by encircling him with his coils, and covering his head with his seven expanded hoods. The great enemies of the Nagas are the Garudas (monstrous birds); but the Garudas can only conquer the weaker members of the family. For further remarks on the Naga, see remarks on the Phrabat, in this volume. I should add, that the Waruna above mentioned is not the Indian deity Varuna, but is probably the same as Vârunda.

136.

Regarding but the small space of earth close around him.—This is a reference to the Buddhist rule that a monk must keep his eyes on the ground close before him, and not gaze around. Most Siamese monks are provided with a screen to assist them in this duty.

137.

Banthawa hills (Pali, Pandawo).—Identified by Cunningham with Ratnagiri, a hill close to Rajagriha.

138.

Seated himself in a position of contemplation.—This is the general attitude of seated idols of Buddha, and is called Samathi (Sanscrit, Samâdhi). The term means a state of meditation, in which the mind is shut up in itself, and insensible to that which is passing around it. It is, as it were, the first exercise preparatory to entering on the various sciences of meditation called Kammathan, Dhyâna, &c., &c. Its first meaning, according to Benfey, is "composing or reconciling differences;" whence arises the meaning, "restraining the senses, and confining the mind to contemplation on the true nature of spirit."

139.

Hermits Alara and Kuddhaka.—Turnour, in his "Pali Annals," gives their names as Alarakalamo and Uddakaramo. In the "Lalita Vistâra," they are called Arâta Kâlâma, and Rudraka. They are not supposed to have lived and taught together, but to have been visited in succession by Buddha, whose ready comprehension of their teachings led each in turn to invite him to remain as joint-teacher.

140.

Dhyâna meditation.—I have endeavoured, by the words in brackets, to explain the Pali words of the Siamese text, which are, that they taught the seven Dhyâna Samapatti from the first to the Akinya chayayatana Dhyâna, but could not reach to the Newa sanyana newa Dhyâna. For an account of Sampatti and Dhyâna, see Notes 38 and 65.

141.

Uruwela, by the Nairanjana river, supposed to be near Bodh-Gaya, about forty miles south-west of Rajagriha.

142.

Severest asceticism (in Siamese, Maha pathan; in Pali, Mahapadhanan; explained by the Siamese as endurance, Phien).—It is not the mortification of self-inflicted pain, but of patient self-denial.

Maha means great, and Pathan probably represents the Sanscrit Pradhana, which has the meanings "primitive matter," "nature;" "chief," "principal," &c., &c. So that the conjoint word only means "something very great;" and it is possible that the Siamese translation of endurance is incorrect, and that it should be translated, he devoted himself to the "highest object," that is, the Buddhahood.

143.

The five Wakkhi (Bencha Wakkhi).—The "Lalita Vistâra," and other lives of Buddha, all contain an account of these first pupils of Buddha, but in none of them do I find the term "Wakkhi" used. I presume it to be the same as the Sanscrit word Varga, a class—compounds of which, Tri-varga, and Chatur-varga, mean respectively an "assembly of three things, and of four things." Bencha Wakkhi would in this case stand for Pancha(n)-varga, "an assembly of five (men)."

Dr Bastian refers to them as the five Chaphakhi. See p. 406 of his third volume "Reisen in Siam."

144.

Self-achieved.—The Siamese is Sayamphu, which is probably the same as the Sanscrit Svayambhu, "self-existent," and which, as an epithet of Buddha, is considered to mean that he of himself, without mastery or guide, brought himself to a state of perfection.

145.

I give a list of the Siamese-Pali names of these eight generals of the evil one, giving the Sanscrit in brackets where I know it :—Kâma (Kâma), Thoso (Dvesha), Sepha (Çepa), Tanha (Trichna), Thinnamittha, Utthacha, Wichikitcha (Vichi Kitsa), and Lop hlu khun. The last word is not Siamese-Pali, but common Siamese.

146.

Angel of tree.—As I mentioned in Note 118, the Siamese recognise not only angels of the heavens, but also angels who live in trees, &c., on earth. To these they commonly make offerings, hanging the offerings on the branches, or placing them on a stand or altar beneath the tree. They often object to cut down trees, lest the angels of the said trees should be angry. The superstition was probably rooted in the minds of the people before they ever heard of Buddhism. It prevails also in Burmah, where these angels are called Nat, a term applied by the Siamese to a beautiful woman.

Some years ago, when I employed my spare energy in showing the Siamese how to make roads in the, till then, roadless suburbs of Bangkok, I had to cut my lines through villages, temple groves, orchards, and plantations, and patches of jungle. For the "wicked" duty of cutting down the trees, a gang of the lowest criminals was placed at my disposal; and, moreover, the Government, which allowed me to interfere as I thought fit with private property, specially interdicted the removal of any holy building or sacred tree.

147.

The story of Suchada (Sudjâta) is somewhat differently told in the "Lalita Vistâra." According to that work, the great ascetic found by the servant of Suchada sitting under the tree accepted an invitation to follow her to her mistress's house, there to receive his meal. Nothing is said about the angel of the tree.

148.

Kala, the Naga, or Snake King.—See Note 135. This Kala, or Maha Kala, is thus mentioned in the "Mahawanso," as teaching King Asoka the appearance of Buddha.

"The supernaturally gifted Naga King, whose age extends as long as a creation of the world, and who had seen the four Buddhas, was brought in to King Asoka, and seated on the royal throne, and having been adored with an offering of flowers, he, at the King's request, caused to appear an enchanting image of Buddha."

I quote this passage because it seems to me to illustrate the mixture of Naga-worship with Buddhism in the fourth and fifth century, the period assigned by Professor Ferguson to the later sculptures of the Amravatti Tope, in which sculptures remarkable prominence is given to figures of the Naga.

149.

The former Buddhas mentioned in the text, whose bowls clashed against Gotama Buddha's, are Kakusandha, Konagamana, and Kasyappa, the three Buddhas of the present creation who preceded Gotama. See Note 24.

150.

The white umbrella, or staged parasol of royalty, the chowrie or fly-flap, and the chank-shell used as a trumpet, are figured on the Phrabat, and described in the list of figures on the Footprint.

151.

The three daughters of Mara.—Raka (Sanscrit, Raga) personifies love; Aradi (Sanscrit, Arati, discontent) is said by the Siamese to personify angry passion; Tanha (Sanscrit, Trichna) personifies desire.

152.

Death.—Mara is referred to, one of his titles being King of Death.

153.

Thirty Barami (or Paramita), described in Note 40 as consisting of ten classes, each divided into three grades. Hardy calls them the ten paths in which he who would be a Buddha must walk, but this meaning is hardly sufficient. The word seems to imply power as well as merit, and I take it as the virtue of accumulated merit of the highest kind.

154.

Chakkra—The disc—weapon of Indra and universal Emperors, also the wheel of the law, or the teaching of Buddha. See Note 12.

155.

Neither spirit nor understanding.—The words in Siamese are Chitr and Winyan. I believe there is no doubt about the translation of Winyan (Sanscrit, Vijnâna) as understanding; but the translation of "chitr" may be questioned. Our only Siamese dictionary (Bishop Palligoix's), though excellent for ordinary purposes, is a dangerous guide in the translation of recondite words, used in religious and metaphysical treatises. In this case I adopt one of the conventional meanings given in the dictionary, where Chitr is translated as "spirit, life, soul, intelligence." "Idea" ought to have been added to this list.

In tracing Chitr to the Sanscrit, one finds the letter *r* at the end (preserved in writing, but mute in pronunciation), indicates that the word is derived from Chitra, "visible," or "a surprising appearance," and not from Chitta, "thought," which is reproduced in the Siamese word "chitta." This derivation does, however, help us, for it shows that the word does not refer to an actual spirit, or soul, but to an "appearance," "manifestation," or "idea" of the same.

156.

Pouring water on the earth.—This ancient Brahminical ceremony is frequently mentioned in Buddhist works—for example, when the King of Magadha presents his pleasure garden, Weloowoon, to Buddha as a site for a monastery, he ratifies the gift by pouring water from a shell upon the earth. In chapter viii. of this "Life of Buddha," when the village maid Suchada is about to present to him, whom she believes to be an angel, the offering she had prepared with vast care and expense, she, as a preliminary, pours scented water on his hands.

In Colebrooke's "Essays on the Religious Ceremonies of the Hindoos," we find that almost all the Brahminical ceremonies for sacrifices, marriage, &c., consist in part of outpourings of water, and that those who make offerings to Brahmins pour water into the hand of those to whom the offerings are given. As an example read the following passage:—"In making a donation of land, the donor sits down with his face to the east, opposite to the person to whom he gives it. The donor says, 'Salutation to this land with its produce; salutation to the priest to whom I give it.' Then, after showing him honour in the usual form, he pours water into his hand, saying, 'I give thee this land with its produce.' The other replies, 'Give it.' Upon which he sprinkles the place with water."

In one of the ancient bas-reliefs figured in Ferguson's "Tree and Serpent Worship," we see a Rajah pouring water from a long-spouted vessel, presumably in confirmation of a grant. The vessel used by the Rajah is very like the teapot which the King of Siam bestows on his officers. The teapot is very useful to them, serving to hold tea or brandy to refresh them while waiting for weary hours at their stations in the King's audience-hall. That ancient sculpture, however, suggests the idea that perhaps originally the teapot of a King's officer was not merely a very convenient utensil, but had a significance connected with the custom of pouring water on the ground.

157.

Angel of the earth (in Siamese, Phra Torani, or Nang Pha sunthari).—In the much finer account of the contest between Buddha and the Evil One given in the "Lalita Vistâra," the goddess of the earth (Sthâvarâ) appears as Buddha's witness, but the flight of Mara's army is caused by an earthquake. In that account the intervention of the angels of the Bodhi-tree is also very noticeable.

158.

The teacher Satsada.—One of the ten great names of Buddha, meaning he who teaches the way of heaven to angels, men, and animals.

159.

The state of meditation which gave him the power of remembering his former existences (Siamese, Buppheniwasayan).—Turnour, quoting from Pali classics (Buddhistical Annals, No. 3, p. 5), defines this power of Pubbeniwâsanânan, from which I extract the following:—"This power six descriptions of beings exercise, viz., heretical teachers (or rather teachers of other religions); ordinary disciples of Buddha, the eighty principal disciples; the two chief disciples; Patyeka Buddhas; and supreme Buddhas. These possess the power in different degrees, the heretics remembering the least, while the memory of the supreme Buddhas has no limit."

This is the fifth of the supernatural powers, of which a list is given in Note 38.

160.

The state which conferred angelic right, &c. (Thipha chaksuyan).—One of the five supernatural powers. See Note 38.

161.

The laws of cause and effect (Paticha samubattham; in Sanscrit, Pratitya samutpada, "the production of the successive causes of existence").—This is commonly known as the theory of the twelve Nidanas. Hardy gives it as Paticha-samuppada, the circle of existence. The translations I give differ in some cases from that he quotes (taken from Gogerley), and also from other translations I have seen. In order to help my readers, I have in the text given a carefully arranged abstract of the Siamese text with my own explanations, and have placed a free translation in Note 173. To make this free translation, I first made a literal translation, but it was so confused that I thought it advisable to remodel it. In so doing, I have, however, only presented the material of the original, and not deprived it of its value by inserting any of my own ideas.

162.

Thorough investigation (Siamese, Wipassana panya).

Panya represents the Sanscrit Prajnâ, "wisdom."

Wipassana, a Pali word, I suppose to be derived from the Sanscrit Praçna, (prachh, "to ask"), "a question."

163.

Contemplation (Siamese, Samathi).—Explained in Note 138.

164.

Patient perseverance in good deeds.—The Siamese is Sammapathân, defined by Siamese as "well-directed endurance of four kinds." It is more correctly defined by Spence Hardy as "four great objects of endurance." I suppose it to be derived from the Sanscrit Samyak (Sam̃yañch), "correct," and Pradhâna, "chief, principal."

The objects are—(1.) To obtain freedom from previous demerit; (2.) to prevent the rise of fresh demerit; (3.) to procure new merit; (4.) to improve previously acquired merit.

165.

Unstable, painful, and illusive.—This triple formula is of very frequent occurrence in Siamese religious writings; indeed, is so well known, that instead of being written at length, it is often written Anichang, &c. The words, which are Siamese-Pali, are Anichang, Thukkhang, Anatta. They correspond to the Sanscrit Anitya, Duhkha, and Anâtma. A-nitya is "inconstant, or perishable." Duhkha is "pain." An-âtma is "that which has no self."

The formula is known as the Phra Trai Laksana, or the three characteristics of existence.

166.

Meditation on all things in due sequence Anulomyan, *cf.* Sanscrit Anulomana.—"Putting in due order."

167.

Khotraphuyan (Gotraphu-gnyana).—The meditation which reveals Nirwana to the mind, which enables the saint to see Nirwana. *Vide* Hardy's "Monachism," 281.

168.

The first path, &c.—In this explanation of the effects of the four paths, the paths are designated as those called (Pali) Soda, Sakkitha, Anakha and Arahatta. See Note 14.

169.

Contamination, &c.—The word is Kilet, which is the same as the Sanscrit Kleça and Pali Klesha (or perhaps rather the participle Klishta, or Kilittha, meaning "what is spoilt").

170.

Samma samphotthi yan.—Somphotthiyan is the complete omniscience of a Buddha. Samma is the Sanscrit Samyak, "properly," "completely." Sam is a Sanscrit prefix, here implying completeness; Photthi is Bodhi, "the intelligence of a Buddha," explained in Note 1. Connected with this term is the second of the Siamese list of the ten great titles of Buddha given in the "Traiphoom," which is Samma samphutho, defined in that work to mean, "knowing of himself the laws of nature and all creatures surely, truly, clearly, and distinctly."

171.

Perfected by, &c.—The Siamese text merely has "perfected by the four Wesara khun." I have stated the four Wesara (Sanscrit, Vâiçâradya) according to the list in Burnouf's "Lotus de la bonne Loi." They may be stated as "confidence" resulting from—(1.) his having a knowledge of all law; (2.) his having freed himself from all vice; (3.) his having recognised the obstacles to contemplation; (4.) his having discovered a law by which sorrow could be destroyed. They seem intimately connected with the four pre-eminent truths.

172.

As I have no materials at hand to complete the Life of Buddha from Siamese sources, I in this note give a short memoir of his further career, compiled mainly from Turnour's "Pali Annals," and Bigandet's "Life of Gaudama," from the Burmese.

After spending four weeks under and around the Bodhi-tree, Buddha passed three weeks more in meditation under three other trees.

While under one of these trees there occurred a violent storm, during which he was sheltered from the rain and wind by the Naga or Snake King, who coiled his body around him and expanded his seven hoods to shelter his head. This is a favourite subject with Buddhist artists, and may be seen painted or sculptured in many Siamese temples.

After these seven weeks of ecstasy, Buddha required food, and the honour of being his first almsgivers and first lay disciples fell to two traders who chanced to be passing by.

Although he had become the Buddha, he doubted his power to do good by teaching, and only accepted the task of enlightening mankind on the special intercession of the Great Brahma.

His first thought was to teach those two masters with whom he had studied, but his omniscience making him aware of their death, he decided on proceeding to Benares, there to convert the five men who had dwelt with him during his struggles to attain the Buddhahood by fasting and self-mortification.

Thus did he first teach his doctrine, or turn the wheel of the law, at Benares; and there he spent his first Wasa or Lent.

This Wasa is the three months during which Buddhists abstain from travelling, and devote themselves to religious duties in the neighbourhood of their own monasteries. Monks count their seniority by Wasas, not by years, though of course it comes to the same thing.

During this first year he converted not only his five former companions but many others, especially the great Kasyappa and his brothers and their numerous disciples, for they were great teachers.

He then kept the promise he had made to King Bimbisara, by teaching the law in his capital, Rajagriha. The pious King accepted his doctrine, and pouring water from a shell, offered his garden for a monastery. The gift was accepted, and the Weluwana (or Weloowoon) monastery was thenceforth a favourite residence of Buddha.

Among the numerous disciples made at this time were two students named Upatissa and Kalita; they became ardent converts, and changing their names to Sariputra * and Moggalana, were elevated to the dignity of disciples of the right and left hands.

His father sent many messengers to beg him to visit him. One after the other was seized with religious zeal, became a disciple, and forgot the object of his mission, but finally the companion of his boyhood, Kaludari, came and persuaded him to visit his parents.

On his way from Rajagriha to Kapila, his father's city, he

* Siamese, Saributr and Makhalan.

passed through the territory of the Malla Princes. They became converts, and the occasion was taken to show how utterly Buddhism ignores caste. Their barber, Upali, a low caste man, was ordained just before them, and they, as postulants, had to do reverence to him, a priest.

Buddha visited his family, but only as a teacher. His wife, his father, and others became converts, and his half-brother and his son relinquished the world and were ordained priests.

Buddha's second, third, and fourth Lents were spent in the Weluwana monastery at Rajagriha. The intervening seasons were employed in travelling and teaching in the neighbouring countries, Srâvasti and Vaisâli. In the fifth year he again visited his father, then lying on his deathbed. After the King's death, his Queen, Buddha's foster-mother, desired to be ordained, and though her request was at first refused, it was subsequently granted on the intercession of Ananda. Thus was founded the Buddhist order of nuns.

His sixth season he spent in retirement on the Makula mountain, and shortly afterwards engaging in public contest with other teachers as to their relative superiority in knowledge and power, he worked miracles which utterly confounded his opponents, and drove their leader, Purana, to drown himself in despair.

I should here mention that, according to our authorities, Buddha was ever wont to illustrate his teaching by parables, most commonly asserted to be narratives of what actually occurred in pre-existences of the persons to whom they were applied. The following was told in reference to his favourite, Ananda, who for a time felt a wish to leave his holy profession and return to his neglected bride, the half-sister of Buddha, subsequently a nun :—

"Once upon a time, a pedlar named Kappaka, strapping his pack on the back of a donkey, set off on a journey. The donkey was well fed and kindly treated, and for a while all went happily. But one day they encamped close by a field where a good-looking she-ass was tethered, and Kappaka's donkey was smitten with love. Vainly his master endeavoured to make him leave the place by expostulations and blows; he would not stir. At last, smarting with his punishment, and sore with love, the donkey told his master the reason of his strange behaviour. Kappaka forthwith promised him that, if he would but continue his journey, he should at the end of it have as many fair asses as he could desire, each one more lovely by far than the creature that had stimulated his passion.

"The donkey accepted the proposal, and at the end of his journey was again addressed by his master: 'I will now keep my promise to you; you shall have as many fair asses as you desire, but you will have to maintain them and their little ones. I shall allow you no more food than I have been accustomed to do, and I shall expect you do your work as usual.' Kappaka's donkey reflected on the comfortable life he led, and was cured of all love for the fair ones of his kind. The donkey has now in course of transmigration become Ananda, and that she-ass his bride."

The seventh Lent is the most celebrated of all. Leaving Moggalana to teach in his place on earth, Buddha rose into the heavens to teach the law to the angels, particularly to his mother (who it will be remembered died seven days after his birth). To the angels he taught the Abhidharma, "the superior truth," or metaphysics of Buddhism; and according to one school of Buddhists, this, which forms the third part or Pitaka of their law, was unknown on earth until revealed some five hundred years later to Nagarjuna by the Nagas; but according to the Siamese, it was known simultaneously with the other two Pitakas, having been repeated to Ananda by Buddha.

The descent from heaven at Sankisa is one of those events in describing which the Buddhist writers have let loose their gorgeous fancy. From heaven to earth extended three flights of steps, of jewels, of gold, and of silver, by which, in radiant glory, descended Buddha the conqueror, attended by a vast host of angels of all degrees.

The narrative of Buddha's life during the first twenty years of his teaching is copiously given in the Burmese version. They were spent in travelling over Central India, living on alms collected day by day, and rewarding the almsgivers by teaching them the law. All classes of people were among his converts, which were of two kinds—lay converts, who kept to their usual avocations, and monks and nuns, who renounced the world.

The Ceylonese, Siamese, and Burmese all claim that Buddha also taught in their countries; but they do not even profess that he visited them by ordinary travel. He visited them supernaturally by flight through the air.

Buddha's teaching during these years was not unopposed. Failing to equal him in science and miracle-working, his opponents tried to ruin his character. Twice they leagued with wicked women to charge him with unchastity. On the first occasion the woman showed herself to the assembly as if she were with child, and taxed Buddha with the paternity; but hardly had she told her story ere a little mouse gnawed the string which fastened a pillow to her waist, and the pillow falling down, exposed the plot. Again, a woman was bribed to accuse Buddha of misconduct with her; and when she had proclaimed her story, was murdered by her bribers, in order that Buddha might be suspected of the act. This plan also failed, for the plotters, in drunken revel, boasted of their craft, and acknowledged their villainy.

In the twentieth year of his teaching, and fifty-sixth of his age, Buddha appointed Ananda as his personal attendant, an admission that age, penance, and exertion had began to tell on his constitution. From this time to the forty-fourth year of his teaching the life or romance lacks details. Presuming that the story is based on a groundwork of fact, we may ascribe this failure in the narrative to confusion caused by political events in the city of Bimbisara, his patron, who was murdered by his son, Adjatasattru. Adjatasattru was at first opposed to Buddha, but afterwards supported him. It is also probable that the age ascribed to Buddha is too great. His remaining Wasas were mainly spent in the Jetawana monastery at Srâvasti, and the Pubhârâms monastery at Sâketa (Ayodhya); but he is described as constantly travelling and preaching, even to the very last.

In the forty-fifth year of his preaching, he lost his two principal disciples, Sariputra and Moggalana, the first by natural death, the second by assassination.

His own end was at hand. "He died," says a missionary writer, "of dysentery caused by eating pork." There is a quaintness about the Pali account of his decease which induces me to narrate the circumstances at greater length than the missionary I have quoted from.

Travelling and preaching his divine law, Buddha came to the garden of Ambapali, an eminent courtesan, of great wealth and high estimation, in a country where, as in ancient Greece and Rome, men of character and wisdom were not afraid of at times openly seeking relaxation in the company of ladies remarkable for their wit, learning, accomplishments, and boldness of thought.

Hearing of his arrival, Ambapali, accompanied by her retinue, proceeded to the garden, and having done homage to Buddha, sat by his side while he preached the law. Comforted by his teaching, she invited him to her house, that she might there serve him and his disciples with a repast. The Princes of Wesali vainly contended for the honour of entertaining Buddha in her stead. He had accepted her invitation, and would make no change. Next day he went to her house, and after she had with her own hands served him and his disciples, she concluded her offering by presenting her garden for the use of the Church. Her offering was accepted, and again Buddha preached the law.

During the ensuing Lent (the forty-fifth) Buddha suffered agonising illness, significant of his approaching end.

After predicting the time of his death to Ananda, and addressing some final advice to the priesthood in various places, he accepted his last meal from Chundo, a goldsmith, who invited him as the courtesan had done.

On reaching the goldsmith's house, Buddha addressed him: "Chundo, if any pork is to be dressed by thee, with it only serve me; serve to the priests from any other food or provision thou mayest have prepared." Chundo having replied, "Lord, be it so," Buddha again called him, saying, "Chundo, if any of the pork prepared by thee should be left, bury it in a hole; for indeed, Chundo, I see not any one in this universe, angels, ascetics, or men, who could digest it, if he ate the same, excepting only myself." Chundo accordingly buried it.

From this meal followed the predestined attack of dysentery. Hastening, as much as his malady permitted, to the city of Kusinagara, attended by Ananda and his disciples, he gave some further instructions on various points, including the ceremonials of cremation. Reclining between two lofty Sala-trees in the garden of the Malla Princes, close to Kusinagara, he spoke his last words: "Transitory things are perishable; qualify yourselves (for the imperishable)!" Absorbed in ecstatic meditation (Dhyâna), he remained until the third watch of the night, and then expired.

Then was there a great earthquake, and the pious who had not yet the perfection of saints wept aloud with uplifted arms; they sank on the earth, they reeled about, exclaiming, "Too soon has the blessed one expired, too soon has the eye closed on the world." But those more advanced in religion calmly submitted themselves, saying, "Transitory things are perishable; in this world there is no permanence."

173.

In accordance with the promise given in Note 161, I now give a more detailed translation of the chain of causation, than I thought advisable to insert in the text of chapter x.

Ignorance (Awicha) * is the cause of predisposition (Sangk-

* Sanscrit, Avidyâ.

han.) * Predisposition is the cause of a controlling influence such as can give it effect, that is, an intelligent spirit or active intelligence (Winyan). † This active intelligence gives rise to distinction and the expression of distinction (Nama rupa). ‡

Each of these follows on the other, perfect in their continuity as a stream of water, the continuity of which remains undisturbed, whatever waves may arise on it.

Ignorance is the not knowing what is good, the disposition to think wrong right, and evil good; the obscuration of the intellect so that it cannot see the four truths. It is that which induces the grasshopper to look on a flame as cool, and seek its own destruction. When it is powerful in any nature, it must cause darkness and error, it must hide intelligence, and prevent the recognition of "change, sorrow, and illusion."

This powerful error was what the Grand Being referred to by the term ignorance.

Predisposition (Sangkhan) is the term applied to "arrangement." It is that controlling power or disposition which causes the birth, fruit, or result to be consistent with the merit and demerit (which cause it). It is not the actual product, but the disposer. Neither is it the actual cause, for it gives no fruit of itself. It is but as the architect of a city, who is by no means the master of it, but prepares it for its master the king.

It is classed under three heads, Bunyaphi, Abunyaphi, and Anenchaphi.

Bunyaphi (meritorious) is of two kinds. First, the meritorious predisposition which will lead to birth in one of the six sensual heavens. This is the state of every one who, without attaining to the ecstatic meditation (Dhyâna), is nevertheless eminently pious, a practiser of almsgiving, an observer of the commandments, a perseverer in the simple meditations (Bhawana), and an attentive listener to religious teaching,

* Sanscrit, Saṁskâra: the translation usually given is "conceptions."

† Sanscrit, Vidjñâna, knowledge.

‡ Sanscrit, Nâmarûpa, name and form.

and a follower of that teaching to the best of his ability. Second, the meritorious predisposition of those who have attained the four states of Dhyâna, which will cause their re-birth in the heavens of the Brahamas who have form.

Abunyaphi (demeritorious) is the predisposition which will lead to birth in one of the four states of sorrow, viz., existence in hell, existence as a Preta, existence as an Asura, and brute existence; and which will cause the object of it, after having endured one of those states, to be born in some degraded condition as a man—as an evil, poor, stupid, unfortunate, sickly, wretched fellow. This is the state of every one who is wicked, and particularly of those who have taken life, or committed theft.

Anenchaphi is the predisposition of those who are steadfast in the higher Dhyânas, the Dhyânas of the formless. It will cause re-birth in one of the four worlds of the formless Brahmas, the angels who have neither form nor materiality, and have but spiritual faculties (Chit-chetasik), fixed and subject to no disturbance.

Intelligence (Winyan), which is the result of predisposition, may be defined as the spirit (Chitr), whose office it is to undergo conception or birth, and to realise fruits or effects. It may be also defined as "thought and knowledge of causes and effects." It is that spirit (Chit) which understands the qualities (Arom)* of all things. It may be likened to the monarch who rules over and governs the city which the architect has prepared for him.

Distinction, and the expression of distinction (Namarupa),† which must exist simultaneously, are the result of intelligence. They are divided into classes, of which there are twenty-eight Rupa (distinctions), and three, or originally fifty-two, Nama (expressions), which are called Chetasik.

The twenty-eight Rupa are as follows: — Four Mahaphutharup, which are the elements, earth, water, fire, and air.

* The Arom are—appearance, sound, scent, flavour, feeling, and nature known by reason.

† Literally, name and form.

Five Pasatha rup, which are the organs of the senses of sight, hearing, scent, touch, and feeling.

Four Wisai rup, which are the qualities of visual appearance, sound, scent, and taste, their size, and nature, which the Pasatha rup appreciate.

Two Phawa rup, which are the distinctions of sex.

One Hatthai rup, which is the heart.

One Chiwitr rup, which is life, that which gives freshness to all the other Rupa, even as water nourishing lotuses.

One Ahan rup, which is food of all kinds, grain and water being the principal.*

Nama is divided into three classes, called Khan, or Kantha. Formerly it was divided into fifty-two Chetasik (modes of expression).

The three Khan are:—

1. Wethana khan, or Wethana chetasik, which has the control of the realisation of pleasure, pain, and indifference, which are essentials of all Chitr (spirit or idea).

2. Sanya khan, or Sanya chetasik, is that which enables us to distinguish colours and kinds. This also occurs in all Chitr.

3. Sangkhara khan comprehends all the remaining fifty Chetasik (or modes of expression of the idea or spirit).

The six seats of the senses (Ayatana),† which are the result of distinction and its expression, are—1st, The eyes, the only place where form is manifested; 2d, The ears, the only places where sound is manifested; 3d, 4th, and 5th, The nose, tongue, and whole body, where respectively are mani-

* My manuscript contains only the eighteen Rupa, translated as above. To make up the number of twenty-eight, there should be added—space, power of giving and receiving information by gesture, the same by speech, lightness, elasticity, adaptation, aggregation, duration, decay, impermanency. Spence Hardy, in his "Manual of Buddhism," states these, with details. They are so different in character to the first eighteen Rupa, that I cannot help thinking that the Siamese writer omitted them deliberately.

† Sanscrit, Ayatana.

fested odour, taste, and touch; 6th, The heart, as a seat of knowledge (Manas).

These six are, as it were, six branches on which the six birds—appearance, sound, scent, &c.—perch themselves, flying on and off them.

Contact (Phat, or Phasa)* is a necessary result of the (existence of the) six seats of the senses. Its property is to assemble, arrange, and bring into contact with the seats of the senses the six objects of the senses (arom), which are appearance, sound, scent, flavour, nature of touch, and effect known by the heart. It may be likened to an officer whose duty it is to make arrangements for an assembly; or it may be likened to the owner of (fighting) rams, who sets his rams, the seats of the senses, and the objects of the senses, to butt at one another.

Sensation (Wethana),† which results from contact, is of five kinds:—

1. Suk, when the absorption of a sensation causes physical pleasure and happiness.
2. Tḫuk, when the same causes sorrow.
3. Somanat, where the same causes joyousness.
4. Thomanat, when the same causes vexation.
5. Ubekkha, when the same causes neither pleasure nor pain, joy nor vexation, but an equable frame of mind.

Desire (Tanha)‡ results from sensation. There are as many as one hundred and eight divisions of desire, ranked under three heads. The first embraces two principal subdivisions, one being desire for voluptuous pleasures, greed for praise and rank, and ambition to excel all others; the other is desire for wealth. The second head embraces those desires in which the desire for sensual pleasures is accompanied by the false belief that beings are stable, and the world stable, that all beings die, and are re-born everlastingly, and never are destroyed. The third head embraces those

* Sanscrit, Sparça. † Sanscrit, Vêdanâ.
‡ Sanscrit, Trichnâ.

desires in which the desire for sensual pleasures is accompanied by the false doctrine that on death all beings are utterly extinguished, and not born again.

Each of these three classes is subdivided into six internal and six external desires, making thirty-six; and each of these thirty-six is again subdivided into desires of the past, of the present, and of the future, thus bringing the total to one hundred and eight.

Attachment, or firm adherence (Upathan),* results from desire, and causes it to flourish. It is of four kinds:—

1. Attachment to lust and greed.

2. Attachment to belief in the permanence of existence,† or to belief in there being no re-birth after death.‡

3. Attachment to false religions, such as those of Brahmins, Mussulmans, and Europeans, and the belief that self-torture can destroy lust and vice, and procure remission of sins.

4. Attachment to the belief that I and mine exist.§

General formal existence (Phop) ‖ results from adherence. It is of two kinds—material and apparitional. It is of three characters – Kama, Rupa, and Arupa. The first (Kama) is the existence of the four places of misery, the human world, and the six lower heavens (Kamawachara); in all, eleven worlds addicted to sensuality. The second and third are the sixteen heavens of the formed (Rupa) Brahmas, and the four heavens of the formless (Arupa) Brahmas.

Individual existence, or condition in being (Chat),¶ is the result of general existence, and is the state of circulating existence, living and dying in the said general existence or worlds.

Decrepitude and death are the consequences of individual existence.

* Sanscrit, Upâdâna: by some translated conception.

† In Siamese-Pali this belief is termed Sasasa thritthi.

‡ In Siamese-Pali, this belief is termed Uchetha thritthi.

§ This belief is termed in the text, Attuwathu.

‖ Sanscrit, Bhava.

¶ Sanscrit, Djâti.

Such are the steps by which we may perceive that decrepitude, death, and sorrow are but the consequences of individual existence. That individual existence is dependent on general existence, and that general existence springs from and is regulated by firm adherence to that which is desired. That desire cannot arise without sensation, and that sensation cannot arise without contact or conjunction of the idea which is to be felt, and the means of feeling it. That contact cannot be without a place of contact—that is, is dependent on the six seats of the senses. That the six seats of the senses are a result of the pre-existence or co-existence of distinction and the expression of distinction (otherwise translated form and name). That these exist because an intelligent influence gives rise to them, and that this intelligent influence springs from a predisposition to action. And lastly, that this predisposition results from ignorance or folly, the want of knowledge of that which is good and evil, the non-appreciation of the four great truths.

By extinguishing ignorance, the predisposition is extinguished; and that being extinguished, each of the other steps also fails, and all sorrow is done away with.

These steps the Lord (Buddha) classed under four heads:—

1. Ignorance and predisposition.

2. Intelligence, distinction, and its expression, the seats of the senses, contact, and sensation.

3. Desire, adherence, and general existence.

4. Individual existence, decrepitude, and death.

The first two are past causes: they first existed. The third to the eleventh are present causes. The last is the future awaiting all beings.

If classed according to character (Akan), there are twenty divisions—that is to say, five past causes and five present effects; five present causes, and five future effects.

The five past causes are—ignorance, predisposition, desire, adherence, and general form of existence; which five originated in preceding individual existence, and reproduced themselves as five present effects. In relation to the future, these five present effects become causes which will again produce the ignorance, &c., which are the five future effects.

If we look for elementary roots (Mula), we find two—one being ignorance, and the other desire.

These two are the axis of the wheel, which has predisposition for its spokes, and decrepitude and death for its tire. Its axle is the ever-circulating Phop, or general existence. Whatever man drives the chariot, the wheel will turn so long as all its parts are perfect.

174.

In this note I give the key to the expressions used on page 39 of the "Modern Buddhist."

The four Satipatthan, or applications of reflective power, are explained in Note 72.

The four Sammapathan, or reasonable objects of continued exertion, are explained in Note 164.

The four Itthibat, or effectual causes, are explained in Note 66.

The five Intri (Indraya), moral powers, are—holiness, persevering exertion, reflection, tranquillity, and wisdom.

The five Phala (Bala), or forces, are—the force of holiness, force of persevering exertion, force of reflection, force of tranquillity, and force of wisdom.

The seven Photchangkas (Bôdhyaggas), or principles of all knowledge, are explained in Note 67.

PART III.

THE PHRABAT;

OR,

SIAMESE FOOTPRINT OF BUDDHA.

THE PHRABAT.

CHAPTER I.

GENERAL ACCOUNT OF THE SUPERSTITION.

In the "Modern Buddhist" an attempt is made, by the aid of translations from the writings of an eminent Siamese philosopher, to give a glimpse of the reasonable religious teaching and beautiful morality which lie buried among the superstitions of corrupted Buddhism; and prominence is given to Buddha's Sermon on Faith, to show how strictly he charged his disciples to believe in nothing that their reasoning powers did not commend to their belief.

The present essay will show how far Buddhists have strayed from the course they acknowledge their great Teacher pointed out to them.

The canonical traditions always acknowledge that Buddha was but a man, a prince who had given up his royal state and devoted himself to the acquirement of omniscience, in order that he might teach men how to escape from sorrowful existence.

Yet the popular superstition, dissatisfied with mental and moral qualifications alone, insisted on adding to them a number of the most absurd physical characters. Thus it is that even the earliest written legends of Buddha's life (which probably reproduce the oral traditions accepted by the members of the third Buddhist Council in 246 B.C.*) contain both the statement that Buddha was a man, subject to the same laws as other men, despised by them until he had, in public contest, shown his superior strength and skill, and, like them, subject to stomach-ache, and deriving benefit from medical advice; and also the statement that he had peculiarities of body enough to have frightened all adversaries, and to have deterred physicians from regarding him otherwise than as a *lusus naturæ.*

The Sanscrit "Life of Buddha," "Lalita Vistâra," tells us that Buddha was born with certain peculiarities of person, which, according to Vedic tradition, indicated a man who would become either a supreme Emperor of the world, or a supreme Teacher. The same story, with Siamese developments, will be seen in chapter iv. of our "Life of Buddha." These personal peculiarities

* The Buddhists of the North have their Scriptures in the Sanscrit language; those of the South, in the Pali language. Some of the Siamese are said to believe that their Scriptures were written in Sanscrit, at the First Council, held immediately after the death of Buddha. Others believe that Pali (which they call Makhot, *i.e.*, the language of Magadha) was the vernacular language of Magadha, the Holy Land of Buddhism, and was that in which the sacred books were first written. It is reasonable to believe this, for otherwise we cannot account for the Pali language being used at all. Sanscrit, the ornamental classical language of India, would have been used, as it was by Northern Buddhists, had not tradition been on the side of Pali. The Pali Scriptures, as they now exist, are supposed to have been first edited by Buddhaghosha, in the fifth century.

are called the thirty-two principal and the eighty secondary characteristics of a grand man, and are for the most part those characteristics which, in the works of Indian poets, are ascribed to the most beautiful men and women. Strange indeed are some of the ideas of beauty. We fail to appreciate the loveliness of a tongue "long enough to reach and enter the ears;" and though we see the practical advantage of "long arms reaching to the knees," we cannot help regarding as ungainly a characteristic which reminds us so forcibly of our ancestors, the gorillas and orang-outangs.

I give an account of the thirty-two characteristics in an Appendix, so need not weary my readers by inserting a list of them here. It will suffice for present purposes to state those relating to the feet, which are, "the toes are marked with a network of lines," and "the soles are soft, flat, and delicate, richly decorated, and marked with the beautiful wheel Chakkra.

The "Lalita Vistâra" does not mention the numerous figures of animals, &c., which are described in our "Life of Buddha," and in Pali works of probably no great antiquity. The mention in the "Lalita Vistâra" of a representation of the wheel Chakkra existing on the sole of the foot, is confirmed as an ancient idea by the sculptures which formerly adorned the Topes or holy relic mounds of Sanchi and Amravatti in India.

The Sanchi Topes, situated between Bhopal and Saugor, in Central India, are described in General Cunningham's interesting work entitled "The Bhilsa Topes." They were carefully examined by him and Colonel Maisey, and from them were extracted a few small inscribed boxes, some of them of crystal and soapstone, containing relics,* declared to be those of the two principal disciples of Buddha.

The sculptures of the great Sanchi Tope have been made known to us by several splendid photographs (taken by Lieutenant Waterhouse) published in Professor Fergusson's "Tree and Serpent Worship."

On one of the gate pillars of this Tope, which, on architectural grounds, Professor Fergusson ascribes to the early part of the first century of our era, there is a sculptured representation of a footprint marked with the wheel or Chakkra. The footprint is large, but not gigantic, being, so far as I can make out by the photographs, about twenty inches long. It is not unshapely, as is the Siamese design of modern days, but is fairly natural and human in outline. It is consistent with the record of the "Lalita Vistâra," and to a certain extent supports the antiquity of that work.

The ruined Tope of Amravatti, situated near the mouth of the river Kistnah, on the East Coast of India, affords numerous illustrations of the footprint.

Some of the bas-reliefs from Amravatti may be seen in the court of the India Office. They may also be studied in Professor Fergusson's book above named. In these bas-reliefs, which are supposed to vary in date from the second to the fifth centuries of our era, there are numerous representations of altars, on or before which are a pair of footprints marked with the Chakkra, but with no other figures. On a fragment, whose position in the building is not yet ascertained,

* The Maisey collection is now on view at the South Kensington Museum. The authorities of that museum have also conferred a favour on students of Buddhism, by procuring casts of some of the most interesting sculptures.

is cut in low relief a large pair of footprints, marked not only with the Chakkra, but with several other mystic emblems. It is thus described by Professor Fergusson :—" In the centre of the soles is the Chakkra ; above it the Trisul * emblem reversed, with a Swastika on each side. Below the Chakkra is the Swastika again, with an ornament like the Crux Ansata on each side. On the great toe is the Trisul. On each side of the others a Swastika."

The Professor ascribes these feet to the best age of sculpture—the fourth and fifth centuries; assuming which date, we see that for about nine hundred years after Buddha's death the people of India regarded the Chakkra as the important sign of the sacred foot, and in all that long period only added to it a few mystic emblems.

After that time, the ornamentation of the footprint was slightly developed in India, but it never attained the elaboration described in so-called sacred books of the Siamese, Burmese, and Ceylonese.

Mr Hodgson inserted in vol. xxi. of the "Asiatic Researches" a drawing of the footprint obtained by him from Nepaul. The accompanying text describes the footprint as marked with the eight mangala, signs of good augury, or royal emblems, to wit: the Crivatsa, lotus, standard, water-pot, fly-flap, fish, parasol, and chank-shell. The text, most strangely, makes no mention of the Chakkra, which, however, I believe to be

* The Trisul is a figure of which the simplest form may be represented as . Swastika is thus formed 卍. For particulars, consult Cunningham's "Bhilsa Topes."

The Crux Ansata, or cross, with a handle, is a T with a ring on the top. It is generally held ring downwards.

represented on the plate by a large blotch that seems to have puzzled both engraver and describer.

The extreme development of the idea in India is, so far as I have been able to ascertain, represented in a drawing of unknown date lent me by Mr C. Horne of the Indian Civil Service, in which are two pairs of feet resting on lotus flowers, and marked with the Chakkra, and fifteen or sixteen other figures, including a palace, temple, elephant goad, standard, parasol, chank-shell, fish, bow, and other figures unknown to me. These plates, however, are not supposed to represent the footmarks of Buddha, but of Radha and Krishna.

I should here mention that veneration of holy footprints is not a peculiarly Buddhist idea, but is also found in other religions, and particularly in Vishnuism.

I shall now turn from considering the documents and stone records bearing on the belief that the sole of Buddha's foot was characteristically marked, and advert to that which is indeed a distinct belief—I mean belief in the existence of rock impressions which are actual footprints of Buddha.

So far as I have heard or read, this belief is not sanctioned by the ancient Scriptures of Buddhism; and the earliest books which mention it were not written until about a thousand years after the date given by Siamese and Singhalese, as that of Buddha's death.

Three works written in the fifth century of our era refer to footprints of Buddha. These works are the Travels of Fah Hian the Chinaman, written and preserved in China; and the Commentaries of Buddhaghosha, and the Mahawanso, or History of Ceylon, both written and preserved in that Island. All these works mention the existence of a footprint of Buddha on Adam's Peak, and their agreement amounts to proof that the superstition was established in Ceylon at the time of Fah Hian's visit (about A.D. 400), and being established, must have originated at some earlier period. I see no particular reason to discredit the Ceylonese tradition that their footprint was discovered at the beginning of the century before Christ, and venerated from the time of its discovery.

Fah Hian's mention of a footprint at Sangkashi * is not so well supported, and in fact seems to refer to a vaguer superstition. He tells us that "a tower is erected where there are certain marks and impressions left on the stones by the feet of the different Buddhas." And Sung Yun, another Chinese pilgrim, who visited India about a hundred years after Fah Hian, writes, "There is a trace of the shoe of Buddha on a rock. They have raised a tower to enclose it. It is as if the foot had trodden on soft mud. Its length is undetermined, as at one time it is long, and at another time short." With respect to this strange footprint, that seems to have depended so much on the imagination of its visitors, we should bear in mind that Sangkashi was the spot where, according to the legends, Buddha first set his foot on earth, after a three months' visit paid by him to the heaven of Indra.

Fah Hian mentions two footprints in Ceylon. "Buddha, by his spiritual power, planted one foot to the north of the royal city, and one on the top of a mountain; the distance between the two being fifteen yoganas (say a hundred miles)."

* Identified by General Cunningham as Sankisa, on the river Kalindri, about 250 miles W. by N. of Benares.

The Ceylonese "Mahawanso" twice mentions the footprint on Adam's Peak with great distinctness. In it we read, "The Comforter of the world, the divine Teacher, the supreme Lord, having there propounded the doctrines of his faith, rising aloft into the air, displayed the impression of his foot on the mountain Sumanekuto (*i.e.*, Adam's Peak)."

In Buddhaghosha's Commentaries * on the sacred books of the Buddhists, written in Ceylon at about the same date as the earlier portion of the "Mahawanso" was written, it is stated that there are three footprints of Buddha—one in Ceylon, and two in India.

The footprint on Adam's Peak, referred to by these three authors, is the celebrated Sri Pada (beautiful footstep), which still attracts travellers to the summit of a mountain, striking in appearance, and most difficult of access. It is a hole in the rock, about five feet long, and represents a very rude outline of a foot; but its unshapeliness has not prevented Buddhists from claiming it as made by the foot of Buddha; Sivaites, as made by that of Siva; Mahometans, by that of Adam; and Christians, by that of St Thomas.

An interesting account of it has lately been published by Mr Skeen, a resident in Ceylon, who has paid several visits to the locality, and has studied the book-lore bearing on its history.

The Sri Pada is supposed to have been discovered

* These Commentaries, known as the Attha Kathâ, are said to have been first written in Pali, by Buddhaghosha, from the Singhalese Commentaries written in Ceylon by Mahindo immediately after the third Buddhist Council. It is evident that the footprint on Adam's Peak could not have been mentioned in Mahindo's Commentaries, as it was not discovered until long after his death.

about 90 B.C., by King Walagambahu, who, when out hunting, was led on and on, by following a beautiful stag, to the very summit of the mountain, where the stag, which indeed was an angel, vanished, and left the fortunate monarch to discover the holy footprint.

So far I can gather from Mr Skeen's book, and the observations of the Hon. R. Marsham, who visited it a few years ago, there is no vestige of any ornamentation on the Sri Pada, and there is nothing in the little building which covers it, or in the monastery below it, to show that the Ceylonese attribute any importance to such marks. All Mr Skeen tells us of such marks is, that on his way to Adam's Peak he saw a drawing of a footprint, marked with a hundred and eight figures of lotuses.

Ceylonese books mention the figures on the footprint, much as the Siamese books do; but as the Ceylonese have copied their religious works extensively from the Siamese, it is possible that the high development of the marks on the footprint is due to Siamese fancy, and not to Ceylonese.

The Ceylonese Sri Pada is the most celebrated of all footprints of Buddha, and, of those now to be seen, by far the most ancient. I am told that there are others in Thibet, Canton, the Malay Peninsula, and the Laos country north of Siam. I know nothing of these, and so pass on to the Siamese Phra Bat or Holy Footprint.

According to Siamese records, their footprint was discovered by a hunter named Bun, in or about A.D. 1602, in the reign of Phra Chao Song Tham, who, on the news being brought to him, sent a number of learned monks to examine it, and compare it with the description of Buddha's foot in the sacred books. The examiners reported that it was genuine, whereupon the King erected a shrine over it, and the place has remained to this day as the great Siamese memorial of Buddha.

On the few fragments of history which I have stated, I venture to base a theory as to the origin and development of the superstition.

The idea that a very superior man should be distinguished by extraordinary physical characteristics, probably existed before Buddha was born.

Peculiar features and marks on the body, ascribed by ancient poets to their heroes, may have been collected into lists, and formulated as the thirty-two characteristics of a great man, previous to the age of Buddha, or shortly afterwards, when, as Mr Childers* has suggested, people assisted their memory by classifying everything in numbered lists.

Until I saw this suggestion of Mr Childers, I looked with great impatience on the numerous lists I met in every Buddhist book,—such as, five commandments, eight commandments, ten commandments, four virtuous dispositions, ten powers, &c., &c. Regarded individually, they seemed to be nonsense; but now that a reasonable object for them has been pointed out, one can regard them with more tolerance.

Among the poetical characters attributed to great men in those ancient days, fleetness of foot would have been naturally one of the most important. Nothing could have conveyed the idea better than a wheel under the foot. This would have been depicted in drawings by a wheel marked on the sole of the foot.

* The Pali scholar, not Mr Gladstone's late colleague.

A symbol so easily comprehended would naturally have been a favourite one with the sculptors who decorated the earliest Buddhist buildings. They adorned the gateways of the Sanchi Tope with huge footprints marked with the wheel—an unmistakable chariot-wheel.

Probably Sanchi was not the only place where pilgrims looked on gigantic carvings of feet thus marked. It is not improbable that some pilgrim from Ceylon, struck by these huge designs, and perhaps, also, hearing some vague stories of actual footprints, such as that I quoted above from the travels of Sung Yun, should have returned to his own country, and there given an incorrect account of what he had seen, describing them not as sculptures, but as actual footprints; and this may have led to some man of vivid imagination discovering on Adam's Peak an indentation, so much in accordance with floating rumours, that he believed he had found a real footprint.

Such a belief would have rapidly spread among people in a low state of civilisation. Thus, while in India the belief retained, for the most part, an imaginative and symbolical character, in Ceylon the actuality of the impression on the rock may have led to the symbolical character being less thought of. In a similar manner I account for the superstition in Siam.

It is reasonable to believe that some pilgrim who had seen the Sri Pada on Adam's Peak, afterwards wandering to the jungle-covered hill in his own country, now called Phrabat, and there having pointed out to him a hole in the hard rock similar in appearance and size to that which he had adored in

Ceylon as the footprint of Buddha, should have believed that his discovery was a footprint also.

A discovery so gratifying to the vanity of the Siamese people would havè met with easy credence. The examiners sent by the King were probably rather credulous than critical, and found little difficulty in recognising, in the centre of the hole, an irregularity or discolouration answering to their idea of the one sign of importance—the Chakkra; and they may have perhaps also discovered other marks which they considered to represent mystical signs. The copyists then came in, and, instead of reproducing facsimiles of the original marks, they set their imaginations free to make what they could out of the discoloured patch of veined rock; and as we in the glowing cinders of a fire can see pictures as varied as our imaginations, they, in the veins and stains and irregularities of surface, found all the many emblems which were subsequently developed into the elaborate design represented in our plate, full accounts of which may have soon worked their way among the received classics of the Siamese and Singhalese.*

Traditions resting on so weak a basis naturally varied; and it is not surprising that there should be a discrepancy in the accounts given in various books. The plate we now print, the list in Burnouf, taken from the Singhalese "Dharma Pradipika," the list given by Colonel Low in the "Transactions of the Royal

* There was quite sufficient intercourse between the Siamese and Singhalese monks to account for Siamese additions finding their way into Singhalese books: indeed, at the beginning of this century, a so-called complete set of copies of the Pali Scriptures was taken from Siam to supply the place of works which were no longer extant in Ceylon.

Asiatic Society," which he copied from a Siamese work—the Siamese list in chapter iv. of the "Life of Buddha;" in fact, all the lists with which I am acquainted differ in various details, though they all agree in the main.

In all of them we find the centre of the foot occupied by the Chak or Chakkra; no longer the simple chariot-wheel of the ancient sculptures, but the destroying wheel or quoit of the Hindu Vishnu, and Indra, king of angels; the disc which, flying from the hand of its fortunate possessor, and rapidly revolving, utterly exterminates those against whom it is directed, and which, as one of the insignia or emblems of Buddha, refers to the extermination of ignorance and sin.

In every account we find grouped around this Chakkra a variety of figures, partly the insignia of royalty, and partly mythological objects. The foot is, in fact, made an index to the prevalent mystical, mythological, and cosmographical ideas. We are introduced to the sixteen heavens of the formed Brahmas, and the six heavens of the inferior angels, Thewadas or Dewas. We have Mount Meru, the centre of each system of the universe; we have the seven annular mountains which surround it, and the seven belts of ocean between them, with monstrous fishes and water-elephants disporting in the waves; and we have the eighth ocean, the great ocean, in which are the four Thawips, Dvipas, or human worlds. The Thawips themselves are depicted separately—one for men such as we are; another for square-faced beings; another for circular-faced beings; and another for semicircular-faced beings. We have Mount Chakrawan, the wall of the world, the crystal annular mountain which encircles the system.

We have a group of stars which may refer to the principal constellations, or the signs of the zodiac. In every description we find the half-mythical Himaphan or Himalaya mountain, with its seven great lakes, in which grow the red-blue rose and white lotuses; we find the five great rivers which flow from the Himalaya, and the various fabulous animals and birds which are associated with its forests—the Kinon, half-human and half-birdlike; the kings of elephants, lions, and tigers; the Insi, or king of eagles; the Hongsa, or royal goose of the Burmese; and the Karawek, the sweet-voiced bird of paradise, whose melodious singing charms all the inhabitants of the forest; the royal Naga, the seven-headed king of serpents, who, in the fables of Buddhism, bears an excellent character for piety; and Phya Khrut, or Garuda, the enemy of the race of Nagas, but not otherwise evil-disposed.

The evil-disposed animals, the demons, yaks, and prets, are absent; the holy foot is not supposed to have borne the figure of anything so ill-omened.

Every description also includes a palace, a flag, a throne, a royal sword, a white parasol of several stages, a crown, and other insignia of royalty; a golden ship, a jar full of water, and other designs of less importance. All these will, by the aid of the following numbered list, be identified in the accompanying engraving, which, however, omits some figures quoted in other lists, such as the golden beetle and the tortoise, and inserts a rabbit, which none of them mention, and also the very significant designs of "a book" and "a bundle of priest's garments," which may, perhaps, be taken as symbols of the law and the church, which, with Buddha, constitute what is called the Buddhist Triad.

I did not myself copy one of the golden plates at Phrabat; but on my return to Bangkok, after a visit to it, requested my friend, the Phya Rat Rong Muang, the Lord Mayor, as he is often called, to procure a copy for me. He had a copy taken from the facsimile placed in the great Wat Po temple at Bangkok, which is that from which the plate illustrating this book is photographed.

The plate accompanying Colonel Low's article in the "Transactions of the Royal Asiatic Society," cannot be identified with his own description of it—is unlike any drawing of a Phrabat which I ever saw in Siam, and seems to have been drawn expressly for foreigners, some of its figures being not only modern, but European. Indeed, Low, to whom very great credit is due for his labours in Siamese literature, only gave it as the fanciful composition of a priest of his acquaintance; and there is no wonder that M. Burnouf should have been puzzled when he compared it with his more classical Singhalese list.

I give a detailed explanation of the figures on the plate in chapter iii.

I shall now quote from Bigandet's translation of the Burmese "Life of Buddha," two stories, illustrating the importance attached to the sacred feet in Buddhist histories. I am sorry I cannot quote from the Siamese version, as my Siamese "Life of Buddha" ends with the attainment of omniscience, and I cannot find the continuation in England.

The first story is thus rendered by Bishop Bigandet:—

"During all the time that elapsed after the rain, Buddha travelled through the country engaged in his usual benevolent errand, and converting many among men and Nats. In the country of Garurit, in a village of Pounhas,* called Magoulia, the head man, one of the richest in the place, had a daughter, whose beauty equalled that of a daughter of Nats.† She had been in vain asked in marriage by princes, nobles, and Pounhas. The proud damsel had rejected every offer. On the day that her father saw Gaudama, he was struck with his manly beauty and meek deportment. He said within himself: 'This man shall be a proper match for my daughter.' On his return home he communicated his views to his wife. On the following day, the daughter, having put on her choicest dress and richest apparel, they all three went with a large retinue to the Dzetawon monastery. Admitted to the presence of Buddha, the father asked for his daughter the favour of being allowed to attend on him. Without returning a word of reply, or giving the least sign of acceptance or refusal, Buddha rose up and withdrew to a small distance, leaving behind him on the floor the print of one of his feet. The Pounha's wife, well skilled in the science of interpreting wonderful signs, saw at a glance that the marks on the print indicated a man no longer under the control of passions, but a sage, emancipated from the thraldrom of concupiscence."

The story continues with a further offèr on the father's part, and a sermon from Buddha, who leads both parents to a holy frame of mind; the rejected damsel becomes the chief Queen of the King of Kothambi, and retains a warm hatred for him who refused her love.‡ Further on in the same work, in a

* Brahmins. † Angels.

‡ The same story, with some interesting variations, occurs in chapter v. of Captain Rogers's lately published translation of "Buddhag-

description of the great saint Kathaba's* arrival at the pile erected for the cremation of the body of the deceased Buddha, the mystic symbols on the feet are morely clearly referred to.

"Standing opposite to the feet, he made the following prayer: 'I wish to see the feet of Buddha, whereupon are imprinted the marks that formerly prognosticated his future glorious destiny. May the cloth and cotton they are wrapt with be unloosened, and the coffin, as well as the pile, be laid open, and the sacred feet appear out, and extend so far as to lie on my head.' He had scarcely uttered this prayer when the whole was suddenly opened, and there came out the beautiful feet, like the full moon emerging from the bosom of a dark cloud."

This subject is sometimes represented by images in Siamese temples, the two feet projecting from the end of a coffin towards a standing figure of Kathaba or Kasyappa.

The idea of rock footprints was not confined to Asia, and Mr Lesley, in his "Lectures on the Origin and Destiny of Man," regards the manufacture of such prints as the next stage in sculpture to that of the flint tools and rough carvings of the prehistoric stone age. I take the liberty of closing this chapter with an interesting extract from his eighth lecture:—

"The next stage of sculpture was, probably, imitations in stone of the marks of wet feet and hands. These would first be made at river fordings, and afterwards on the tops of look-out mountains. Such sculp-

hosha's Parables," and I think it also occurs in Hardy's "Manual of Buddhism."

* Kasyappa.

turings are described in books of travels all over the world. The savage crosses a stream by swimming, and dries his dripping body on some sun-lit rock. Then he waits for his companions, or for his prey, or for his enemy. Meanwhile he pecks away at one of the damp footsteps on the rock. Others notice what he has left undone, and finish it. The footprint becomes a permanent landmark. Some battle there in subsequent days shall make it famous; some deified hero shall be propitiated there by sacrifices. The footprint becomes a symbol of worship. You have all heard of the two footprints sculptured on the summit of Mount Olivet, and worshipped by pilgrims as the marks left when Jesus sprang into the sky at His Ascension. There is another footprint of Jesus preserved on a stone in the Mosque of Omar, at the extremity of the eastern aisle. At Poitiers, in France, the traveller may see two footprints of the Lord upon a slab enshrined in the south wall of the church of St Radigonde, made when He stood before her to inform her of her coming martyrdom.

"The prints of the two feet of Ishmael are preserved on a stone in the temple of Mecca, which, tradition says, was the threshold of the palace of his father-in-law, the King of the Dhorhamides. Others say they are the prints of his father Abraham's feet, when Ishmael's termagant wife drove the old patriarch away from the threshold of her husband's house.

"There are two immense footprints, 200 feet apart, on the rocks of Mägdesprung, a village in the Hartz mountains of Germany, which, tradition says, were made when a huge giantess leaped down from the clouds to save one of her beautiful maidens from the violence of a baron of the olden times."

CHAPTER II.

JOURNEY FROM BANGKOK TO PHRABAT.

I VISITED Phrabat in December 1868, having been provided by the Ministry in Bangkok with very excellent letters of commendation or command to the authorities of the towns I was likely to stay at *en route*.

Be the season wet or dry, there is only one way of travelling from Bangkok, that is, by water; for even when the floods have left the rice-fields, the numerous canals and branches of the river which reticulate the flat alluvial plain of the Menam effectually prevent land-travelling. The travelling boats generally used are propelled by four to sixteen men, who stand and push the oars, which are attached to high standing rowlocks. These posts or rowlocks have to be high, as the men do not stand on the bottom of the boat (as in the gondolas I have seen in the Mediterranean), but on a deck. The middle of the boat is covered by a house or cabin, in which the traveller lives. The stores and luggage are all stowed away under the deck, and the cook generally makes his kitchen just at the back of the house. On this trip, as my wife was with me, we took two boats, one to live in, the other for cook and servants.

The first part of a journey from Bangkok is always rather tiresome to old residents—they have seen the same things so often—they pass the temples, the palaces, and floating-houses of Bangkok, then a mile or more of teak and bamboo rafts moored for sale just above the city, and then village after village of poor-looking bamboo shanties, all very similar, and none very picturesque. If the start is made in the afternoon, soon after nightfall one is interested in passing a village of sugar-cane sellers; a row of small stalls, built over the water, in each of which sits a girl with a heap of large bundles of sugar-cane, lit up by a flaring torch, hailing every boat that passes to purchase her "oi chin," the thin yellow cane, which is a favourite sweatmeat among the Siamese.

The reader can picture our progress—the two boats keeping pretty close, the boatmen, in high spirits, singing catches or chaffing passers-by, and now and again indulging in a race, or dropping their oars and enjoying a smoke; for when I go on a pleasure excursion, I always let my men do much as they like, provided they don't do what I dislike. My wife and I are comfortably reclining in the cabin on a heap of cushions, uttering perhaps an occasional growl at the mosquitoes, but otherwise very comfortable. I smoke contemplatively, and do not disturb myself much with moonlight effects and darkness visible, but my wife, who has never made such a journey before, is full of lively enjoyment, and thinks every fresh bush that flashes with fireflies more lovely than the one she has praised just a moment before. She is charmed with the water rippling past the boat, she finds life and change in the plash of the oar and the merriment of the boatmen, and she thinks that she never knew so fine a night for travelling, though indeed, in Siam, almost every night is fine from October to May.

A little before midnight we stop for the night at a Wat, or Buddhist monastery, just below Samkhok, which is the largest village between the old and new capitals. The monks' dwellings and temples are hidden among thick trees, but we find two Salas or travellers' rest-houses built on piles by the shore, and in one of these we spread our beds, and pitch our mosquito-curtains. As the erection of resting-places for travellers is a recognised means of merit-making among the Buddhists, there is no lack of them in the populous parts of Siam. Every temple has two or three of them, and others are placed at the mouths of frequented canals and in other convenient spots. They are almost always quite simple buildings, consisting of a plank-floor raised above the ground, with a tiled roof supported on wooden columns, and no walls, for in so warm a climate there is no need for walls. Some are more solidly constructed with bricks.

Before daybreak we hear the monastery bell waking the inmates, and as soon as it is light we see two or three boats, canoes, paddled each by one or two monks, who are starting off to collect their day's supply of food. Two of the canoes are larger, and hold monks who have some pretensions to scholarship, and who, instead of paddling themselves, are paddled by their pupils. All these monks have shaved their heads and eyebrows, and wear the significant yellow robe said to have been originally adopted by Buddha, because it was the dress of outcasts, and so its use would be a standing declaration against caste; but I do not know whether this story has any foundation; I have not yet found good authority for it.

According to strict rule, the monks ought to sweep their monastery before going out to collect food, but I have not observed this to be the practice.

As we pass along the river we notice the monks' boats stopping before the houses on the banks, and at each stoppage their food-pans receive a ladleful or more of rice and condiments, the donor, generally a woman, raising her joined hands to her forehead as a mark of respect and gratitude to the representative of the priesthood—the "khun,"* or benefactor, as she calls him who has given her an opportunity of making merit. He, for his part, looks stolidly, as if unconscious that he has gained anything by the merit the other has made. It is not now the custom, as, according to the legends, it was in Buddha's time, to reward the donor by preaching the law to them; in fact, very few of the monks, except in the greater monasteries in the towns, know much of the law, or could preach it with any effect. Only a few of the number have any idea of remaining monks all their days, and the majority relinquish, after a few months, or at most a few years, the orders they have taken on them, not from any preference for a monastic life, but in compliance with their religious idea that every man should be a monk for some part of his life.

We presently stop at another monastery, and breakfast in its Sala. Our appetites have been invigorated by the cool morning air, and by a short walk in the Wat grounds, where we have shot some pigeons.

* Both this word Khun, and the word Sala, used a few lines above, are Sanscrit words, very slightly changed. Khun is Guna, which, among other meanings, has those of "excellence" and "quality," both which are also meanings of Khun. Sala is Sâlâ—a house.

It is altogether improper to shoot birds in temple grounds, but on this occasion one of the monks has invited us to shoot the dark birds, as he only wishes to have white ones. We are very glad to avail ourselves of his proposal, but we cannot help thinking him a very bad Buddhist. Two or three sad fights have arisen from foreigners ignorantly or wilfully shooting in temple grounds against the wish of monks; and I am sorry to say that, in the last of them, not only were the monks punished, as their cruelty probably justified, but the foreigners, who had brought their thrashing upon themselves, had a large compensation obtained for them by their Consul. The case I refer to was not English.

After breakfast we push on until nearly noon, and then rest for a while at another Sala. There is no difficulty in finding one, for we pass an astonishing number of temples. The monks are now taking their last meal for the day, as they must not eat after midday. Once the sun has begun to fall, they must be satisfied with tea and cigars until the next morning. In regard to this matter of fasting, as also in regard to continence, I believe that most Siamese monks carry out the rules of their order very creditably.

Some of the villagers come in while we are taking our rest, and having been obliged by an inspection of my breechloader, which they believe to be a gun that requires to be loaded with shot only, and has no need of powder, they are easily led into conversation. They are not Siamese, but the descendants of Peguan captives. I ask them whether they are any better off now than they were before foreigners frequented the country, that is, before the treaty of 1856; and they say, much better off; that in former times they used always to go in person when called on once every three months for the *corvée*, or service of one month, to which they are all liable, and that their crops were often ruined in their absence; but now they can get a good price for their produce, so they attend to their fields, and pay a composition in money for non-attendance at the *corvée*, and thus grow richer every year. They neither know nor care much about state affairs, and are even unaware that their King died nearly three months ago.

During the afternoon we pass from the winding river, with its fringe of trees, which has almost constantly, from the time we left Bangkok, limited our view; and entering a narrow canal, make a direct course for the former capital of Siam, Yuthia, through the still flooded rice-fields, a wide, open, treeless plain, in some parts bounded by low jungle, in others level to the horizon, which is backed by a few very distant chains of hills.

The many temples of the old capital next rise into view. First, one or two conspicuous spires tower over the horizon, and presently afterwards the whole city appears, a crowd of spires of varied forms, but mostly ruinous, lying in the midst of luxuriant jungles, fruit and shade trees.

The Siamese call this place "Kroong Kao," the old capital, or simply "Meuang Kroong," the capital town; but among foreigners it is better known as Yuthia, a corruption of Ayutthaya, or Ayodhya, "the unassailable," a part of the long state name which belongs as much to the whole country or the present capital as to the old one. The old capital belied this part of its name by being captured, and in great measure destroyed, by Burmese invaders in 1767, since which it has ceased to be the seat of the Government. It is now a large, populous, and flourishing town, though half-buried among jungle and ruined temples, which present a most desolate and melancholy appearance. These temples, having been built on a scale only suitable for a capital city, and endowed with extensive lands which cannot be re-granted for secular purposes, are necessarily, many of them, deserted and covered with dense jungle. It is a remarkable transition to pass from some canal, half-choked with weeds, and bordered by masses of ruins and tangled jungle, directly into the main street of the town, a wide canal about a mile in length, crowded with boats, with a line of floating-houses on each side, and behind them on the banks numerous well-kept temples and houses. The whole length of the street is a bazaar, and such of the boat-shops as cannot find room in it are moored in close lines on one of the smaller canals running from it. These boats serve both as dwellings and shops for the traders, who lay in a stock worth one or two hundred pounds at Bangkok, and then quietly journeying to Yuthia, wait there until they have disposed of their goods. No European trader lives at Yuthia.

We stay a day at Yuthia, that I may show my wife the three sights which all travellers thither are supposed to see. Two of them are temples situated some five miles apart, and the third is a place of elephant-catching, some distance from either of the others, so that the three together give a good day's work. The first is the "Mount of Gold," the highest of the spires, which differs from most Buddhist towers in having three accessible terraces round it. The highest terrace commands a view over most of the tree-tops. From it we count about fifty spires, so there may be some truth in a native assertion, that Yuthia had two hundred temples. There is nothing very elegant about the spire to justify its grand name; and its height, which I judge to be about a hundred and fifty feet, is nothing very great; but as a good illustration of one of the forms of Buddhist spires, it is worth describing.

Upon an extensive square base rises a pyramidal tower in three parts, tier above tier, separated by wide terraces. Cornices of many forms, round and angular, encircle it in close succession. Deep flutings and re-entering angles reduce the squareness of the four corners. Two flights of steps on the north and south sides lead to the terraces.

From the highest terrace, which is about sixty feet from the ground, the tower rises for about thirty feet more in the same pyramidal form as described for the lower part. In this portion are two niches containing images of Buddha about seven feet high. Above the niches the still tapering tower is without cornices and quite smooth for about fifteen feet; and thence changing from a square pyramid to a cone, it rises about forty feet to a point. The upper part of the spire is ornamented with narrow beadings or rings, lying close one over the other.*

The tower is built of brick, and seems to be almost

* Some Buddhist spires are supposed to represent or symbolise, by their various tiers and cornices, the various tiers of the Dewa and Brahma heavens; and possibly the three stages of this temple may

solid, excepting only a small chamber, to which access is obtained from the highest terrace. We find nothing but bats in the chamber, which seems to have suffered from fire. Previous to the Burmese invasion, it probably contained some idols or relics. I know of no other large spires, or Phrachedi, as they are generally called, which have an accessible chamber, though such are found in a few of the smaller spires.

Leaving this, we, after some time, pass a temple newly built or repaired, and ornamented with a mosaic of broken bits of coloured crockery set in plaster, and representing flowers and other fanciful designs, with gay saucers let into the walls, bright china birds on the cornices, coloured and glazed tiles for the roof, and all the usual accessories of the modern Siamese florid style—a style which has an excellent effect at a little distance, the form, and often the colour, being good, but is most disappointing on close inspection, the materials being too common and perishable.

The second great sight is Wat Cheuen, built, I am

have been meant to typify the world, the Dewa heavens, and the heavens of the formed Brahmas. In other temples I have counted the rings of architectural ornament, but have seldom found them tally with the number of heavens. The temple above described is of the form called Phra Chedi, which represents the primitive Tope or relic mound. The nearest approach to the form of the old Topes is shown in some Chedis or Sathups, which are bell-shaped, with a small pointed spire rising from their crown. The Phra Prang differs from the Phra Chedi or Sathup in being terminated, not by a pointed spire, but by a straight column rounded at the end, a form said to be derived from the Linga, and therefore not really Buddhistic. Great confusion exists as to the proper application of the terms Phra Prang and Phra Chedi, the words being often misapplied. Thus the spire of Wat Cheng at Bangkok, though a Phra Prang, is often called Phra Chedi. This misapplication is, to a certain degree, warranted by the derivation of Chedi, viz., Chaitya, "a holy place;" and it is to be observed, that though Chedi is used for all relic spires, Prang and Sathup are seldom misapplied.

told, by a Princess Cheuen. We land at a small Chinese josshouse, with fantastic roof, and great red placards of unimpeachable morality on the outside, and within darkness, dirt, tinsel, and peacock's tail offerings, flaring tapers, sickly-smelling pastilles, and an old gray-bearded, long-nailed, filthy Chinaman in charge of it; everything, in fact, as I have seen it in Hong-Kong. Behind it is a well-kept Buddhist monastery, with a large "wihan," or idol-house, and "bort," or most holy building, *i.e.*, the building where take place the assemblies of the monks, consecrations, &c. The "bort," according to invariable custom, has not far from its walls eight "sema,"* or boundary stones, cut in a shape somewhat like the leaf of the *ficus religiosa*, or Po-tree, which mark it out as the most sacred part of the temple; and in the same courtyard are also numerous small spires. In an adjoining court is the idol-house, and in close vicinity are the monks' residences and preaching-hall. Not far distant is the part of the ground set apart for cremations, the recent use of which is proved by two or three heaps of fresh ashes. The hall for idols I judge to be about one hundred and twenty feet in length, square, and about eighty in height; perhaps this is an overestimate. Externally it is an ugly building—a Chinese pagoda spoilt—but internally it is very effective. The

* The Sema, or Bai sema (Sanscrit, Sîmâ, a "boundary" or landmark), are eight stones placed, one at each point of the compass, round the most holy part of a temple. When the ground is first dedicated, eight "luk nimit," or round marking-stones, are sprinkled with holy water and buried, to mark the limits from which evil spirits are warned off. Over these Luk nimit are built small platforms, supporting the heart-shaped Bai sema, generally covered by an elaborately carved or mosaic-worked canopy.

walls are pierced with a fretwork of pigeon-holes, in each of which is a gilt idol about a finger in length. All around, on hundreds of pedestals, are figures of Buddha and his disciples in various attitudes, from a few inches to six feet in height; and in the centre, on a broad pedestal or throne, between six huge red pillars, whose capitals are lost in the darkness which hides the roof, is seated a colossal image of Buddha, in what Buddhists call the position of contemplation, the legs crossed, the right hand clasping the right knee, and the left lying palm upwards across the thighs. The head is indistinct, as there are no lights in the upper part of the building. The general expression is that of profound meditation, and the effect decidedly grand. The size we cannot judge with any accuracy, the only clue we have being that a priest, who has ascended as far as the hand to dust it, seems no larger than the thumb of the image. The idol is, I believe, made of brick and plaster, covered with lacquer, and then gilt.

On the right and left of this great seated figure are two standing figures about twenty feet high, representing Sariputra and Moggalana, the disciples of the left hand and the right hand.

The third sight is the stockade for elephant-catching, a strong enclosure into which once a year are driven the elephants from the neighbouring jungles, that the King may select such as he desires to have domesticated for use. Elephants are supposed not to breed in confinement, and are therefore kept in this half-wild way.

The nearest route from Yuthia to Phrabat is by a branch of the river flowing from the east; but as our object is to see Nophburi, we take a smaller branch, and keep a northerly course. The main river lies to the west of us. Our channel, which is about the size of the Thames at Richmond, is more picturesque than the broad river below Yuthia, the trees on the banks not being dwarfed by too wide an expanse of water. The floods being still over the country, enable us to avoid many a bend of the river, and make short cuts across fields, and along what, in a month or two hence, will be cart-roads. The white paddy-bird is very abundant; there are a good many large herons, and occasionally we find teal, water-hens, plover, and other birds fit for the table. My wife is charmed with a bright blue plume of kingfishers' feathers, and, in fine, the gun has quite a good day of it. In the evening, we put up at a Sala, one side of which looks over a wide lake, and the other looks on the river, overhung with graceful clumps of bamboo, all bright green and golden in the lights, and a rich brown in the shadows—an exquisite picture. I try fly-fishing, at which the natives smile pityingly, as they never saw fish eat feathers; but they seem just as pleased as I am when a number of little, dace-like fish fall victims to the new guile. In the meantime my wife adds another pretty sketch to her collection. With darkness comes dinner, then a chat with the monks, and early retirement within our mosquito curtains; for the mosquitoes are both numerous and virulent. We are unfortunate in not having any *pyrethrum roseum*, which, infused in alcohol, makes a varnish for the body which effectually keeps the vermin away. The friend who taught me the use of it found only one fault with it—it was expensive; so each coat had to be made to last as long as possible; and, in short, he could not afford to wash oftener than twice a week.

Our night is rather disturbed, not only by the mosquitoes, but by a number of dogs, who swarm about our quarters, and are made restless by our presence. Buddhists are forbidden to kill animals; so, whenever their dogs, or any other domestic animals, have the mange, or otherwise become a nuisance in the house, they take them across a river, and leave them to pass the rest of their lives in some monastery, whence it arises that almost every temple is infested with diseased and half-starved dogs; and in some cases, pigs and other animals add to the nuisance.

Despite such little inconveniences, we pass very agreeably the two days occupied in journeying from Yuthia to Nophburi, the Louvo of old French writers on Siam. The correct name is Lophaburi, which means "the new city." We first take up our abode in the Kambarien of a monastery—that is, a large enclosed building used for preaching. My experience of these preaching-halls has been, that they are invariably large and dirty, and that their furniture consists solely in a chair or pulpit for the preacher, who, on great days of the church, recites a number of sentences in the Pali language to a prostrate crowd, mainly consisting of women, not one of whom understands a word that is said. A corner of the hall is generally used as a lumber-room for articles used as ornaments at the cremation ceremony of people whose friends are ready to go to some expense on the occasion; and among this rubbish will usually be discovered a litter of puppies, with a savage mother, who never will be quiet. We are very glad to be rescued from such a place by the Governor, who at once calls on us, and installs us most comfortably in a large and clean floating-house. In front of this house there is nearly eighteen feet depth of water; yet we are assured that, soon after the floods abate, all the water in the river will disappear, no boats will be able to approach the town, and water will be only obtainable by digging wells in the sandy bed.

My wife is charmed with our quarters; there are two lovely views up and down the river, and within a few hundred yards are many more "perfect pictures" than she will ever find time to transfer to paper.

We are not far from the old palace, the favourite residence of the King of Siam in the days of Louis XIV., when a Greek, Constantine Falcon, by sheer ability, rose to be Prime Minister of Siam, and would probably, had he not been assassinated, have succeeded in handing over the country that had used him so well to the Jesuits and soldiers of the French monarch. His story, a very romantic one, can be read in Sir John Bowring's "Siam;" so I shall not repeat it here. The ruins of his house and chapel, which are European in style, still exist, and traditions of him, by the name Chai Yin, or Phya Wichaiyen, survive among the people. He is said to have built an aqueduct to bring into the palace water collected on hills some eight miles distant. Whether the work was ever completed and in action, I cannot say; but its remains do him much credit as an engineer; and the large earthenware pipes or tubes are excellently made. He also built smelting furnaces, and began to work the neighbouring copper mines, a work which it might pay to try once again; for such surface specimens as I obtained were very promising.

The palace outer walls are very extensive, and the gates handsome; but the beauty of the place has been much destroyed by the late King building a new and ugly palace on the site of the old one. The old ruins were picturesque; but now there is a labyrinth of whitewashed, prison-like dens, which are quite an eye-sore. Even the old gates have mostly been spoilt with whitewash.

We spend several days in Nophburi, seeing the sights, and feasting on Pla Tepo, a rich and delicious fish, the pig of the waters, as the Siamese call it, which is rather an uncommon luxury in Bangkok, but so abounds here, that a fish of four pounds weight, which is an average full-sized fish, costs less than four pence.

The obliging Governor seems to take a pleasure in exceeding the courtesy our letter of commendation demands from him. He waits on us several times a day, to learn what more can be done for our comfort; he escorts us on walks and rides; for we have now escaped from the flooded lowlands, and only use our boat to land from our floating-house. He is as kind as it is possible to be, and we find that every one else is also civilly disposed.

In country places I have almost always found the Siamese of all ranks a kindly people, though sometimes shy; but in Bangkok, where they are more used to foreigners, and see many bad specimens of them, and where also the worst conducted and most drunken natives congregate, the lowest class does not always show such good feeling.

Nophburi has a considerable trade in limestone and

lime, and also in a white clay called Din siphong, used as a medicine, cosmetic, &c. This clay is dug up near the river side, in a very soft, plastic state, and, being moulded into lumps, and dried in the sun, it becomes like a lump of chalk. Plastered over children, it is believed to keep them cool; it whitens the young ladies' dusky faces, and foreigners find it convenient to pipe-clay their white boots, and to chalk the tips of their billiard cues.

The rides and walks about the town are very pretty. The distance of the town walls from the palace appears to prove that it was formerly a populous place, though now no longer so. Much of the space inside the walls, and some ground outside, is covered by plantations of custard-apple trees; but we do not notice any other fruit-trees as particularly abundant.

We, of course, visit the copper mines already spoken of—that is, we visit the hill where the copper ores are. The only traces of work that we see are the ruins of a furnace, and the inclined plane on the hill-side, down which the ore seemed to have been rolled. We pick up several heavy stones, covered with verdigris, and from a cave one of our men extracts a little copper pyrites. The place certainly looks promising. The Governor, who is very anxious to see his province become of more importance—and to that end desires to have the mines worked—visits them with us, and points with regret to the camping-ground of an English mining engineer, who, some twelve years ago, devoted himself to the task of re-opening the mines, and unfortunately died of jungle fever within a few days after discovering specimens of very rich ore.

After two or three days spent rambling about Nophburi, we start for Phrabat. Our friend the Governor has provided us with seven elephants and guides; the cook has packed his pots and kettles; and my wife and her maid have, by aid of a ladder, been placed in a howdah, about as comfortable as a washing-basket, on one of the elephant's backs, there to remain until the end of the journey. I, unwilling to be made a prisoner of, learn at once to mount my animal in Siamese style, that is, to clamber up by the aid of the elephant's knee, for Siamese elephants do not, like the animal which the fellows of the Zoological Society of London exhibit at fourpence a ride, kneel to be mounted, but simply raise one knee a very little, to be used as a step.

We have a choice of two roads. One is a well-made road which follows the high ground, so as to be serviceable in all seasons—a work dating from the time of Nophburi's greatness; the other is a track across the lowland, much more direct than the former, and as the country it traverses is now dry, we determine to follow it. Our great difficulty is to tell when we are in it, and when not; for where it crosses fields, the farmers have obliterated all trace of it, run their dikes across it, and planted their rice over it; and in other parts it is so covered by long grass, and a thick jungle of young trees, and fresh shoots of old trees, that only a practised guide can recognise it. It has probably never been really cleared. A body of men with axes, swords, and bill-hooks has, may be, some three or four years ago, cut a fairly straight track through the jungle, avoiding large trees, and from that time to this, the road has never been retouched, and scarcely ever used except by an occasional foot-passenger. We consequently lose our way two or three times, and even when on the track, our progress is slow, the leading elephant having to stop continually, while the way is cleared of bamboos and awkward branches. Part of this clearance is done with swords, but the elephants help considerably with their trunks, breaking off great branches, and throwing them aside. My elephant, which is the tallest, shows surprising accuracy of judgment in knowing when he can safely pass an overhanging branch without damage to his howdah, and when it is necessary for him to stop and break away the obstacle with his trunk, or select another passage.

Our journey is said to be about twelve miles in length, and by the time half that distance is accomplished, which we know by finding a rest-house in the jungle, I get thoroughly tired of being shaken upon an elephant, and take to my legs, which I find enables me to make quicker progress, although it is very hard work brushing through grass higher than one's head, and struggling away from the bamboo thorns which every now and then make one a prisoner. We see one little deer cross our path, but no sign of the tigers, which are said to be numerous.

After a while the stilless of the jungle is broken by the sound of a bell, tolling probably as a summons to the monks to get inside their houses before nightfall. The increasing gloom of the undergrowth, and the rich golden fringes of the tops, is a further sign of the approach of sunset, and we hurry on to our destination, having by some lucky chance lost our jungle track, and found a good road on which fast walking is practicable.

Just before sunset, I and two men who have kept up

with me, emerge from the bamboo jungle on to a grassy plot on the skirts of the monastery. Before me on a heap of rugged rocks is a small but very elegantly designed temple of the kind called Maradop, a square building with carved columns round it, supporting the projecting cornices of a most elaborately decorated pyramidal roof, terminating in a tapering spire, surmounted by the symbol "Chat," or royal parasol in stages. I judge it to be about a hundred feet high. The whole roof is richly gilt, and the last rays of the setting sun resting on it make it gleam like a mass of flames. Behind it is a dark limestone hill, whose rugged side and many peaks are dotted with numerous little white spires, on some of which hang yellow cloths, the offerings of pilgrims. Near the Maradop are residences for monks, idol-houses, numerous rest-houses for travellers, and an unusual number of large bells, each covered by a small roof. Most of the rest-houses are of wood, but we are introduced by an official of the place into a brick one. Having selected quarters, I anxiously await the arrival of the elephant party, which has evidently got lost in the jungle, and in the meantime the men make as much noise as they can on the bells by way of signal to the lost ones. At last they arrive, a full hour after dark; the cook sets to work at the fires we have made ready for him, our dirty quarters are illuminated and swept, and we make ourselves fairly comfortable for the night.

First thing in the morning we take a walk. We find the monastery well kept, several slaves being attached to it in order to sweep it, cut the grass, &c. There seem to be no residents in the neighbourhood except the monks, officials, and servants of the temple.

Of monks, only ten are now in residence, others having gone off travelling. Most Siamese monks travel a great deal, only remaining in their monasteries for the three months of the rainy season known as the Buddhist Lent,* during which time residence is imperative.

We are struck by the unusual number of Salas, or rest-houses, erected to shelter the crowds of pilgrims—men and women—who resort hither in the month of February each year. A very pleasant house has been erected for the King. Passing from the courts of the temple, with their crowd of spires, idol-houses, preaching-houses, and bells, we ascend the hill-side, a mass of jagged rocks, and climb to one of the points, on which there is a spire. Some heavy body is heard crashing through the grass and brushwood, evidently in flight; and we step on to a smooth lair, still smelling strongly of a tiger, whose white and tawny hairs lie there in some quantity. We look about for the footprints of all kinds of animals which an old traveller (Bishop Paligoix) assures us he found imprinted there in the hard rock, but we only find many little hollows, due apparently to fossil shells. We also search for what he describes as the butterfly-plant, but do not find any. I once had some of the plants brought to me from Phrabat, and

* The Buddhist Lent lasts from the middle of the eighth to the middle of the eleventh Siamese months, corresponding roughly with the time from July to October, the worst part of the "rainy season." The custom of remaining in one place during this time is believed to be an imitation of the practice of Buddha himself. The Siamese word for it is Wasâ, which is a form of the Sanscrit Varsha, meaning "rain," and also "a year." The time of Wasâ is spent in the monastery, or Wat. This word Wat is rather curiously derived. It represents, I believe, the Sanscrit Vâta, "an enclosure, grove," &c., which is derived from Vâta, the *ficus Indica*, one of the Buddhist sacred trees. If Wat does not come from Vâta, it may come from Vâsa, a dwelling-place.

found their leaves indeed very like butterflies, with green wings striped with red. I have never seen any specimens except from Phrabat.

On our return to the monastery, the monks invite us to see the Phrabat. We mount a flight of steps to the rocky platform on which stands the before-described Maradop. Its walls are all covered with a common but brilliant mosaic; the large double doors are very elaborately and beautifully inlaid with mother-of-pearl figures set in black lacquer. The inner face of the walls is painted * with scenes from the life of Buddha, &c. The floor is covered by a mat of plaited silver-wire. Some incense-sticks burn before a small image of Buddha, and a most miscellaneous collection of offerings is heaped around, comprising European and Chinese toys, bottles, .pictures, mirrors, common jewellery, and odds and ends of all sorts, for the most part neither beautiful, useful, nor valuable. The more valuable gifts are probably taken care of elsewhere. On the walls are fixed two large gold plates, one jewelled, which are full-size representations of the design supposed to have formerly existed in the Phrabat itself, a collection of figures which I shall describe in the next chapter. These figures are more curious

* The inner faces of the walls of Siamese temples are frequently painted with scenes not only taken from their religious histories and mythologies, but also from European drawings. There is a very good example in Wat Bowora Niwet, at Bangkok, where, by compounding native and European drawings of different dates, the artist has introduced us to a scene of ladies and gentlemen of the time of Louis XIV. having a picnic and dance on a hill, under which is a railway tunnel with a train about to enter it; and not far off a contemplative Buddha is pondering on the mutability of human affairs, or, perhaps, on the change of fashions. In some cases, a whole story is depicted in a series of tableaux.

than beautiful, excepting the central disc (see the engraving), which is really very handsome.

We next examine the actual Phrabat, which is in the centre of the building, and find it to be a hole in the rock about five feet long by two broad, perhaps a monster relative of the fossil shells we have seen outside. The grating which usually covers it is removed to enable us to see the bottom, but the temple is so dark that we cannot see much of it. We move aside some of the offerings lying on it, but can see nothing of the pattern except the five marks of the toe-nails—five grooves in the rock, which some declare to have been made with chisels; and on inquiry we are told that the other marks were long ago destroyed by an accidental fire. Likeness to a foot there is none.

Yet to this holy footprint year after year crowds of Siamese flock with varied offerings, and even the most enlightened among them—the late King for instance—have observed and encouraged the practice. Whether the King considered it politic to encourage the delusion that there existed in his country a mark of the special favour of the founder of his religion, or whether he merely supported it as a formal duty, or whether he had himself, if not a belief in it, yet a respect for it as one of the generally received symbols of his religion, we cannot tell, but probably the latter was the preponderating reason. Probably he made offerings to the Phrabat monastery in the same spirit that he raised spires in conspicuous places, the summits of hills and headlands—in the same spirit that he built images of Buddha; not that he wished the Phrabat, or the spires, or the idols to be worshipped, but that he believed in the utility of everything which attracted the thoughts of men, even but for a moment, to the great Teacher of the law of the avoidance of sorrow—to the Prince who, in the prime of manhood, gave up a throne, and a life of luxury and honour, and became a wanderer and mendicant, that he might teach men by example as well as precept that a life of conscious virtue, a life free from anxiety as to the future, is the life of the truest happiness, and that freedom from anxiety can be obtained by a man's own efforts; that he is not a toy or puppet, exposed to be victimised by malignant spirits unless saved by an intervening deity, but that he is the absolute ruler of the destiny of his own soul, controlled only by the law of perfect justice.

CHAPTER III.

DESCRIPTION OF THE PLATE.*

THE drawing of the footprint is surrounded by an ornamental border, the design of which is derived from the lotus (*nymphæa*). This lotus-pattern is found everywhere in Buddhist architecture, and notably is used for the capitals of columns, and for the decoration of the "lion seats" or altars on which images of Buddha are placed.

The toes are three-jointed, and each joint is marked with a spiral pattern, "the network" of the books. The great-toe is on the left side, showing this to be a print of the right foot.

The CHAK or Chakra occupies the central square of the print. It is sometimes described by the Siamese as the beautiful Chakra with its thousand rays or flames, also as the beautiful Chakra with its thousand spikes, adorned as it were with emeralds. In Indian drawings we find the Chakra, disc, or quoit, as the weapon of Vishnu. In Siamese mythology, it is the irresistible weapon of Indra, the king of the lower heavens, with which he can, at his pleasure, drive his adversaries from any part of his dominions. In Siamese religious writings we find it described as the wheel of the law, the teaching of Buddha, the means of exterminating

* The plate, being a photographic reduction, should be examined with a reading-glass or other magnifier.

sin and misery. European writers commonly regard it in its mystic reference to the circle of transmigration.

I have, in chapter i., suggested that the Chakra marked on the foot was originally a poetical way of expressing fleetness. This suggestion is supported by examination of the most ancient Indian sculptures, those of Sanchi, in which the Chakra is evidently a chariot-wheel. But at the same time that I offer this explanation of the original meaning of a wheel on the sole of the foot, I do not suggest it as the only meaning of the wheel in the first five centuries of Buddhism. The Sanchi sculptures show it in positions in which we can only regard it as having some mystic signification. In one bas-relief, from the Tope, called by Professor Fergusson, No. 2, there is a Chakra, also exactly like a chariot-wheel, with two figures standing by it, and perhaps about to make it revolve, while other people around are offering it adoration. This design may represent the Chakra as described in the "Lalita Vistâra," or it may represent the teaching of Buddhism in a manner I shall presently indicate. In the "Lalita Vistâra" we read of it as the most marvellous of the seven extraordinary possessions of an emperor of the whole world. Turned by his hand, it rolls before him and his armies, causing all to bow down to him and acknowledge his righteous rule. It seems to me that this rolling wheel originally referred to the advantage possessed by the first possessors of chariots; in course of time poets and priests made a mysterious emblem of it.

During a few centuries preceding, and just after the Christian era, while Buddhism was flourishing in India, and the monastic system developed itself extensively, mysticism prevailed greatly, and the Chakra was probably regarded no more as a poetic image, but as one of the most holy emblems of religion; it might naturally have been first applied to Buddhism, from Buddha's treatment of life. Buddha, as I have tried to show in other parts of this book, did not attempt to teach of the beginning of existence, but assumed it as a rolling circle of causes and effects. This was his circle or wheel of the law.

In the same way that the early teachers of Buddhism adapted their doctrines to their disciples, by formulating them in easily-remembered lists, five kinds of this virtue, four kinds of that, &c., &c., they may have met the difficulty of professing to teach everything without being able to show either a beginning or end, by setting up a wheel in their schoolrooms, and showing that which is perfect in itself and may revolve eternally, without beginning or end. Such a practice on their part would have accounted for the expression used in the sacred books to denote Buddha's teaching, viz., "turning the wheel of the law;" and would also have naturally led to the mystic wheel becoming what Professor Fergusson considers to have been an actual object of worship.

This religious meaning, applied to the Chakra, did not result in a distinct word being invented for it, or for its other sense mentioned above, *i.e.*, the emblem of an emperor. The same word was retained for both ideas, but in its religious use, Dharma (law or right) was prefixed to it.

As time rolled on, the chariot-wheel of the emperor lost that which I have supposed to be its original significance, and became the discus or quoit, the most powerful of all weapons. Indra, the good king of angels, had but to hurl it from his hand, and the heavens against which it was cast were depopulated. Mara, the devil, the bad king of angels, hurled his Chakra against Buddha; and though he could not injure the object of his rage, his weapon clove the mountains in its course. Buddha, with his Chakra, the Dharma chakra, exterminated ignorance and sin. Thus, in the modern drawing of the footprint of Buddha, the simple wheel of the Sanchi sculptures has given place to the radiant weapon so beautifully drawn in the original from which our plate is taken.

The smaller compartments of the plate, of which there are one hundred and eight, I shall describe by numbers. The upper left-hand corner, adjoining the great-toe, being No. 1, and the numbers running across the plate, from left to right, viz.—six lines of eight figures each (1–48); four lines of four figures each (49–64); three lines of eight each (65–88); one central line of two (89–90); one curved line of four (91–94); one curved line of six (95–100); and one curved line of eight (101–108).

This arrangement will separate some of the figures, which ought to be taken in groups; but that is unavoidable.

I should mention that the number of compartments, one hundred and eight (Attra sotawara rup), agrees with the Siamese account in the Life given in this volume, although neither Low nor Burnouf seem to have found this number stated in the native works quoted by them. It also tallies with the number in the Burmese footprint now in the British Museum, and in a Ceylonese drawing mentioned in Mr Skeen's account of "Adam's Peak."

This number, one hundred and eight, also occurs in the "Lalita Vistâra," not applied to marks on the footprint, but to a list of the "Evident Gates of the Law;" that is a summation of one hundred and eight things especially to be remembered by Buddhists.

I believe it to have been a number selected somewhat fancifully by some Buddhist mathematician. I see that it is composed of unity, duality, and trinity. It consists of one one, two twos, and three threes, all multiplied together, thus:—

$$1 \times 2 \times 2 \times 3 \times 3 \times 3 = 108.$$

In the same way I find that thirty-two, which is the number selected for the signs of a great man, is composed very simply of the square of two multiplied by the cube of two.

These numbers seem to show that the early Buddhists were a mathematically-minded set of men, or at least studied the science of numbers.

I will now describe the compartments as numbered:—

1.

The royal spear. Literally the crystal spear, but the word crystal (Keou) is applied to anything gemlike, or beautiful, or royal.

2.

A palace (Siamese, Prasat; Sanscrit, Prâsâda). The projecting, flame-like points of the roof are marks of royal and sacred buildings in Siam. The Siamese call them flowers of heaven, or gems of heaven. They are of two forms, according to their position as terminals of the ridge of the roof, or ornaments of the eaves. These latter, I feel little doubt, represent the heads of hooded snakes, and are a modification of the snake-heads which occupy a similar position on the roofs of ancient Cambodian temples.* The Siamese acknowledge that they obtained the alphabet of their religious literature from Cambodia, and it is probable that some of their architectural ideas were also derived thence. I believe the Siamese derived their civilisation from the ruling race of ancient Cambodia, and that ancient Cambodia† derived its civilisation from Central India. This would account for the number of Sanscrit forms in the Siamese language, and for the use by the Siamese of Brahmin astrologers and Brahmin ceremonies. I have above remarked that the sacred books of the Siamese are written in the alphabet of ancient Cambodia, the Kawm character, which is, at least, in part the source of the modern Siamese character, and which is allied to the Devanagari. The neighbours of the Siamese lying on the west and north —the Peguans, and Avanese, and Laos—are also Buddhists, but the character in which they write seems to me to show that Ceylon gave them their teachers.

3.

A trident (Tri), the weapon of Siva. The insertion of this emblem illustrates a point I referred to in the preceding note—that is, the occurrence of Brahminical ideas among the Siamese. Buddhism, emphatically a

* See Thompson's photographs of Cambodian ruins, published under the title "Antiquities of Cambodia." Edinburgh, 1867.

† See Fergusson's "Tree and Serpent Worship" as to a conquering race from India being the builders of the great temples and palaces of Cambodia.

religion of peace, ought to have nothing to do with warlike weapons, still more should it avoid as an emblem that which is a special emblem of one of the great Hindu divinities.

4.

A golden vase supporting a prince's hair-pin. The pattern of the vase is derived from an expanded *nymphœa* (lotus). These vases are used by the Siamese in offering anything to the King, or carrying any object entitled to peculiar respect. When the King of Siam is informed of the arrival of a letter from any foreign sovereign, he sends his state barges, and has the letter conveyed to him in one of these golden vases, placed on a royal throne, and screened by a state umbrella.

The gold and jewelled hair-pin is worn in the top-knots of princes and other wealthy Siamese children. The top-knot is a tuft of long hair left uncut from infancy on the centre of the head, all the rest of the head being kept clean shaved. When the child reaches its ninth, eleventh, or thirteenth year of age, this top-knot is shaved off with much ceremony, and the hair left to grow all over the head until it becomes thick enough to be cut and shaved into the brush worn by adults. It is considered very unfortunate that a child should attain puberty before its top-knot has been shaved. More on this subject will be found in the description of figure 24.

5.

The flower Montha (Mandara). There is in Siam a sweet-scented flowering tree called by this name, but

I believe the Montha of the figure is a flower of heaven.

6.

A royal candle or torch stand (Sao tai).

7.

A book resting on a vase.

8.

The royal elephant goad (Kho chang); the hook with which the driver, sitting on the neck, controls the elephant.

9.–15.

The seven annular belts of ocean which separate the seven annular mountains from Mount Meru and each other. They are supposed to be inhabited by immense fish.

An account of the Buddhist idea of a system of worlds is given in page 10. Mount Meru is the centre of each system, round it are seven alternate belts of ocean and mountain; then an eighth (the great) ocean, at the four cardinal points of which are the four great human worlds or continents (Siamese, Thawip; Sanscrit, Dvipas), one inhabited by men, the other three by half-human beings. Each great continent has around it five hundred islands. The system is bounded by the walls of the world, the crystal mountain Chakkrawan.

16.

A palace of the angels (Wiman; Sanscrit, Vimâna). Vimâna means also a chariot or any vehicle; and if we in this place suppose (as is permissible), the

Siamese Wiman to mean "litter" or "palanquin," then our figure will answer to one of the symbols mentioned in the Ceylonese list, which I cannot otherwise identify.

The usual meaning of Wiman is "palace of the angels," and the idea attached to that meaning is shown in the following translation from the "Book of Indra," one of the most ancient of the Siamese law books:—"There is a celestial abode in the Dewa heavens, an aerial dwelling covered with gold and gems, with roofs shining with gold and jewels, and roof points* of crystal and pearl; and the whole gleams with wrought and unwrought gold more brilliant than all the gems. Around its eaves plays the soft sound of tinkling golden bells. There dwell a thousand lovely houris, virgins in gorgeous attire, decked with the richest ornaments, singing sweet songs in concert, with a melody whose resounding strains are never still. This celestial abode is adorned with lotus lakes, and meandering rivers full of the five kinds of lotus, whose golden petals, as they fade, fill all the air with sweet odours. And round the lakes are splendid lofty trees growing in regular order, their leaves, their boughs, their branches, covered with sweet-scented blossoms, whose balmy odours fill the surrounding air with heart-delighting fragrance."

My object in translating this passage is to show the Siamese idea of a sensual heaven.

17

The great ocean (Maha samut), in which are the *four* continents mentioned in Nos. 9–15.

* These points are the projections mentioned in No. 2.

18.

The royal ox Usupharat; the humped Brahmin bull, otherwise called king of the white oxen.

19.

Erawan, the three-headed elephant of Indra, sometimes a conspicuous ornament of Siamese temples.*

An Indian drawing in Moor's "Hindu Pantheon" (plate 79), shows Indra riding on this three-headed elephant.

Burnouf applied the term Erawan or Airavana to a one-headed elephant, and considered the three-headed elephant to be that named Chatthan, which he identified as Chaddanta, the elephant of six defences or tusks. We find Chaddanta (or Chatthan), represented in our plate as one-headed (No. 42).

20.

The dragon Mangkon (Makara), or sea-serpent. The name of the Chinese dragon. The Indian Makara is, I believe, a fish.

21.

The golden junk or ship. In the "Life of Buddha" we read of "the lustrous vessel of the true law," by which Buddha would enable men to cross the ocean of transmigrating existence, and reach the other shore, *i.e.*, Nirwana.

The symbol is probably connected with the Hindu legend of the precious things recovered by churning

* Wat Cheng at Bangkok is an instance. The elephant's head may be seen high on the principal spire.

the ocean, in the tortoise incarnation of Vishnu. The ship was one of the precious things.

22.

The cow and calf. Probably the Hindu cow of plenty, one of the precious things referred to in the previous note. The cow is a symbol of the Buddha Gotama, as the Naga, hen, and crocodile are of preceding Buddhas.

23.

This figure of water and lotuses, seven times repeated (31, 39, 47, 51, 55, 59), represents the seven lakes of Himaphan, or Himalaya, named Anodat, Kannamuntha, Rotaphan, Chatthan, Kunala, Manthakini, and Sihapat. Of these, the only two whose names I have read more than once, are Anodat, the source of rain, and Chatthan, the home of the king of elephants and his dependents.

In these lakes grow the five kinds of *nymphæa* or lotus (Bencha prathum).

The lotus, the emblem of vitality and symbol of Buddha, holds a very foremost position among Buddhist symbols.

In Siam (and judging from drawings, it is much the same in India) one can scarcely see a Buddhist building, figure, or drawing, but what has some part of its design taken from the lotus (*nymphæa*).

In Hindu mythology it may be especially noticed in connection with Brahma and Vishnu.

In the Siamese Traiphoom we read, that on the formation of a new system of worlds (their theory being that worlds are from time to time destroyed and reproduced) some of the Brahma angels from the highest heavens, who have escaped the destruction which has long previously overtaken the lower heavens and the abodes of men, come upon the new world, and anxiously seek to discover whether a Buddha, a teacher of the law of escape from sorrow, will be born in it. The lotus is the sign. If there is no lotus, there will be no Buddha. If there are lotuses, the number of flowers foretells the number of Buddhas. Thus for this present world there will be five Buddhas, for the Brahmas found five flowers growing on one stalk.

Another pretty story anent the lotus, which I got from the Laos of Chiengmai, north of Siam, is, that the alphabet was taught by a fairy, springing from a lotus, on each of whose expanded leaves appeared one letter.

24.

This is a figure of what the Siamese call Bai si and Wen wien thien, used in the ceremony of top-knot-cutting. The Bai si is a pyramidal construction of plaintain-leaf, designed to hold what may be called sacrificial rice and flowers. The "Bangkok Calendar" for 1864, in an article on the top-knot-cutting of a prince, thus describes the Bai si and ceremony of Wien thien :—

"After the shaving is over, the priests, princes, and noblemen are sumptuously fed; and that being ended about midday, two standards called Bai see are brought and set within the circle of concourse. They have something the appearance of the Siamese Sawekrachat, or royal umbrella, one of the five insignia of royalty peculiar to the Kings of Siam. These standards are about five cubits high, having from three to five stories. The staff is fixed on a wooden pedestal, light and portable. The different stories of the Bai see are made of plantain-leaves, interspersed with silvered and gilt paper. Each story is circular in form, with a flaring and deeply-serrated brim, and has a flat bottom. Within these receptacles, custom places a little cooked rice, called Khao khwan, a small quantity of cakes, a little sweet-scented oil, a handful of fragrant flowers, young cocoa-nuts, and plantains. Other edibles of many kinds are brought and arranged round about the Bai see, and a beautiful bouquet adorns the topmost story of each. A procession is then formed of the princes, noblemen, and others, who circumambulate the standards nine times. There are three golden candlesticks, holding each a large wax-candle, which, being lighted, are carried by different princes and other dignitaries in the procession, and handed from one to the other as they move around the standards. Meanwhile the royal son or daughter, for whom the festival is held, is seated on a kind of throne between the two standards, arrayed in splendid costume. The persons holding the candles wave them when passing in front of the prince, and fan the smoke of them into his face, as the influence of this has much to do in conferring the desired blessing upon him. This moving of the procession around the Bai sees is denominated Weean theean, literally, circumambulating with candles. There are nine of these evolutions for a child of a king, and five for a child of a subject."

25.

The chank-shell with reversed spiral; a shell something like a large whelk, much prized in the East when it is white, and has its convolutions turned the contrary way to what is usual in shells. Among the King of Siam's presents to Her Majesty was one of these shells. The Brahmins, or royal astrologers, carry them in state processions, and blow shrill music from them on great occasions. One of them, richly decorated with gold and jewels, is among the chief insignia of kings.

In Hindu mythology, the chank is generally borne by Vishnu, and is one of the precious things recovered from the sea of milk in the tortoise incarnation above referred to.

26.

The Burmese goose or swan, Hongsa; the bird which gave its name to Hongsawadi, the capital of Pegu. Representations of it, carved on the tops of high columns, are common in the temples of those Siamese villages where live the descendants of captive Peguans. It is probably the same as the Hindu Hanasa, the bird which carries Brahma, and from it the common goose of Siam has derived its name, "han."

27.

The four-faced Brahma. Sixteen squares will be found to contain four-faced Brahmas, with very slight differences in dress. These sixteen squares represent the sixteen heavens of the formed Brahmas (Siamese, Phrom), the meditative angels. Their distribution is treated of in Note 65 to the "Life of Buddha."

28.–29.

Are the same as the preceding.

30.

A Kinon, or Kinara, a figure half-man and half-bird, one of the inhabitants of the Himalayan fairy-land.

31.

One of the Himalayan lakes. See No. 23.

32.

The royal umbrella, or white parasol of several tiers, called Sawetrachat, the principal insignia of the Kings of Siam. Seven or nine tiers are usual in the Sawetrachat of Buddhas or kings.

33.

A Dewa angel (Siamese, Thewada), of the lower or sensual heavens. As these are elsewhere depicted, this may be intended for the Universal Emperor.

34.

A king of Nagas (Siamese, Phya nak). The Naga of Siamese mythology is a hooded serpent, possessed of various supernatural powers, such as ability to change its form and assume any desired appearance; to dart through the earth, fly through the skies, and indeed to move anywhere instantaneously; also to cause death by a glance or a breath. In the "Modern Buddhist," the Naga is alluded to as causing epidemics by poisoning the air. In the "Life of Buddha," we read of the Naga King Kala, who wakes only when a new Buddha is about to illumine the earth, and who, having risen from his subterranean abode, honours the Buddha with innumerable songs of praise, and then returns to sleep. Another great appearance of the Naga, in connection with Buddha, is one, often depicted in Siamese temples, in which the seven-headed King of Nagas shields the teacher from a storm by encircling him with the coils of his body, and spreading over his head his seven expanded hoods. The Naga's appearance is not confined to religious literature; Nagas are important characters in novels. For example, in the story of "Prince Phin Suriwong," we read that the young Prince, lost in a forest, and sleeping under a tree, is awoke by a loud noise, and sees that the mighty bird Garuda has pounced on a King of Nagas, and is about to carry him off. The Prince claps his hands, and so alarms the bird, that he drops his prey and flies. The Naga glides into his hole, but mindful of the service rendered to him, sends his son, transformed into a man, to escort the Prince to his dominions, and present him with a ring, enabling him to take any desired appearance, or become invisible. The novel continues with an account of the way the Prince makes love to a Princess by help of this ring.

The Naga was the symbol of Konagamana, the Buddha next but one before Buddha Gotama.

In my description of No. 2, I mentioned that an ornament, derived from the snake-head, decorated the roofs of Siamese temples and palaces; and that the design had apparently been adopted from Cambodia, some of the grand religious buildings of which country are richly ornamented with carvings of the seven-headed snake. Professor Fergusson regards Cambodia as having been a great seat of serpent-worship; but although his fascinating writing did for a time make me inclined to agree with him, my agreement was but transitory, and I am inclined to believe that the temples of Cambodia were Buddhist temples; the Brahmin element, so marked in Siam, being perhaps even more marked in Cambodia; and the Naga-worship, probably, no more than that indicated in the before-quoted passage of the "Mahawanso," where Asoka is represented as obtaining his knowledge of Buddha's appearance by the aid of a wonder-working serpent, who was treated with royal or divine honour.

Professor Fergusson refers to the formation of the courts of the temple at Nakhou wat, and pictures them flooded for the ceremony of serpent-worship. He even points out the pipes used for flooding them. Those pipes seem to me to be mere drains for carrying off rain-water from the courts; and if the courts had intended to be flooded, I hardly think the rich carvings would have been carried down to their very pavement; they would surely have ended at the water-line. There can, however, be no doubt that the old Cambodians attached an importance to the Naga which it has now lost; and it is most interesting to follow the learned Professor in tracing the position of the Naga in various ages as shown by architectural remains. From the ruins of Cambodia (date, fifth to thirteenth centuries), we pass back to the Tope of Amravatti, where the Naga appears as the protector of altars, and also as the sign of some family or race; and thence, going back three hundred years, to the date when the Sanchi Rail was carved, we still find the protecting Naga.

Professor Fergusson, in his elaborate work, indicates the respect paid to the snake among almost all ancient people. I cannot enter into that subject here, and must refer those interested in it to the "Tree and Serpent Worship," or if they cannot borrow, and cannot afford to buy that very expensive book, I can commend to them an "Essay on Tree and Serpent Worship," which they can obtain by forwarding six penny-stamps to Mr Thomas Scott, Mount Pleasant, Ramsgate.

35.–37.

Brahmas. See No. 27.

38.

A Kinari or female Kinara. See No. 30.

39.

One of the seven lakes of Himaphan. See No. 23.

40.

The royal sword (Phra khan) on a vase. This is one of the five great insignia of kings.

41.

This and the three similar figures below it must represent the four Thawips or Dvipas; that is, worlds of the square-faced, round, semicircular, and human-faced beings, whose worlds respectively partake of the contour of their inhabitants' faces. See also No. 9.

The figures, which are those of female angels, probably represent the angels of the earth, mentioned in the "Life of Buddha."

42.

Ubosot (Uposâtha), one of the two kings of elephants of the Himalayan fairyland. On the saddlecloth is the mystic sign described by Burnouf as Çrîvastaya.

The general meaning of the word Ubosot is described in the notes to the Life.

43.–45.

Brahmas. See No. 27.

46.

The bird Insi, king of eagles.

47.

One of the seven lakes of Himaphan. See No. 23.

48.

The fan used by monks. This is not so much a fan as a screen; something to cover the eyes of the monk, and prevent his attention being diverted by what is passing around him. It helps him to avoid seeing the dangers of the bewitching ladies he may meet on his journeys. It does not prevent his fixing his eyes on the ground before him, and watching, lest he break the great commandment, not to destroy life, by treading on one of the myriad creeping things which are ever present in the prolific East.

49.

This probably represents the Thawip or Dvipa of semicircular-faced beings. See No. 41.

50.

Chatthan, or Chaddanta, a king of elephants, who, according to Siamese legends, lives in a golden palace on the shores of the Himalayan lake Chatthan, attended by eighty thousand ordinary elephants. See also No. 19.

51.

One of the seven lakes of Himaphan. See No. 23.

52.

The peacock's tail, a mark of royal dignity.

53.

The continent of round-faced beings. See No. 41.

54.

Phalahok (Valahaka), the king of horses. The horse occupies a much more important place among Northern Buddhists than it does among those of the South.

55.

One of the seven lakes of Himaphan. See No. 23.

56.

The Mongkut, or crown, the design of which was, according to the Siamese, taken from the flaming glory on the head of Buddha.

57.

The continent of square-faced beings. See No. 41.

58.

The King of Tigers. The tiger is the symbol of the coming Buddha Maitreya.

59.

One of the seven lakes of Himaphan. See No. 23.

60.

The Batr or pot in which Buddhist monks collect their food. (Sanscrit, Pâtra, a plate or cup.)

61.

The sun, moon, and planets.

62.

Rachasi, the king of lions.

63.

Mountains. Ten mountains are depicted on the plate, seven of them in juxtaposition, the others separate. The seven lying together represent the seven annular mountains surrounding Mount Meru. See No. 9. The three detached figures probably represent—1. Mount Meru; 2. The walls of the world, Mount Chakrawan; 3. Mount Krailat, or some other representative of the eighty-four thousand mountains of Himaphan or Himalaya.

64.

A vase and diamond chain.

65.

A rabbit or hare.

66.

Mountains. See No. 63.

67.–69.

Brahma angels. See No. 27.

70.

A peacock.

71.

Mountains. See No. 63.

72.

River, with lotus. There are five similar figures representing the five great rivers (Maha nathi), whose source is in the Himalayan lake Anodat. They are named Kongkha (Ganges), Yumna, Achirawadi, Saraphum, and Mahi.

73.

Peacock expanding its tail.

74.

The Chamara, chowrie, or mosquito-swish. This useful article is one of the royal insignia—the long hair in that case being properly the tail of the Thibetan yak.

75.–77.

Brahma angels. See No. 27.

78.

The bird Khektao, by some called dove.

79.

Mountains. See No. 63.

80.

River, with lotus.

81.

A palace of the angels. See No. 16.

82.

A preacher's chair.

83.

Brahma angels. See No. 27.

84.-85.

Dewa angels (Siamese, Thewada), holding swords and lotuses. These, with the four adjoining similar figures, represent the six heavens of the inferior or sensual angels. These six heavens bear the names—1. Chatumaharachit, which is level with the summit of Yukhunthon, the circular range next to Mount Meru, and in which dwell the four guardians of the world. 2. Dawadungsa, level with the summit of Mount Meru, in which is the palace of Indra, and in which flourish the Kalpa trees (Siamese, Kamaphruk), whose branches furnish everything that the angels can desire. 3. Yama, which rests entirely on air. 4. Dusit (or Tushita) the joyful heaven, wherein Buddhas and others pass their last existence before being born on earth. 5. Nimanaradi, a heaven in which the mere will of the angels dwelling in it creates for them all they desire. 6. Paranimit wasawadi, in which angels have all they desire, without having to create it by their own will, subsidiary angels gratifying their desires. In this highest of the luxurious sensual heavens, dwells Mara, the angel who takes the place of Satan, the tempter in our legend of Buddha.

86.

The Karawek bird of fairyland, whose sweet song charms all the inhabitants of the forest.

87.

Mountains. See No. 63.

88.

River, with lotus. See No. 72.

89.–92.

Dewa angels. See No. 84.

93.–94.

Peacocks. There are too many peacocks on our plate, owing probably to the copyist not being able to distinguish between the peacock and other birds. The plate omits the jungle-fowl, Karieng (stork), Chakphrak, and Krachip (two small birds), and gives the royal peacock in their place.

95.

The flag of victory.

96.

An alligator, the symbol of the Buddha Kasyappa.

97.

The King of the Garudas (Siamese, Phya khrut). The Garudas or Suparnas figure in Siamese writings mainly as the great enemy of the Nagas. With the Hindus, Garuda is the vehicle or Vahan of Vishnu.

98.

Deer.

99.–102.

Mountains. See No. 63.

103.

The golden fishes; or perhaps the Pla anon, the huge fish in the waters beneath the earth, whose movements, shaking the world, give rise to earthquakes.

104.

Pha krai or Trai chiwara, the three robes of a monk.

105.

A (full) water-jar. In Indian Buddhist architecture the overflowing water jar is a conspicuous figure, but the idea does not seem to have passed on to the Siamese.

106.

Mountains. See No. 63.

107.–178.

River, with lotus. See No. 72.

APPENDIX.

THE THIRTY-TWO CHARACTERISTICS OF A GREAT MAN.

In predicting the glorious future of the young Prince, born to be a Buddha, the Brahmin soothsayers, skilled in Vedic lore, relied on the appearance of the thirty-two principal, and eighty minor, characteristics of a great man; the marks which were a sure sign that their bearer would be either temporal or spiritual Lord of the whole world, that is, either a Chakkravartin Emperor, ruler over all the continents, or a Buddha, teacher of all beings.

According to the Siamese account, Brahma had previously descended from heaven, and appeared in human form, merely to teach men the signs by which they might recognise the Great Being who would be born for their salvation.

These signs probably are the various characteristics ascribed to or possessed by different Indian heroes, and exaggerated by the fancies of Indian poets; and we may suppose that they have been formulated in a list, as "the thirty-two great signs" for at least twenty-two centuries.

M. Burnouf, in an appendix to the "Lotus de la bonne Loi," treats of these signs almost exhaustively. They interested him under two aspects—one as illustrating the authenticity of Buddhist classics, evidenced by the concurrence of the records of the Northern and Southern Buddhists, the other in connection with a theory that they showed the race to which Buddha belonged—certain persons having, on account of the curled hairs described in the list, and shown in idols, supposed Buddha to have been a negro.

The list has lost its interest in connection with these points; no one now supposes Buddha to have been a negro, and the age of Buddhist books is established by something better than the similarity of the lists contained in Northern and Southern records.

The concurrence of these lists only carries us back to the beginning of the fifth century; for Buddhaghosha, the commentator and translator into Pali of the Singhalese sacred works, learned his Pali in India, and would naturally have made the lists in his translations agree with the Indian lists, which he must have learned.

We have in the sculptures of the Sanchi Tope a better proof of the antiquity of Buddhist records than any afforded by comparison of Northern and Southern books, for these sculptures are evident illustrations of stories contained in the books, and it is manifest that the age of a story must be greater than that of its illustrations. The researches of scholars in China have also given us some valuable dates, considerably anterior to the days of Buddhaghosha.*

I will now quote the list as given by Burnouf:—

1. His head is crowned with a protuberance of the skull.
2. His curly hair is of a brilliant black, shining like the tail of a peacock, or sparkling collyrium (eye-salve), and each curl turns from left to right.
3. He has a broad and regular forehead.
4. Between his eyebrows is a circle of down, brilliant as snow or silver.
5. His eyelids are like those of a heifer.
6. He has brilliant black eyes.

* See Introduction to the Rev. S. Beal's "Travels of Buddhist Pilgrims."

7, 8, 9. He has forty teeth, all equal, set closely together, and of the most perfect whiteness.
10. His voice is like that of Brahma.
11. He has an exquisite sense of taste.
12. His tongue is broad and thin, or, according to the Thibetan version, "long and thread-like."
13. He has the jaw of a lion.
14. His shoulders or arms are perfectly rounded.
15. He has seven parts of his body filled out, or with protuberances (*i.e.*, soles of feet, palms of hands, shoulders, and back).
16. The space between his shoulders is covered.
17. His skin has the lustre or colour of gold.
18. His arms are so long that when he stands upright his hands reach to his knees.
19. His front is lion-like.
20. His body is perfectly straight, tall as a banyan-tree, and round in proportion.
21. His hairs grow one by one.
22. And their ends are turned to the right.
23. The generative organs are concealed.
24, 25. He has perfectly round thighs, and his legs are like those of the King of the Gazelles.
26. His toes or fingers are long.
27. The nails of the toes are well developed.
28. His instep is high.
29. His feet and hands are soft and delicate.
30. His toes and fingers are marked with lines forming a network.
31. Under the soles of his feet are marked two beautiful, luminous, brilliant white wheels, with a thousand rays.
32. His feet are even and well placed.

Such is the list given by M. Burnouf. In the fourth chapter of the "Life of Buddha" is the Siamese list. The differences between the two are very trifling. Scarcely one character of importance is wanting in the Siamese list, and the only additions of consequence are four large canine teeth (which M. Burnouf places among the eighty secondary signs), and a peculiar attachment of the feet to the body—such that, while they remained still, the whole body could move round on them as on a pivot.

INDEX.